AAKAR BOOKS CLASSICS

CLARA ZETKIN

Clara Zetkin, ca. 1928

AAKAR BOOKS CLASSICS

CLARA ZETKIN
Selected Writings

Edited by
Philip S. Foner

Foreword by
Angela Y. Davis

Introduction to the Indian Edition
Tripta Wahi

AAKAR

Clara Zetkin: Selected Writings

First Published in India 2012
Reprinted 2024

ISBN 978-93-5002-132-3

Published in agreement with International Publishers, New York for publication and sale only in the Indian Subcontinent.

Published by
AAKAR BOOKS
28 E Pocket IV, Mayur Vihar Phase I
Delhi 110 091, India
www.aakarbooks.com

Printed at
Mudrak, Noida

CONTENTS

ILLUSTRATIONS

FOREWORD BY ANGELA Y. DAVIS

Almost one hundred years ago, Clara Zetkin began to work out many of the central concepts associated with the Marxist analysis of women's oppression, concepts which are no less relevant today than they were during her era. Along with Frederick Engels and August Bebel, she emerged as a pioneering theorist of women's status in capitalist society and a strategist who illuminated the way toward a social order delivered from the effects of institutionalized oppression of women and male supremacist ideology. Like her heroic contemporary, V.I. Lenin, she sought to understand the special oppression of women by placing it within the larger context of the socioeconomic evolution of humankind and consequently attempted to analyze most of the major events within the history of the class struggle of her era. In exploring contemporary social issues, she was hardly a dispassionate observer—indeed, she was a deeply committed activist, a woman who became one of the outstanding Communist leaders in the decades surrounding the Great October Revolution. A central figure in German Social-Democracy for many years, she later disassociated herself from the Party—as did Rosa Luxemburg and Karl Liebknecht—because of its failure to take a firm stand against World War I as imperialist in character and injurious to the interests of the German workers as well as to the international working class. Clara Zetkin was always a staunch defender of the proletariat. She never failed to rely upon a class approach in her theoretical deliberations as well as in her practical political actions. Her theoretical and practical contributions shed light not only on her own historical period, but today they can assist us to better comprehend the relationship between the fight for socialism and the struggles against racism, for women's equality and for peace.

Zetkin's first major analysis of the condition of women in capitalist society was presented in a speech she delivered in 1889 at the Paris International Workers' Congress. Emphasizing the centrality of female labor in her presentation, she argued that "the question of women's emancipation . . . in the final analysis is the question of women's work. . . . " (see p. 45). Zetkin was in agreement with Engels, who, in examining "the peculiar character of the supremacy of the husband over the wife in the modern family" and "the necessity of creating real social equality between them", concluded that "the first condition for the liberation of the wife is to bring the whole female sex back into public industry."[1] Emphasizing the same point, Lenin would later make the following observation:

> The chief task of the working women's movement is to fight for economic and social equality, and not only formal equality, for women. The chief thing is to get women to take part in socially productive labour, to liberate them from "domestic slavery", to free them from their stupefying and humiliating subjugation to the eternal drudgery of the kitchen and the nursery.[2]

In order effectively to validate her claim that women could only achieve their liberation via the path of participation in economic production and by thus achieving economic independence, Clara Zetkin had to challenge the prevailing notion that the entrance of women into the labor force militated against the interests of the proletarians.

> The Socialists must know that given the present economic development, women's work outside the home is a necessity, that the natural tendency of women's work is either to reduce the working hours that each individual must render to society or to augment the wealth of society, that it is not women's work per se which in competition with men's work lowers wages, but rather the exploitation of female labor by the capitalists who appropriate it (*see* p. 45).

On several occasions during her speech, Zetkin emphatically pointed out that women ought not be compelled to bear the blame for a process of exploitation for which the capitalist class alone was responsible. If, in fact, the large-scale employment of women had led to a longer rather than shorter work day and if female labor had been used to bring about a decline in the wages of male workers, the solution did not lie in lending support to the prohibition of female labor but rather in recruiting women workers to struggle alongside their male comrades for the ultimate elimination of the capitalist system of production.

Clara Zetkin's arguments in support of women workers contain a logic which can be effectively employed today in defense of stronger affirmative action programs, not only for women but for the racially and nationally oppressed as well. A weakness in her early analysis (which she later corrected), was a failure to acknowledge the need to fight for special protective provisions for women workers in order to guarantee their ability to labor and struggle on an equal basis with men. Nonetheless, she made an important appeal to the male members of the German Social-Democratic Party (SPD) to comprehend what a massive involvement of women workers would mean for the battle for socialism and she issued a passionate call to women workers to recognize the SPD as the authentic bearer of the women's liberation banner. In other words, the participation of women workers would be as indispensable an element in the battle for socialism as the victory of socialism would be in the struggle for women's emancipation.

The title of a speech Clara Zetkin delivered some years later was: "Only in Conjunction with the Proletarian Woman will Socialism be Victorious." In this presentation to the 1896 Social-Democratic Party Congress at Gotha, she argued that the woman question could not be formulated as a single, homogeneous theory, transcending considerations of social class. Bourgeois feminists today who still insist that their strategies for emancipation which reflect their own class positions are also valid for working class and racially oppressed women have a great deal to learn from Zetkin's analysis. From one class to another—from the grand bourgeoisie to the middle and petit bourgeoisie to the proletariat—the structure of women's oppression varies significantly. She pointed out, however, that all these classes were creations of capitalism and that only women of the particular classes which are associated with the capitalist mode of production had developed a historical need to emancipate themselves.

> It was only the capitalist mode of production which created the societal transformations that brought forth the modern women's question by destroying the old family economic system which provided both livelihood and life's meaning for the great mass of women during the pre-capitalist period (*see* p. 72).

Here, Zetkin raised the important question of the historical genesis of social consciousness. Although women may have been severely oppressed during the pre-capitalist era, they had not yet encountered the objective circumstances which permitted them to develop an awareness of their suppression. "The women's question . . . is only present within those classes of society who are themselves the products of the capitalist mode of production." She pointed out that among peasants still possessing a natural economy, there was no systematic consciousness of the need to emancipate the women of that class. But "there is a women's question for the women of the proletariat, the bourgeoisie, the intelligentsia and the Upper Ten Thousand." For the haute bourgeoisie, it was a question of women fighting to "dispose of their property in an independent and free manner," whereas for the other bourgeois strata, whose women were not already in possession of property, the demand focused on equal professional training and equal access to the respective professions (*see* pages 74-75). The passage in which Zetkin described the way that the suppression of women and their conscious drive for liberation manifested itself among the working class is important enough to cite here in its entirety:

> As far as the proletarian woman is concerned, it is capitalism's need to exploit and to search incessantly for a cheap labor force, that has created the woman's question. . . . She went out into the economic life in order to aid her husband in making a living, but the capitalist mode of production transformed her into an unfair competitor. She wanted to bring prosperity to her family, but instead misery descended upon it. The proletarian woman obtained her own employment because she wanted to create a more sunny and pleasant life for her children, but instead she became almost entirely separated from them. She became an equal of the man as a worker; the machine rendered muscular power superfluous and everywhere women's work showed the same results in production as men's work. And since women constitute a cheap labor force and above all a submissive one . . . the capitalists multiply the possibilities of women's work in industry. As a result of all this, the proletarian woman has achieved her independence. But verily the price was very high and for the moment they have gained very little. . . . In former times, the rule of a man over his wife was ameliorated by their personal relationship. Between an employer and his worker, however, exists only a cash nexus (*see* pages 76-77).

The primary distinction as Zetkin saw it, between working class women's fight for equality and the struggles of their bourgeois sisters was that the latter pitted themselves against the men of their class, while the women proletarians needed to join together with their husbands, brothers, fathers and sons in order to wage a common battle against the capitalist class. Moreover, what the bourgeois women perceived as ultimate goals, the proletarian women should have interpreted as weapons in the battle to participate in the class struggle on an equal basis with men. Zetkin developed this notion most systematically in her analysis of the relationship between the woman suffrage campaign and the struggles of working class women. This analysis is significant not only because of its important historical value, but also because of the lessons to be gleaned from it with respect to the class nature of such contemporary women's struggles as the campaign for the Equal Rights Amendment in the United States. In a paper read before a 1906 Social-Democratic Women's Congress in Mannheim, Zetkin asserted that middle class women perceived woman suffrage as a natural right to participate in the political processes of an equally natural and immutable bourgeois society. For working class women the ballot was, on the contrary, a social right, a demand which had arisen as a clear consequence of the emergence of the capitalist economic system. Moreover:

> The middle class women really wish to obtain this social reform because they think it is a measure which will strengthen and support the whole of middle class society. The working women demand the suffrage not only to defend their economic and moral interests of life, but they wish for it as a help against the oppression of their class by men and they are particularly eager for it in order to aid in the struggle against the capitalist class.

Thus, women's right to vote assumes entirely different dimensions among women of opposing social classes. As Zetkin pointed out in a resolution she introduced during the international Socialist Congress at Stuttgart (1907), Socialist women could not place as much weight in suffrage as did bourgeois women because the achievement of the right to vote would not fundamentally affect the underlying cause of women's oppression, i.e., private property. After all, the male proletariat which was permitted to exercise the franchise remained nonetheless severely exploited. In other words,

> the granting of suffrage to the female sex does not eliminate the class differences between the exploiters and the exploited from which the most serious obstacles to the free and harmonious development of the female proletarian are derived (*see* p. 99).

If, however, woman suffrage emerged as a significant demand in working class women's battles, it was because the ballot was potentially a powerful weapon to be wielded in the larger class struggle against capitalism. In fact, it was a weapon required not only by female workers, but by their class brothers as well. As increasing numbers of women entered the ranks of labor, becoming an integral part of the working class, the fight for woman suffrage would increasingly become "a struggle for the capture of political power by the proletariat."[3]

Considering the recent defeat of the Equal Rights Amendment in the United States and the escalation of anti-E.R.A. propaganda by organized right-wing forces, the protracted nature of the struggle may well be comparable to the long fight for woman suffrage. What Clara Zetkin said about the campaign to extend the ballot to women might well be said today about the E.R.A. campaign:

> We know that we shall not obtain the victory of woman suffrage in a short time, but we know, too, that in our struggles for this measure we shall revolutionise hundreds of thousands of minds. We carry on our war, not as a fight between the sexes, but as a battle against the political might of the possessing classes; as a fight which we carry on with all our might and main without hatred of the other sex; a fight whose final aim and whose glory will be that (one day) the proletariat in its entirety, without distinction of sex, shall be able to call out to the capitalist order of society, "You rest on us, you oppress us, and, see, how the building which you have erected is tottering to the ground."[4]

Clara Zetkin emphasized again and again that the larger historical context of the battle for women's liberation was the working class drive for socialism. A contemporary feminist theorist with distinct anti-Communist leanings writes that

> ever since the existing socialist societies dawned on this earth disillusionment with socialism, which results from revolution, has been an impetus to the emergence of feminist theory.[5]

Had she, like Clara Zetkin, more seriously examined the real relationship between socialism and the women's movement, she would have realized that the birth of socialism, since the triumph of the October Revolution, has acted as an inspiration and a beacon of light to countless working women across the globe. When the face of history was transformed by the Russian Revolution, Zetkin joined millions of workers throughout the world in enthusiastically greeting this triumph.

> The Bolsheviks have reached their goal in a bold assault which has no parallel in history. Governmental power is in the hands of the Soviets. What has transpired is the revolutionary dictatorship of the proletariat (*see* p. 138).

When she wrote about the impact of the revolution on the Moslem women of the former colonies of Tsarist Russia, her observations could be applied, many years later, to the situation in the United States with respect to the struggles waged by Black working class and other racially and nationally oppressed women. The active strivings of Moslem women for their freedom

> confirm the fact that the proletarian revolution will indeed turn out to be a world revolution in which even the last suppressed and enslaved individual will free himself by his own strength (*see* p. 158).

Implied in Zetkin's discussion of the liberation struggle among Moslem women is a message that is clearly relevant to the women's movement today. Working class and racially oppressed women confront sexist oppression in a way that reflects the real and complex objective interconnections between class exploitation, racist oppression and male supremacy. Whereas a white middle class woman's experience of sexism incorporates a relatively isolated form of this oppression, working class women's experiences necessarily place sexism in its context of class exploitation and Black women's experiences further incorporate the social factor of racism. These are by no means subjective experiences; rather there is an objective interrelationship between racism and sexism in that the general context of both forms of oppression in our time is the class struggle unfolding between monopoly capitalism and the working class.

It is of special importance to progressive people in the United States who understand the extent to which racism is interwoven in the history of this country and the extent to which it has been used as a tool to set asunder the unity of the working class, that Clara Zetkin had an important role in the extension of international solidarity to the struggle for Black equality in the United States. As the head of the International Red Help, she appealed in 1932 to progressive people throughout the world to defend the nine Scottsboro youth who had been fraudulently convicted of raping two white women in a small town in Alabama. She specifically called upon the international movement to prevent the executions of the eight who had been sentenced to death. Of course, the struggle against the death penalty—and especially as it focuses on the racist implication of capital punishment—is very much alive fifty years after Clara Zetkin called for a defense of the Black youth in Scottsboro, Alabama. In 1983, approximately 1200 people are on death row in the United States and almost half of them are Black. A campaign similar to that which was organized around the Scottsboro case has taken shape around the case of another Black youth—Johnny Imani Harris—

fradulently convicted through Alabama's judicial system. Certainly Clara Zetkin's successful appeal in 1932 holds important lessons to be applied in the case of Johnny Harris and many others.

The most crucial struggle of our time focuses on the global necessity to prevent our planet from being consumed in the fires of a nuclear disaster. Before anything else, Clara Zetkin was a woman of peace. While she never capitulated in the midst of the battles of the working class, she always emphasized the importance of the struggle for peace as a factor in the class struggle itself.

> Imperialist wars are directed against the workers; they are the inevitable expression of the very being of capitalism. The first decisive step toward demolishing the system of blood-sucking capitalism must be strong and inexorable recognition that the workers are against imperialist wars.[6]

Indeed the efforts to counter monopoly capitalism's stronghold in those countries which have not yet joined hands for peace with the Soviet Union and the the socialist community of nations are inherently tied to the struggle to end the threat of nuclear annihilation which looms over us all. Peace among nations, as Clara Zetkin repeatedly insisted, is always in the interests of the working class.

CLARA ZETKIN AND THE WOMEN'S QUESTION

An Introduction to the Indian Edition

The publication of an Indian edition of the book *'Clara Zetkin: Selected Writings'* is an historic occasion. This publication for the first time brings the principal speaker for Europe's working class women of her times, Clara Zetkin, to the Indian public. Leader of the revolutionary international movement of the Socialist women, her speeches, letters and articles included in this publication throw a remarkable light on her views on the women's question and her relentless struggle against the reformism of the social democratic movement. Indeed, her views on the women's question and her struggle against the revisionism of social democracy are inextricably interlinked and they are the obverse and reverse of the same coin. Her views and struggles on both these issues, which were central to her life and politics, are as germane to our times, perhaps even more, as they were to her own times. They have an underlying universality which makes them relevant to our own times particularly in societies like India.

In this introductory note to the Indian edition of *Clara Zetkin : Selected Writings* an attempt is being made to present Clara Zetkin's understanding of and contribution to the women's question. This is being sought to be done through her speeches, articles and letters included in this volume, a substantial part of which deals with questions pertaining to women in the last quarter of the nineteenth century and the first few decades of the twentieth century. Almost all pieces included in this work are speeches delivered or articles written by Clara Zetkin for specific occasions on issues in which she was deeply involved. Grappling with issues confronting her times, be it the question of women's right to work, their conditions of work, or their wages or the question of women's franchise, Clara Zetkin was deeply involved in struggles at multiple levels both for raising these issues and seeking their resolution. Her basic understanding of the women's question emerges clearly from her views on these issues, the agendas that she strongly advocated and firmly stood by and the struggles she engaged in and organised for their realisation. Through these she also enables us to have a deeper insight into those questions as well as the period itself.

Born as Clara Eissner in a small weaver's village in Saxony in 1857, her interest in the women's question was part of her social inheritance. Her mother Josephine Vitale Eissner, was one of the earliest activists in the women's movement in Germany. Imbued with the ideals of the French Revolution and believing in the complete economic equality for women, she kindled in her daughter Clara a deep interest in the cause of women's rights. This interest was further reinforced by August Schmidt and Louis Otto Peters two leaders of the German women's rights movement, during her secondary schooling at the Steyber Institute in Leipzig. Under Schmidt's direction Clara Eissner received the finest secondary schooling then available to women in Germany, the country where women had practically no social, political and economic rights.

During the course of her stay in Leipzig while pursuing her studies, she came in contact with a circle of revolutionary socialist students and émigrés from Russian Poland. It was her younger brother and a Russian school mate who first introduced her to socialist ideas. Her exposure to socialist ideas and her involvement with the revolutionary socialist students and émigrés was to deeply influence the course of her intellectual development, political activity and her personal life.

She not only read and discussed Marx, but also started moving among workers with Ossip Zetkin who later became her life partner and whose name she adopted and had two children by him. However, they did not get married formally. This arrangement was meant to circumvent the discriminatory marriage laws whereby a German woman marrying a foreigner lost her German citizenship.

By 1878, the year of her graduation, Clara Eissner had become closely associated with the German Social Democratic Party (SPD), although as a woman she could not become a member of any political party under the prevalent laws in Germany. A year later the Anti-Socialist Law under Bismarck was to outlaw the SPD, but Clara continued to participate in the party's illegal activities. However, in 1881 when her partner Ossip Zetkin was expelled from Germany as an 'undesirable alien', she was forced to take the path of political emigration and she then adopted Zetkin's name and became Clara Zetkin. During this period she participated in the socialist movements of France, Austria and Italy. During her sojourn in Switzerland she edited the illegal newspaper *Der Sozial Demokrat* and helped to organise its distribution in Germany. The Zetkins subsequently shifted to Paris, had two children and unable to secure a steady job, they lived on the verge of poverty. Their miserable living conditions took a toll of the couple's health, Clara stayed with her mother for a few months for recuperation despite the fact that the mother had severed ties with Clara after her involvement in revolutionary socialist politics. After her recovery she joined her partner in Paris and nursed him for several years. Ossip Zetkin died in 1889 of spinal tuberculosis after having been confined to bed for three years. During their stay in Paris Clara Zetkin drew close to Laura Lafargue, the daughter of

Karl Marx, as also to the prominent leaders of the French socialist movement such as Paul Lafargue and Jules Guesde.

The second half of the 1880s proved crucial for Clara Zetkin's political development to be on her own. Her responsibility of being the sole bread-winner of the family with two small children, and Ossip Zetkin's political responsibilities devolving upon her due to his illness, circumstances obliged her, as she wrote in her letter to Karl Kautsky in March 1888, 'to make [her] way in the world like a man'. In the process she overcame her lack of confidence, shyness before crowds and a reluctance to make decisions on her own', 'psychological handicaps common to her sex'. Recovering from her personal loss, maturing to be politically on her own, Clara Zetkin emerged on the international scene in July 1889.

The first piece entitled 'For the Liberation of Women' included in this volume is a speech delivered by Clara Zetkin at the International Workers' Congress in Paris in July 1889, the centennial year of the French Revolution. This was the founding congress of the Second International of which Clara Zetkin herself was an organiser. She was one of the eight women among the four hundred delegates elected to the Congress. Apparently she was chosen to deliver the first policy statement of the European working class on the women's question in recognition of her political activities and of the fact that she had been writing on the issue of women's emancipation for the socialist press. Her speech 'For the Liberation of Women' contains the essence of Clara Eissner Zetkin's understanding of the women's question both with regard to the underlying causes of women's situation in society as also the way forward for their emancipation.

In her speech Clara Zetkin chose to 'illuminate the general principles of women's work' and not about the situation of female workers for 'their situation was no different from that of male workers'. She had taken up the theme of the general principles of the women's work since that question was 'surrounded by a great deal of confusion' and hence it was 'incumbent upon this workers' Congress to address itself clearly to this topic by probing the underlying principles'. The 'confusion' referred to the then prevalent notion that women's work should be abolished, the notion which was present in the Socialist camp too. Clara Zetkin was here addressing the question of the influx of the female labour force in industry, its causes, consequences and its socio-political implications, perceived or real. The entry of women into the industrial workforce tended to lower the wages of male workers and hence the idea of legislation abolishing women's work was gaining ground among male workers including socialist-led trade unions. Clara Zetkin was addressing this ugly reality, this 'erroneous concept' that women were responsible for depressing male wages.

Clara Zetkin argued, cogently and forcefully, that women were not responsible for the lowering of male wages and that it was the capitalist system which was responsible for it. Her argument was that women were compelled by force of historical developments to come out of their homes to work because their house-hold production – they were in the earlier times producing almost all items of family consumption/use – was no longer economically viable in the machine age of production. Their husbands' income was not enough for the survival of their families as machine production had killed their household production. Women came out to work to supplement their husbands' income. The machines also created the basis of women's activity in society by making it possible for women to work in factories since physical power was no longer essential for working in industry. Their work should have reduced the working hours of their men and created more social wealth, but their joining the industrial work force had exactly the opposite impact of increasing the working hours of the male labour force without any addition to the social wealth either. Clara Zetkin was unequivocal in her view that it was capitalism and not the female industrial labour that was responsible for the longer hours and the lowering of male workers' wages. She argued that the capitalists increasingly employed female labour because it was particularly attractive to them 'not merely for its lower price', but also because of 'the greater submissiveness of women'. As female labour was used to lower male wages, child labour was used to lower female wages. Lower wages and longer working hours were instruments of increasing the capitalists' profit and there was no increase in social wealth since the profits were pocketed individually by the capitalists.

Fully aware of the facts that women workers' wages were abysmally low and their working conditions abominable, Clara Zetkin still regarded their coming out of their homes to work as an essential step towards their emancipation. Knowing that 'the slave of the husband' had become 'the slave of the employer' she still regarded women's work outside of her home as 'a transformative step' for women because through this they acquired their economic independence from men and thereby they 'no longer remained mere economic appendices of men'. From here Clara Zetkin went on to defend the women's right to work; she underlined the fact that since the 'quintessential pre-requisite for their economic independence is work', women 'with all their might' must protest against the move to outlaw women's work by legislation and protest she did and there was a tremendous response to her speech. However, she had no misgivings that the economic independence under capitalism had no potential of emancipation of the working class women. She categorically asserted that 'the emancipation of women as well as of human kind will only occur within the framework of the emancipation of labour from capital'. For the first time the demand for 'an equal pay for equal work' appeared in the history of the working class.

From the women's right to work the next logical step was their organisation in trade unions. After her partner's death Clara Zetkin returned, in 1890, to Germany where Bismarck's Exceptional Law Against the Socialists had been repealed. Back in Germany, Clara Zetkin worked tirelessly to mobilise and educate women workers to join the socialist trade unions. Herself a member of the Stuttgart Book Binders' Union and particularly active in the Tailors' and Seamstresses Union, she was also involved in the activities of the Brush Makers' Union, the Garment Workers' Union, the Glovemakers' Union, and a few other South German Unions. Zetkin raised and shaped the working class women's movement according to her understanding of the women's question. She did all this not because of any directive of the party but despite the party. It is remarkable that despite her long, rich and varied political experience of working, speaking, mobilising, framing policy statements at multiple levels, 'not even the active support of the party's leader August Bebel and its chief theoretician Karl Kautsky could secure for Clara Zetkin any work within the party more creative than soliciting advertisements for the party press'. Zetkin was here face to face with entrenched male prejudices in the German Social Democratic Party which otherwise theoretically supported women's emancipation. Indeed, she found male prejudices almost in all spheres of activity of the party.

The second piece entitled 'Women's Work and the Organisation of Trade Unions' included in the volume is taken from the November 1893 issue of the *Die Gleichheit*. Starting with the 'indubitable fact that in all capitalist countries women's work in industry plays an ever larger role', Clara Zetkin supports her view with facts and figures culled from the factory inspectors' reports where factories were protected by law and supplemented this information from other sources for factories and work outside the purview of legal protection. From these statistics she surmised that 'the number of women workers had increased, in both relative and absolute terms' and concurrently the number of male workers had decreased, particularly during the recession period that Germany was facing. She added that the numbers given by her did not include 'the myriad of women' working in factories not protected by law. Referring to 'the repeatedly pointed out reasons' for this increase of female industrial labour – the cheapness of the female labour and the improvement of the mechanical means and methods which had rendered muscle power and acquired skills superfluous – Clara Zetkin, using the statistics taken from the records of the Leipzig Chamber of Commerce, shows that the wages of the female workers were half and invariably less than half the wages of their male counterparts. She underlined the fact that women workers were receiving starvation wages, and 'their living conditions correspond to their miserable wages'. The extent of women's industrial labour, their low wages and the wage-depressing impact of female work 'all speak out clearly for the necessity and the significance of organising working women into trade unions.' It was imperative for the success of any movement advocating better wages and shorter working hours etc. that women be brought into the fold of the trade union movement. Otherwise, non-organised women could be easily used by the employers against any trade union movement for better wages, shorter working hours and better working conditions. Clara Zetkin noted that one of the reasons for such low wages for women workers was the fact that they were practically unorganised. The women 'lack the courage, the feeling of power, the spirit of resistance and the ability to resist which is produced by the strength of an organisation in which the individual fights for everybody and everybody fights for the individual'. Hence, the sooner they were organised, the better it would be for both male and female workers. The more women workers were drawn into struggles for better wages, their wages would rise and they would cease to be unfair competitors for male labour. Clara Zetkin clarified that she was aware of the earlier efforts made by the trade unions in this regard, but very little had been accomplished and 'incredibly much remains to be done'. Out of many factors that she enumerated which kept women workers away from the trade unions Clara Zetkin assigned primacy to their 'lack of time' as the main impediment in the way of women's participation in any organisational activity. She argued that time was a major constraint in keeping them back from participating in any organisational activity. This constraint was due to the fact that 'women were forced to bear a double workload'. They were 'house as well as factory slaves'.

Clara Zetkin was of the view that the work done so far to unionise women workers did not reflect 'the urgency and importance of the task'. The majority of the trade unionists were averse to supporting the activity of those who were attempting to unionise women workers. In fact, they mocked at their attempts. Clara Zetkin underlined the need of every single member of the unions to mobilise women workers in factories and workshops. In order to actively mobilise women workers, 'male workers must stop viewing the female worker primarily as a woman to be courted if she is young, beautiful, pleasant and cheerful (or not) and they must stop molesting them with crude and fresh sexual advances'. They must learn to treat them as fellow workers 'as working class comrades fighting class slavery and as equal and indispensable co-fighters in the class struggles'. She had no misgivings that a change in male workers' attitude was a pre-requisite for their activity and ability to mobilise women workers.

Clara Zetkin advocated broadening of the base of the labour movement by enrolling 'broad, amorphous masses', instead of concentrating only on the party cadre and their sympathisers. She regarded the trade unions as the instrument of 'enlightenment, disciplining and education [of all workers] for the class struggle'. She was absolutely clear that in view of the increasing female labour and its subsequent consequences, 'the labour movement will surely commit suicide if, in its efforts to enroll the broad masses of the proletariat, it does not pay the same amount of attention to female workers as it does to male ones'. Through this analysis Clara Zetkin was addressing her own party and the male leadership of the unions of the need and urgency of bringing women workers within the fold of labour movement. Notwithstanding their 'double workload', female workers were getting increasingly organised through Clara Zetkin's constant and relentless efforts. Her efforts were not confined to merely mobilising the women workers, she simultaneously and constantly questioned the position, views and prejudices of her own party leadership and the male workers. In the process, she not only politicised, mobilised, organised women workers and sensitised the male workers to the need of unionising women workers, but also critically evaluated the SPD's position on the issue, and addressed herself to the male prejudices both of the leadership and the ordinary male workers within the fold of the labour movement.

Advocating the women's right to work, herself organising and politicising women workers within the framework of scientific socialism, exhorting the party and the male leadership of the unions to mobilise women workers in their factories and workshops, understanding and pointing out the double burden of women workers and simultaneously emphasising the need to transform male worker's perception of and attitude towards women workers'. Clara Zetkin was deeply involved in the issues confronting the working class women of her times. She also supported the movement for women's suffrage, but strongly opposed any move to restrict the franchise by imposing any qualifying clauses. It was her resolution for universal suffrage that was adopted at the first International Socialist Women's Conference at Stuttgart in 1907 by a vote of 47 to 11. In consonance with the general tenor of her work on the women's question, the universal suffrage demand was not put forward as an exclusively women's demand. Neither was it taken up as an issue on which women alone were to agitate. It was part of the resolution that the socialist parties of all countries were to fight for it both by agitation and by parliamentary means; the demand for universal suffrage was to be made both for women and men. At this International Socialist Women's Congress, an International Women's Bureau was established and while Clara Zetkin was elected its Secretary, *Die Gleichheit* was adopted as the official organ of the socialist women associated with the Second International. Her election as the Secretary formalised her longstanding position as the leader of the international socialist women.

Despite her deep involvement in the women's question, Clara Zetkin was very wary of the feminist movements of her time. She supported their demand for women's franchise, but without any property qualifications whatsoever. Clara Zetkin consistently worked towards protecting the working class women's movement under socialist leadership from being influenced or co-opted by feminism. This is manifest from her views on 'The Women's Rights Petition' in the volume. She stubbornly fought her own party through the pages of the party newspaper *Vorwarts* and the women's paper *Die Gleichheit* over the question of the tacit approval by the party of the action of a few socialist women having collaboration with several womens' rights organisations over the Women's Rights Petition addressed to the Kaiser, about Women's Right to form associations. The petition 'humbly seeks from the monarch' for the grant of this right to women.

Clara Zetkin was furious over this supplication. It is clear from the thrust of her argument that she regarded this petition as demeaning of the proletarian women's struggles over years. She reminded the party leadership that proletarian women over years had been constantly and actively involved in forming associations and coalitions and they had been bravely and courageously fighting and putting up with the state oppression and state persecution. She describes how 'one dissolution of a proletarian women's organisation follows another, prohibition after prohibition of women's assemblies takes place, the expulsion of women for violating the law for the Formation of Associations inundates the courts'. She strongly asserts that their 'bitter poverty' and 'double-burden' of workload notwithstanding, the proletarian women had been 'constantly making sacrifices of their material goods and time' to form their associations and then to support their organisations. She reminds her party that the humbly made petition was unlikely to make any dent if 'the powerful and penetrating message' of the proletarian women's struggles had been lost on the Reichstag and the government. She further argued that the petition made no cogent plea for advocating the women's right to form associations at this time. Further, the procedure and the form of the petition lack democratic credentials; the petition is addressed to the Kaiser and does not ask the Reichstag or any party to submit a bill dealing with the reform. She adds with sarcasm that 'one of the few rights and prerogatives which parliament possesses in this splendid German Empire is the right to submit bills and to make demands in the name of the people instead of begging from the government'. The petition thus 'avoids the only correct way that leads to the Reichstag'. Nor did the originators of the petition deem it essential to consult the class-conscious proletarian women's representatives before drafting the petition. The essence of Clara Zetkin's fight in her own party over the issue of signing a petition originating from bourgeois women's organisations concerning a right which the proletarian women have been using and violating for several years through their struggles, comes out vividly from her comments towards the end of the article. She writes : 'The actual draft of the petition as well as the behaviour of its authors is characteristic of the concepts of bourgeois women and their relationship to the world of proletarian women. One is enough of a humanitarian under certain circumstances to do something for the poorer sisters, one is clever enough under all circumstances to accept their manual labour, but to co-operate with them on an equal basis, no Sir, that is something totally different'. Clara Zetkin zealously guarded the working class women's movement under the leadership of socialist women from being penetrated by bourgeois feminism.

Clara Zetkin was very clear in her understanding that the women's movement was not a homogenous movement. She placed the women's question and the feminist movements within the larger framework of historical developments and social relations and inequalities of a given system. She placed the women's question within the class frame-work of society. Her speech at the Party Congress of the Social Democratic Party of Germany at Gotha on 16th October 1896 'Only in Conjunction with the Proletarian Woman will Socialism be Victorious' and her article 'What the Women Owe to Karl Marx' in *Die Gleichheit* of 25th March, 1903 explicitly and unambiguously show what is implicit in her work and struggles, that Clara Zetkin placed the women's question of her times within the framework of the political economy of capitalism. Her article 'What the Women Owe to Karl Marx' still retains its full relevance more than a hundred years after it was written.

Clara Zetkin introduced the subject by a simple statement that 'to be sure, Marx never dealt with the women's question 'per se' or 'as such'.' Not having dealt with the question per se, how and what Marx contributed to the women's question is what Clara Zetkin discussed in this article. She is absolutely categorical about Marx's contribution; he 'created the most irreplaceable and important weapons for the women's fight to obtain all of their rights'. These weapons were the theoretical framework provided by historical materialism and the knowledge that it was the historic task of the working class to demolish capitalism. She was aware that 'Marx's materialist concept of history has not supplied us with ready-made formulas concerning the women's question', yet 'it has done something much more important. It has given us the correct, unerring method to explore and comprehend that question'. Clara Zetkin emphasised that it was only the materialist concept of history 'which enabled us to understand the women's question' within the broader framework of historical developments and 'the universally applicable social relationships and their historical necessity and justification'. Having studied *Das Kapital*, she was brilliantly applying the dynamics of the working of capitalism to the problems and issues confronting the female proletariat. She used the law of wages to explain and oppose the move, even within the socialist camp and the trade unions, to outlaw women's work. She applied and extended the same logic to the issue of women and the trade unions. Only through the materialist concept of history 'did we perceive forces and the aims pursued by them', so wrote Clara Zetkin, as also 'the conditions which are 'essential to a solution of these problems'. Referring to Engel's 'illuminating study, *The Origins of the Family, Private Property and the State*, Clara Zetkin mentioned that the theories and viewpoints developed in this book are 'derived in good measure from Marx's unpublished work.'

The class framework provided by historical materialism enabled Clara Zetkin to discern, understand and explicate the class dimensions of the women's question. Indeed, the very question itself she placed within the context of larger historical developments whereby the earlier social relations gradually came to be dissolved by capitalist relations of production which bought in its wake new classes, structures, demands and aspirations. Taking her argument back to the period of the Renaissance, 'the period which saw the awakening of modern individuality', which developed in 'most diverse ways', saw the flowering of women's talent in 'social, artistic and intellectual life'. The women's question, 'if it can be so called at that time', wrote Clara Zetkin, was solved by convents, charitable institutions and religious orders. She explained that the women's question, as it is understood in modern times, came with the undermining of domestic production with the coming of the machine age when millions of women came out of their homes seeking livelihood and also new meaning and mental satisfaction in their lives. In her characteristically simple and lucid way Clara Zetkin explains that the moment they came out of their homes 'they became aware of the fact that their social illegality stood in opposition to their most basic interests. It was from this moment on that there existed the modern women's question'. She points out that the women's question exists within those classes who are themselves the products of the capitalist mode of production. She supports her contention by the fact that there is 'no women's question in peasant circles that possess a natural economy' although that natural economy had been severely curtailed. But there certainly exists a women's question within those classes of society 'who are the very children of the modern mode of production'.

With the transformation of society under capitalism there emerged, step by step, 'a growing mass of women who, in a planned and organised way, strove for 'emancipation of their sex from the legal and social domination of men' and for 'the social and human equality between the two sexes'. But the sum and substance of equality is different for different classes. 'There is no such thing as a "women's movement" in and of itself'. Delineating on how the question manifests itself in different forms in different classes, Clara Zetkin points out the issues before each class. The woman of the 'Upper Ten Thousand', thanks to her property, may develop her individuality and live as she pleases. She is, however, still legally subjugated for the family law still maintains 'And he shall be your Master'. These women may develop their individuality, 'but money decides the matrimony. Its motto is : what capital joins sentimental morality must not part.' The family life develops accordingly; the woman 'may devolve her duties as spouse, mother and housewife' upon paid servants – for and to them all is available with money. For the women of this class, if they seek a meaningful life with any serious purpose in life, their control over their property is a pre-requisite for it. Therefore they must, first of all raise the demand to dispose of their property in an independent and free manner. As for the women's question in the circle of the petit-bourgeoisie, the middle class and the bourgeois, it is not the property 'which dissolves the family, but the concomitant symptoms of capitalist production'. The 'formerly respected and profitable societal positions of the members of the professional class are getting eroded due to over production of "mental workers".' This is turn was affecting the marriages of this group with simultaneous worsening of their material position and heightened individual expectations from life. The age limit of setting up the family was increasingly getting higher and higher and the number of unmarried women was continuously on the increase. The women of this strata were getting pushed out in society for livelihood. They had to achieve their economic equality by demanding access to equal professional training and job opportunities for both sexes.

This would entail 'untrammeled competition' between men and women to the demands of professional equality and job opportunities. Clara Zetkin had no misgivings that it was 'pure and simple, the fear of competition. All other reasons given against the mental work of women such as the smaller brain of women or their allegedly natural avocation to be a mother are only pretexts'. Hence the women of this class got pushed towards demanding their political right. However, the women of this class were not solely motivated by their economic consideration; the bourgeois woman 'not only demands her own bread', but also 'seeks higher spiritual nourishment' to develop her personality. Clara Zetkin points out that it is among these women that 'we find these tragic, yet psychologically interesting Nora figures, who are tired of living like dolls in doll-houses'; they were seeking intellectual and cultural development. She concludes that their movement for their, economic, intellectual and political rights was justified for their emancipation.

The women's question of the proletarian woman is rooted in the need of capitalism to exploit and to incessantly search for a cheap labour force. The proletarian woman, came out of her home to supplement her husband's income, but capitalism made her into an 'unfair competitor' of the proletarian male. She became an equal of the man as a worker, but, 'verily the price was very high and for the moment, they have gained very little'. From being the slave of her husband she became the slave of her employer. Despite economic independence, the proletarian woman has had no opportunity to develop her individuality. For the work she does as a wife and a mother 'there remain only the breadcrumbs which the capitalist production drops from the table'. It was apparent that the struggle of the proletarian woman cannot be similar to the struggle of the bourgeois women against the men of their class. Undoubtedly she agrees with and supports the demands of the bourgeois women's movement, but she supports those demands not to fight against proletarian men, but to fight along with the male proletariat for their ultimate emancipation by demolishing capital.

Obtaining political equality by women was unlikely to substantially change the situation for the working class women, but the process of obtaining political equality would lead to their politicisation. For their right to organise themselves they had been 'waging war against police power and juridical stratagem', which only served 'her class consciousness'. It was the 'Anti-Socialist Law which for the first time taught the proletarian woman the meaning of the concepts of 'class justice, class state and class rule'. 'It was this law', so writes Clara Zetkin, 'which taught women the need to learn about the forces which so brutally intervened in their family lives'. This enabled them to establish linkages between the women's question and the larger socio-political forces. The theoretical exposition of such linkages had for the first time been forcefully established by August Bebel's book *Women and Socialism*. Notwithstanding its limitations, of which she was fully aware, Bebel's book 'within the context of its times in which it was written' was 'more than a book' it was an event – a great deed'. For the first time, the book pointed out 'the connection between the women's question and historical development'. For the first time 'there sounded from this book the appeal : we will only conquer the future if we persuade the women to become our co-fighter'. In recognising this, Clara Zetkin clarified that she was 'not speaking as a woman but as a party comrade'.

Clear that the proletarian woman's emancipation could not come without the abolition of capital, Clara Zetkin applied this understanding to her political practice. In putting forward before the party congress concrete suggestions for mobilising women workers, her focus was on taking up the current issues in a manner that would mobilise female proletarians for struggle towards socialism. She categorically maintained that 'Our guiding thought must be: we must not conduct special women's propaganda, but Socialist agitation among women.. Our task must be to incorporate modern proletarian woman in our class battle'. The main task was 'to awaken the women's class consciousness and to incorporate them into the class struggle'. It was this underlying principle which had informed her perspective while leading the women's agitation on the right to organise themselves into unions / associations and in the agitation against the Anti-Socialist Law. With this focus, she underlined the need of unionising women workers as there were at least 700,000 of them in large industrial enterprises. Achievement of a legally fixed work day and higher wages were to be the main demands as well as the pre-requisites for their unionisation. She was fully aware that laws of individual states on unionisation and the right to assembly rendered unionisation among women almost an impossibility. In such circumstances it was not possible for proletarian women to organise themselves together with men; they must struggle to gain their 'right to organise.'

Clara Zetkin grasped the immensity of the task of organising women workers, as also its potential for their emancipation through the liberation of the proletariat from the slavery of capital. This liberation was predicated on a united struggle of the working class without distinction of sex. She repeatedly underlined that 'The incorporation of the great masses of proletarian women in the struggle of the proletariat is one of the pre-requisites for the victory of the socialist idea and for construction of a socialist society'. This fundamental theoretical understanding constantly shaped Clara Zetkin's own political work among women workers whom she politicised and organised for their struggle for their unionisation and for their rights, both political and economic, within the class framework of capitalism and the historic role of the working class in destroying it. In the process, she educated and enrolled them for the cause of socialism.

Linking the struggle of the working class women of her times to raising the level of their class-consciousness, Clara Zetkin aimed at bringing them into the fold of the revolutionary socialist movement. The journal *Die Gleichheit* (Equality) was directed especially to the 'progressive avant-garde' of the working class, whether they were slaves to capital with their hands or with their brains. It was not a journal for the mass of women workers. Focusing on the political, economic and social issues of her times, relating to women workers, Clara Zetkin always tried to bring out the fundamentals of the question under discussion. Raising the women's questions within the framework of capitalism, Clara Zetkin always brought out the class implications of the issue and addressed herself simultaneously to the politically conscious male workers and her own party comrades. This pattern runs through all her articles from *Die Gleichheit* included in this volume dealing with women's political rights, women's work, their wages, their working conditions and the need of organising them in trade unions. The journal covered conditions of work in those branches of industry where women pre-dominated, giving details of factory legislation which could be utilised to the benefit of working women; it covered the activities of the women workers in other countries too. The paper urged its readers to bring up their children in such a manner that girls break out of their traditional gender roles and boys also participate in housework. But in this matter Clara Zetkin was in a tiny minority in the party.

The circulation of the paper in its early years was limited, rising from 2000 to 1891 to 11,000 in 1903-04. Only after 1904 when *Die Gleichheit* came to be distributed free to women members of the SPD and to the wives of the party members did its circulation jump from 75,000 in1907 to 125,000 in 1914. From 1905 onwards the party began to pressurise Clara Zetkin to initiate a series of changes in the content and form of the paper incorporating material for ordinary housewives etc. She started bringing out a supplement at regular intervals so as not to compromise the content of the paper; through these supplements the reading materials on revolutionary writers and writers of fiction reached the working class. With reformism becoming dominant in the SPD, Clara Zetkin's editorial control got increasingly weakened. It is quite remarkable that the gaining of the political right by women in Germany of joining political organisations coincided with the blunting of the militant edge of the women's movement in the party. Clara Zetkin's editorial control weakened and within two years *Die Gleichheit* underwent a metamorphosis; it was carrying dress designing, recipes and articles on fashion and cooking.

Indeed, the right to join political organisations and the changed character of the women's movement in the SPD seem to be integrally linked. The prevalence of the law disallowing women from joining political organisations influenced the content and course of the women's movement within the party; of necessity women had to organise themselves separately from the men in the party. The separate organisation of women under Clara Zetkin's leadership kept it insulated from male interference. As one of its most prominent leaders, Clara Zetkin could shape the movement according to her own understanding and ideas. It has already been discussed above that she placed and analysed the women's question within the theoretical framework provided by historical materialism. From this stemmed her understanding that it was impossible for the proletarian women to be emancipated within the framework of capitalism; her emancipation could come only as a consequence of overthrowing wage slavery jointly with the male proletariat. Hence Clara Zetkin aimed at preparing working class women for their historic role of overthrowing capitalism. This inevitably meant a militant revolutionary women's movement. It was owing primarily to the nature of Clara Zetkin politics and the bi-weekly jounal that she edited from 1892 to 1917 that by 1914 the SPD had a female membership of 175,000, that is, 16% of its total membership. Hence, the force of negative historical circumstances, of the absence of political rights acted positively to free women from the control and prejudices of their male comrades as also the reformism of the party, and build a women's movement which became a training ground for them to grow and mature politically, learning to think for themselves and expressing their own thought, 'which had been lost through centuries of dependence upon men and exclusion from public life.'

Clara Zetkin played a leading role in the international women's movement. On her initiative the first international women's conference, in fact, a Socialist Women's International, was organised in 1907 in conjunction with the Stuttgart Congress of the Second International at which 59 women from 15 countries participated. Already she had been instrumental in the establishment of bi-annual women's conferences in the German Party. She also played an important role as one of the chief advocates both within German Social Democracy and within the Second International of establishing a separate Women's Bureau run by women and designed to act as an interim centre for women's activities between conferences. The first international women's conference, in effect a Socialist Women's International, got organised at Clara Zetkin's initiative under the aegis of the Second International at which 59 women from fifteen countries participated. Differences emerged in the conference on the attitude to be adopted towards universal suffrage and the issue of feminism. The delegations from France, Austria, Belgium and Britain argued that it was more practical to fight for a limited suffrage restricted by property and income qualifications than to demand universal suffrage. The British and French delegations further criticised the 'sectarian attitude' of Clara Zetkin and her supporters in relation to the feminist movement. Obviously, these delegations were ready to sacrifice working class women's rights in order to support feminist movements in their countries. The consistent Marxist view of Clara Zetkin supported by Alexandra Kollontai and others won the day in part due to the preponderant dominance of the German delegation. The resolution noted that 'socialist parties of all countries have a duty to struggle energetically for the introduction of universal suffrage for women' and that the 'socialist women must not ally themselves with the bourgeois feminists, but lead the battle side by side with the socialist men'. Three years later the second international conference held at Copenhagen in 1910 reiterated the demand for universal suffrage and adopted the resolution prepared by Clara Zetkin to establish 8th March as International Women's Day. In this way the demonstration of American socialist women in New York on 8th March 1908 in opposition to the local bourgeois suffrage movement became an annual world-wide event of the socialist movement. In fact, it gradually became the International Women's Day all over the world, the centenary of which has been celebrated only last year. As early as March 1911 a million women and men in Germany, Austria, Switzerland and Denmark participated in mass activities on the International Women's Day.

It is ironical that the women's movement that Clara Zetkin built up with the aim of the final emancipation both of women and men of the working class suffered a serious setback when women got the right to join political organisations and parties. Indeed the new situation brought to the fore the issue whether there was any longer the need to have a separate women's organisations within the party. In this battle Clara Zetkin lost to the male dominated party with its increasingly reformist agenda and practice. The issue has been discussed at length by Karen Honeycutt in her easily available article given in the select bibliography at the end of this introductory note. Clara Zetkin had always supported women's separate organisations so that they would be able to develop themselves politically far more freely and independently than if they were working under the domination of male cadres of the party. Clara Zetkin knew from her personal experience that despite her education and learning it took her time to overcome her social limitations as a woman and to develop herself independently in the political arena; far greater social limitations stood in the way of working class women than Clara Zetkin had ever experienced. She strongly held the view that separate women's organisations and activity would lead not only to their political development, but also through the maximum release of individual and group potential, it would benefit the socialist movement. Her standpoint on the issue led her to advocate the elections of female delegates to party and international congresses in separate women's meetings so long as legal restrictions or male prejudice prevented the elections of women at sexually integrated meetings. Clara Zetkin maintained a constant vigil against discriminatory treatment of women within the socialist camp. She constantly defended with the full weight of her influence and prestige socialist women who got into difficulty with socialist men over the expression of their prejudices.

It was this understanding of Clara Zetkin's that led to the establishment of the bi-annual women's conferences both in the party and the Second International; she was also instrumental in the establishment of a separate Women's Bureau run by women and designed to act as an interim centre for women's activities between the conferences. With the same purpose she was instrumental in the establishment of the International Women's Day. Clara Zetkin's stubborn refusal to compromise on issues affecting working class women stands out on every issue on which she had differences of opinion with the party or with socialist women of other parties. She criticised the women Austrian socialists for refusing to propagate the cause of women's suffrage out of the fear that universal male suffrage might be jeopardised by association with the more controversial demand for women's suffrage, 'Such opportunism and self-abdication', in the opinion of Clara Zetkin, 'made too blatant a concession to reformist thinking and to prevailing attitudes towards the "second", sex'. Although criticised for her 'unsisterly' behaviour towards the Austrian women, Clara Zetkin firmly stood by her position and ultimately won a majority for her resolution in 1907.

In 1908 when the women were given the legal right to organise politically with men, the Executive of the SPD responded to the new situation by advocating the dissolution of all separate women's organisations within its ranks. Although the Women's Bureau was permitted to function for several more years, it lost its independence to function. Agitational work among women could be carried out only with the concurrence and agreement of the male-dominated Party Executive.

To reassure the socialist women that their interests were nevertheless being safeguarded, it was decided to have one woman on the Party Executive although till 1912 she was without voting rights. Significantly, they chose for this post not the acknowledged leader of the German and international socialist women, Clara Zetkin, but Louise Ziets who had been working with Clara Zetkin but lacked her clarity and stubbornness to fight on the issues pertaining to working class women. Clara Zetkin continued to fight for separate women's groups within the party, but increasingly she was marginalised organisationally and the activities of the women in the party came under the total control of the party which for a long period had been increasingly acquiring a reformist character. Soon Clara Zetkin's independence as editor of *Die Gleichheit* was challenged and the bi-annual women's conference was postponed by one year. This postponement proved a mere prelude to its abolition; and in 1912 the Women's Bureau was also dissolved. Over a few years most women active in the party were excluded from positions of actual power and relegated to charity and welfare work of the kind conventionally considered appropriate to the female sex. The percentage of women in positions of genuine responsibility in the party structures relative to their percentage in the party as also the percentage among the delegates to party congress seriously declined. The Party Executive closed down *Die Gleichheit* (from which Clara Zetkin had already been expelled as editor in 1917 because of her anti-war activity) and provided in its place a fashion and family magazine edited by a man. The militant activism with a revolutionary perspective of the socialist women workers got devoured by the reformism of social democracy.

As one of the leading figures amongst the left wing of the German Social Democratic party Clara Zetkin had always carried out a consistent struggle against the revisionism of the epoch. As long back as 1894 she had spoken out against the opportunist draft agrarian programme advanced by David and Vollmar at the Frankfurt congress of the Social Democratic Party. Clara Zetkin jointly with Rosa Luxemburg – with whom she was tied by strong ties of friendship – led the struggle against Bernstein's attempt to divest Marxism of its revolutionary essence in order to induce the working class to renounce the fight for socialist revolution. In conjunction with left socialists such as Karl Leibknecht, Clara Zetkin actively campaigned against militarism, imperialism and colonialism. In 1912 at the Basle Congress of the Second

International she called upon the international workers movement to actively struggle against the threat of imperialist war. With the onset of the war, Clara Zetkin strongly condemned the 'chauvinist and imperialist' policies of the Social Democratic Party. When in opposition to the resolutions to the Second International at Basle for mass action against imperialist war, the German Social Democratic Party voted for military credits to the Kaiser's government in the Reichstag in August 1914, Clara Zetkin in an article in *Die Gleichheit* in August itself argued that the war was only in the interests of the Junker big landlords and big capital, she made an oblique call to revolutionary struggle when writing 'What must be done? There is a single moment in the life of the people when they can wish all if only everyone is set. Such a moment is here. Working women be prepared.' Her article 'To the Socialist Women of all Countries' (*Die Gleichheit*, Stuttgart, November 7, 1914, but blacked out by the censors) she urged : 'We women socialists must call upon the women of all countries to oppose the prolongation of this insane genocide. From a million voices our irrestible cry must arise. Enough of killing, enough destruction. No total war until our people bleed to death! Peace! Permanent peace...It is true that we women have only limited, political rights in practically all countries, but we are not without any social power. Let us make use of every tiny bit of this power... When the men kill, it is up to us women to fight for the preservation of life. When the men are silent, it is our duty to raise our voices on behalf of our ideals.

'Female comrades, sisters! Fulfill the promise which your representative at the memorable Peace Congress of the Socialist International at Basel made : 'It is for this reason that even during a war we will be among those advancing, attacking units that fight against war'.

In the brief period between the beginning of the war and the removal by the Social Democratic Party leadership of

Clara Zetkin from the editorial board of *Die Gleichheit* the journal became the key organ opposed to war. Rosa Luxemberg and Clara Zetkin helped to organise the International Women's Socialist Conference in Berne, Switzerland, against war. For her pains Clara Zetkin was imprisoned for 'attempted treason' by the Kaiser's government and removed from the editorship of *Die Gleichheit* by the socialist party. After her release Clara Zetkin returned to Leipzig where she edited the women's supplement of the *Leipziger Volkszeitung*. The bulk of the women socialists of the Social Democratic Party effected a rapprochement with the feminist movement in support of the war just, as the party itself established a 'civil truce' with the German government during the course of the war. With Rosa Luxemburg, Karl Leibknecht, Frank Mehring and others Clara Zetkin became a founder-member of the International Spartacus League. After the war, together with the revolutionary Marxists, she joined the Independent Social Democratic Party and, finally, joined the Communist Party of Germany and its Central Committee.

In common with the left-wing of the Social Democratic Party Clara Zetkin enthusiastically welcomed the October Revolution and helped to set up a solidarity movement with the new workers' government. It is a tribute to her enormous contribution to the women's question and the correctness of her understanding that Lenin in a one to one personal meeting in the autumn of 1920, with Clara Zetkin discussed the women's question with her. He was absolutely categorical about the importance of work among women; it was a historical necessity. 'We cannot exercise the dictatorship of the proletariat without having millions of women on our side. Nor can we engage in communist construction without them. We must study and search in order to find this way.' Hence, it was perfectly legitimate to put forward demands for the benefit of women. On the question of whether women needed to be organised separately, Lenin was clear that no separate organisations of communist women were needed, but the party must have organs and working groups for mobilisation of women of different strata. He expressed the opinion that the women's question must be seen as part of the social, working class question bound firmly with the proletarian class struggle and the revolution. This was precisely the understanding that had shaped Clara Zetkin's own work among proletarian women. Lenin wanted a clear understanding of the women's question to evolve through an international congress around which the communist women's movement a mass movement must be built. Lenin wanted Clara Zetkin to take charge of the issue of working out the leading theses on communist work among women.

Clara Zetkin's thesis that real emancipation of working class women could only come through a socialist revolution was validated by the work of the Soviet state on the principle of full equality for women, not merely legal equality, but their real liberation and emancipation, right from the very beginning of the seizure of power by the Bolsheviks. The new state under the dictatorship of the proletariat heralded an era of tremendous social reconstruction on the principle of the abolition of exploitation of man by man. Organising the society around the principle of abolishing exploitation of man by man, the Soviet state addressed itself to all forms of economic, social and political inequality, including the social inequality between man and woman that exists in every society divided in classes. The Soviet state addressed itself to all aspects of women's life and emancipation so as to give not merely legal equality to realise their liberation but to help them by creating enabling social structures.

The approach of the Soviet state towards the women's question emerges absolutely clearly and succinctly from Lenin's discussion with Clara Zetkin on the women's issue in the autumn of 1920. He stated 'we hate yes, hate and want to remove whatever oppresses and harasses the working women, the wife of the worker, the peasant woman, the wife of the little man, and even in many respects the women of the propertied class'. He referred to the fact that men and women were absolutely equal before law and 'a sincere desire to give effect to this equality is evident in all spheres'; women were being enlisted in the economy, legislation and the government. All educational institutions were open to them so that they could improve their professional and social training, special training was being given to them in all spheres. The Soviet state was organising community kitchens and public dining rooms, laundry and repair shops, crèches, kindergartens, children's homes and educational institutions of every kind. 'In brief', so said Lenin to Clara Zetkin,

> 'We are quite in earnest about carrying out the requirements of our programme to shift the functions of housekeeping and education from the individual household to society. Woman is thus being relieved from her old domestic slavery and all dependence on the husband. She is enabled to give her capabilities and inclinations full play in society. Children are offered better opportunities for their development than at home; we have the most progressive female labour legislation in the world and it is enforced by the authorised representatives of labour'.

The Soviet state, Lenin goes on 'is establishing maternity homes, mother-and-child health care centres, courses for infant and child care and every effort was being made to provide for the needy and unemployed women.'

Each and every word of Lenin's utterances quoted above is substantiated by the details of legislation, policy and reconstruction of society under the Soviet State. Addressing all questions of oppression, the Soviet state was the first state in history to be based on the principle of the abolition of exploitation of man by man. In addressing the women's question, at the very beginning of its activity, the Soviet government abolished all marriage and family laws that were based on the enslavement of women and created a new legal system founded on the complete equality of women in marriage and the family. The concept of the 'head of the family' was abolished and the woman was no longer obliged to take her husband's name after marriage. Both husband and wife came to have equal rights and responsibility towards rearing and educating their children. Both acquired complete freedom in choice of their life partners and their occupation or profession. Both marriage and divorce became voluntary acts of two parties. If a father deserted the family the state acquired rights to compel him to contribute towards the upkeep of the children until they come of age; the same obligation was imposed for children born out of wedlock. Alimony for children was in proportion to the man's earnings.

Besides complete equality of the sexes in personal civil rights, there existed in the Soviet Union complete equality for man and women in all political respects. According to the Soviet Constitution the right to elect and be elected to the Soviets, the Supreme organs of authority were open to all persons of both sexes above the age of eighteen. The legal equality of men and women in political and civil rights was not enough by itself for women to exercise their equal rights; women had to be given the opportunity of making full use of their rights. To bring the women out of their cultural and social inferiority and from material dependence on their husbands, the Soviet Union was continuously attempting to induct masses of women into industry and other useful public services. Concurrently with their induction in industry and public services, women were able to improve their qualifications by attending training schools of all kinds for their better performance.

To relieve the woman of the 'double burden' of the drudgery of unproductive house work, communal services were being continuously provided and expanded. These communal services comprised of community kitchens and public dining rooms, laundry and repair shops. Without these structural social solutions to the burden of running the household, the women could not have gainfully stepped out of their homes to render socially useful labour.

It is important to bear in mind that the Soviet state paid meticulous attention to detail to make every design of a new factory to satisfy certain sanitary and technical conditions, particularly those conditions affecting women, which in turn facilitated the entry of female labour in industry.

Soviet labour laws on working hours and social insurance were of great importance to the health of workers in general, and of women in particular. The Soviet state had the most progressive labour laws in the world. The working hours varied between six to seven hours, depending on the nature of work. The workers were given a minimum annual holiday of two weeks or more depending again on the nature of their work. But most important of all, women were paid the same wages as men. The principle of 'equal pay for equal work' thus got materialised in the Soviet Union.

The Soviet system of insurance provided help to all workers in illness, accident, physical injury, disability – temporary or permanent. This social insurance was available to all wage-earners whether in town or in the countryside. These benefits extended to include burial expenditure and feeding of a child. In 1935 the budget for social insurance was sixty-five million rubles while in 1934, 340,800 workers and members of their families visited sanatoriums and rest homes at the expense of the social insurance funds.

There were special labour laws for the protection of women workers. In the Soviet Union great attention was paid to protecting motherhood and childhood from within one month of conception itself. Women workers had 16 weeks obligatory leave for pregnancy and infant care with not only full payment of wages, but with several other benefits too.

In a remarkable work, *Red Medicine : Socialized Health in Soviet Russia* by Sir Arthur Newsholme, KCB, MD and John A.Kingsbury, LL.D. published in 1934, the authors who, by no stretch of imagination were inclined towards socialism and whose main purpose was to learn lessons from the Soviet Union to prevent trouble in the capitalist countries, we get details of the pre-natal, natal, infant care, child care provisions and centres which are astounding. A mere reading of the book can perhaps give better insights into the working of the Soviet society than volumes of specialised work. For the Soviet Union the health of the individual was the concern of the society as a whole. Systems and structures were put in place which could make the best of health facilities and expertise available to everyone in society, particularly pregnant women, infants, children and other needy sections.

Besides labour laws there were general laws governing health care. Also in addition to the maternity leave with full wages, there were several other and varied provisions for the expectant mother in the Soviet Union. On attending a prenatal centre the expectant mother received a card, which entitled her to : (a) the right of precedence in tramcars and a sheltered place in them (b) service in shops without waiting in a queue; (c) a supplementary food ration; (d) lighter work in the office or shop in which she was employed; and (e) as already stated, two months' rest without loss of wages.

The authors of *Red Medicine* remarked that their observations on Soviet arrangements for the medical and hygiene care of mothers and their children 'have filled us with admiration and with wonder that such good work, scientific and advanced work, should be undertaken and successfully accomplished in a period when the finances of the country are at a low ebb'. They observed that motherhood and childhood is regarded as a 'first charge on Soviet funds'. Such facilities were being rapidly extended to the rural areas.

For the lactating mothers (breast-feeding was encouraged

in the Soviet Union), half an hour's break was given to feed their babies kept in the well-maintained and well-organised crèches in factories. These breaks were regarded as part of the working hours. Expectant and lactating mothers were given lighter work with special rations. Indeed, the Soviet State created structures and infrastructure which made motherhood easier and self-fulfilling for women without having to sacrifice their jobs. These conditions were an integral part of the socialist construction of society.

The construction of the socialist society by the Soviet people under Stalin's leadership transformed the society so radically that the USSR through its heavy industry acquired the ability to produce its own means of production instead of having to depend upon the capitalist countries for their import. This qualitative transformation of the USSR is reflected in every sphere of activity in society, be it economic, intellectual, cultural or social.

There was the expansion of the positive measures to facilitate further women's participation in work both physical and mental. Women's participation reached a new level with the socialist transformation of society. This brought within its fold the women of poor and middling peasantry through the collectivisation of agriculture. The technological transformation of the industrial production under the first two five-year plans, translated itself for women into more jobs, greater facilities for 'protection of mother and child', and overall development of the infrastructure for scientific research, intellectual, cultural and physical development. The guiding principles which had informed the policy of the Soviet state were given the legal status of rights in the constitution that was framed and adopted after the construction of socialism in the USSR within a historically short period of time. The Article 122 of the *Constitution of the USSR*, popularly known as the Stalin constitution, reads —

'ARTICLE 122, Women in the U.S.S.R. are accorded equal rights with men in all spheres of economic, state, cultural, social and political life. The possibility of exercising these rights is ensured to women by granting them an equal right with men to work, payment for work, rest and leisure social insurance and education, and by state protection of the interests of mother and child, pre-maternity and maternity leave with full pay, and a provision of a wide network of maternity homes, nurseries and kindergartens.'

The principles of guiding policy became women's legislated rights under the Constitution of the U.S.S.R. (1936) with the transformation of society into a socialist society. It was within this transformed society that 'motherhood and childhood', became the first charge on Soviet funds' as stated in the *Red Medicine*. Pre-natal, natal, maternity care, infant centres, child centres for different age groups, kindergartens, schools, youth clubs, professional training institutions, colleges, research institutes for sciences, languages, cultural organisations all reflect the transformed society and, within it the position of women achieved through all protective measures at every level. The best of health facilities and expertise, with full network making these accessible to all was a marvel of the Soviet society.

The Bolshevik revolution and the Bolshevik policy towards women under the leadership of Lenin and Stalin had ensured women in the U.S.S.R. an equal economic and political status with men. If they acquired equal status with the men, the women also had a great share in the victory of socialism in the U.S.S.R. In the course of 'our country's socialist development', as Nina Popova puts it in her remarkable work *Women in the Land of Socialism*, 'hundreds and thousands of women learned to manage public industry and to administer the state'. Construction of a socialist society was not possible without the active participation of women, as Lenin had stated it in 1920 and as Clara Zetkin had maintained all through her life in theory and practice.

The extension of all these activities and protective measures to the countryside was done systematically by the Soviet state. This work was taken up on a priority basis with the collectivisation of agriculture in 1929-30. The emancipatory influence of the collective–farm system awakened tremendous forces latent in the masses of peasant women, 'helped many of them to reveal their hidden talents'. That is why the women collective farmers, in step with women factory workers, were in the first rank of the initiators and heroes of the Stakhanov movement. Women were the first to raise the banner of socialist emulation for a high crop yield. Their initiative was supported by hundreds of thousands of collective farmers and a nation-wide movement developed for 'Stakhanovite harvests'. The collective farm women joined the movement of 'increased labour productivity'. Machines, including tractors, harvesters and threshers, which made women's labour in farming easier and the state ownership of the means of production, which made the machines accessible to the small and middling farmers through collectivisation, liberated the peasant woman. Training centres for using the machines attracted large female participation. We may cite here at length the example of a woman tractor driver, Praskovya Angelina, Member of the Supreme Soviet of the USSR, who was twice awarded the Hero of Socialist Labour medal, who related her story as follows:

> My mother's lot was a bitter one, the lot of the long-suffering peasant woman', relates Hero of Socialist Labour Praskovya Angelina, Member of the Supreme Soviet of the U.S.S.R. 'And her children shared her poverty and her tears. Her older sons had no childhood. All of them went out into the world when still small children, to work for rich peasants at a miserable wage. I was no exception. At the age of eight, I left home and hired out in order to earn my crust of bread...
>
> My father is 70 years old now, yet he does all he can to help with the work on the collective farm. He was awarded a

> medal for valorous labour during the Patriotic War. The Soviet Government has decorated my mother too for having brought up seven children. My oldest brother is an agronomist and has been decorated for his wartime work with the Order of the Patriotic War and several medals. My second brother, Vasili, is a colonel and has earned eleven decorations for valour in active service. My sister, Nadezhda, has been awarded the Order of Lenin for her splendid work on the collective farm and two medals for participation in the Patriotic War. My brother Konstantin is now chairman of a collective farm and also has government awards.
>
> My work as a tractor driver has brought me honour. Twice I have been elected to the Supreme Soviet of the U.S.S.R. and I have been awarded the title of Hero of Socialist Labour for the large harvest our collective farm obtained in 1946.
>
> We owe all this to our Soviet system. It is the Soviet system that has made us what we are today, that has raised us so high.'

The information culled out of Nina Popova's book reveals that in the Soviet state it was quite the usual thing for women to hold leading government positions. Maria Sarycheva, Vice-Chairman of the Executive Committee of the Moscow City Soviet, was also Vice-Chairman of the Supreme Soviet of the R.S.F.S.R. P.G. Radchenko was Vice-Chairman of the Supreme Soviet of the Ukrainian S.S.R. Zoya Andreyeva was President of the Presidium of the Supreme Soviet of the Chuvash Autonomous S.S.R., and also Vice-President of the Presidium of the Supreme Soviet of the R.S.F.S.R. Chimnaz Aslanova was Vice-Chairman of the Soviet of Nationalities of the Supreme Soviet of the U.S.S.R. Fatima Kadrybayeva was Chairman of the Supreme Court of the Kirghiz Republic.

Nina Popova goes on to add 'The Public Health Minister of Azerbaijan is a woman, Kyubra Faradjeva. The Minister of Justice in the Turkmenian Soviet Socialist Republic is Nuri Karadjayeva, Tatyana Zuyeva is Vice-Chairman of the Council of Ministers of the R.S.F.S.R.; Olga Lauristin is Minister of Social Insurance of the Estonian Soviet Socialist Republic; Praskovya Kalinina is Minister of the food Industry of the Chuvash Autonomous Soviet Socialist Republic. Three women, Basti Bagirova, Varvara Vakholdina and Natalya Kuklina, are members of the Council for Collective Farm Affairs under the Council of Ministers of the U.S.S.R. Many women are deputy ministers of the U.S.S.R., and of Union and Autonomous Republics, as well as chairmen of Executive Committees of local Soviets of Working People's Deputies. In the R.S.F.S.R. alone over 27,000 women head village Soviets'.

An especially vivid illustration of women's absolute equality in the U.S.S.R. is the fact that many of them were judges. This was impossible in Russia before the October Revolution. In 1948-49 there were fourteen women members of the Supreme Court of the U.S.S.R. Women comprised 33.9% of the members of Supreme Courts of Union Republics. Many women were presiding judges of regional and territorial courts, and 35% of all people's courts judges were women.

All these facts and figures are an eloquent testimony to the emancipation of women under the Soviet state as also of their contribution to the building of that state and society and its transformation into a socialist state.

Based on the fundamental principle of freeing people from different forms of oppression, the Soviet government approached the women's question in the minority nationalities' regions within the framework of the national question in these regions and its policy of full, genuine equality for women in all fields of economic, government cultural, public and political life.

The Soviet system achieved development in these nationality regions which was 'national in form and socialist in content'. While higher education was out of bounds for women, even the number of males with a higher education could be counted on the fingers of one hand under the czarist regime among the Azerbaijanians, Uzbeks, Turkmenians,

Tajiks, Kazakhs and many other nationalities. One of the finest achievements of the non-Russian Soviet republics of the East was the advancement of the cultural standards of masses and the rise of a national intelligentsia among them – engineers, physicians, agronomists, teachers, scientists, poets, artists, writers, many of them women. Under the Soviet system school attendance was compulsory for boys and girls alike in the formerly backward non-Russian regions of old Russia, which became Union or Autonomous Republics of the U.S.S.R. Universities and colleges, technical high schools and various vocational schools were established in these republics and there came into existence palaces of culture, clubs, libraries and museums.

In pre-revolutionary Turkmenia only seven persons per thousand could read and write. In 1946 the proportion was nine hundred to a thousand. By 1948-49 over 200,000 boys and girls attended public schools in Turkmenia. This number excludes the pupils of factory trade schools, a medical college and an agricultural college. There were about a thousand libraries in the republic. Ashkhabad, the capital of Turkmenia, boasted one of the largest public libraries in the Soviet Union. Turkmenia had over 1,200 clubs and reading rooms, five museums and dozens of other cultural institutions. Before the revolution the theatrical art was unknown to the Turkmenian people. By 1948-49 there were fourteen theatres in Turkmenia, including an opera and ballet theatre.

The extent to which women were represented in the teaching profession in the non-Russian Soviet republics is indicative of their cultural progress. The percentage of women among teachers in primary and secondary schools before the war, in 1941, was as follows : Georgian S.S.R. – 51.3%, Kazakh S.S.R. – 37.8%, Armenian S.S.R. – 30.9%, Kirghiz S.S.R. 30.2%, Azerbaijan S.S.R. – 29.5%, Uzbek S.S.R. – 25.4%, Turkmenian S.S.R. – 17.6%. By 1949 the percentage of women teachers had increased still further.

The number of scientific workers among the non-Russian peoples increased so rapidly that it was possible to organise Academies of Sciences or branches of the Academy of Sciences of the U.S.S.R. in all the union republics. Many women were among the foremost Academy workers. Over 100 women were employed in the Georgian Academy of Sciences, nearly 100 in the Azerbaijan Academy, about 200 in the Kazakh Academy, about 50 in the Turkmenian branch of the Academy of Sciences of the U.S.S.R., 30 in the Tajik branch, 30 in the Kirghiz branch.

The Soviet state's deep solicitude for mother and child had penetrated to the most distant corners of the vast socialist country. A ramified system of maternity homes, obstetrical centres, and nurseries catered to the needs of mothers and children of those republics. These republics saw the unprecedented emancipation of women. With such infrastructural societal systems of support there was a flowering of the female talent in all spheres.

> 'The revolution emancipated our woman, removed the horsehair veil in which she had been wrapped for centuries,' says a letter from the Azerbaijan people to Comrade Stalin. 'Azerbaijan women have become active builders of our socialist society. Women hold positions of responsibility in the government, in factories, in the oil fields, on college teaching staffs and in surgical wards of hospitals. There are women ship's captains and aeroplane pilots.'

In bourgeois Estonia women were kept out of government bodies and their wages were lower than the male wages. Soviet Estonia gave equal rights and wages to women. There were in 1949-50 twenty-four women deputies in the Supreme Soviet of the Estonian SSR among them were included a peasant, a school teacher and worker from Krenholm Textile Mills. In Latvia in the pre-Soviet days, women possessed formal equality, but were paid lower wages, were discriminated in job appointments and scientific work was an unattainable dream for the Latvian women. Educated women ended up working as domestic help in rich homes or as farm labourers for rich peasant farms. The Soviet system had opened all roads to the Latvian women including highest political decision-making structures; seven Latvian women were members of the Supreme Soviet of the USSR.

It is apparent that the Soviet system acted as a liberating force for the emancipation of women of all nationalities and regions within the USSR. It addressed the specificities of oppression and found solutions through mass participation in special women's clubs and classes particularly in the eastern regions with predominantly Muslim population. Clara Zetkin's article 'In the Muslim Women's Club' brings out the transformation of the lives of these women within the transformative framework of Soviet liberation both legally and substantially.

The process of women's emancipation received a serious reversal in the post-Stalinist period with the end of the policies which underlay the construction of a socialist society. Within half a decade of Stalin's death, the state ownership of the means of production in agriculture was gone and planning was decentralised. The profit motive was introduced in the Soviet economy. With the commodification of the means of production and the absence of a centralised planning system, the growth rate got impacted adversely. As a consequence of the slowing of the growth rate, the entire socialist infrastructure sustaining the process of the steady emancipation of all the oppressed, including women, received a setback. The emancipatory superstructures created during the Stalin era were so strong that they retained their efficacy for a considerable period even as the material base supporting those was gradually and steadily eroded. This process is evident from the appearance and increase of fashion magazines etc. in the Soviet Union and the ultimate reappearance of prostitution, which manifests the ultimate degradation of the woman through the commodification of her body. The entire process reveals how inextricably the position of women is intertwined with the nature of the social formation of any society.

As for Clara Zetkin was not just the specificities of women's oppression, but also of other forms of oppression such as based on racial discrimination that deeply concerned Clara Zetkin. An outstanding example of this was her attempt to save the lives of nine black boys who were sentenced to death in the United States on the charge of raping two white girls. With all racial biases, a fast trial without evidence, found the boys guilty. An international campaign was raised to save them and Clara Zetkin as head of the International Red Aid, issued an appeal in April, 1932: 'Save the Scottsboro Black Youth'. This too is included in the present volume and it reveals Clara Zetkin's understanding of racist oppression as distinct from class oppression.

Clara Zetkin made her journey from the Second International to the Third or the Communist International, known as Comintern, through the thick and thin of struggles for women's rights, fights for an understanding of the women's question within the framework of historical materialism and stubborn fight against the reformism of social democracy. After the brutal murders of Karl Liebknecht and Rosa Luxemburg on January 15, 1919 and the death of Franz Mehring, Clara Zetkin was the most important pre-war socialist leader in the German Communist Party. She sat in the Reichstag for the party continuously from the first to the last session of the Weimar Republic. In the spring of 1920, Clara Zetkin was appointed the International Secretary of the Communist Women by the Executive Committee of the Comintern. Partly because of the secretarial work of the Comintern and partly due to health reasons (Clara Zetkin received special medical care), Clara Zetkin lived much of the time in the Soviet Union near Moscow. During her stay in Moscow she interacted with Lenin on the women's question the discussions of two of these meetings she recorded. She lived through the tumultuous and great period of transition to socialism under Stalin. She witnessed the liberation of women in the Soviet Union within the framework within which Clara Zetkin herself understood the entire women's question.

Clara Zetkin's views on the women's question would not be complete without a comment on her view on marriage. With property not forming the basis of marriage and family, Clara Zetkin firmly believed that marriage would acquire a strong new moral fibre to impart new meaning to relationship within marriage. Both Clara Zetkin and Lenin were opposed to promiscuity. Lenin held the view that 'promiscuity in sexual matters is bourgeois. It is a sign of degeneration'.

One of Clara Zetkin's last major speeches in the international arena was delivered in 1932 at the Anti-war Congress held in Amsterdam. After 1920 Clara Zetkin had been regularly elected to the German parliament, the Reichstag, and on 30th August 1932, being the seniormost deputy, she was invited to give the inaugural speech at its opening session. Despite infirmity she journeyed from Moscow to Berlin for this function and in spite of the warnings of the fascist press – which threatened that it would settle accounts with her if she dared to appear in the Reichstag – she delivered a magnificent revolutionary speech against the fascists, exposed the compromising role of the Social Democratic Party and called for the forming of an anti-fascist united front. Zetkin considered that the victory of fascism in German was rooted in the capitulation of German social democracy before the bourgeoisie. She concluded by stating that she was opening the congress in fulfilment of her duties as honorary President and in the hope that despite her current infirmities 'I may yet have the fortune to open as honorary President of the first Soviet Congress of a Soviet Germany'!

The death of Clara Zetkin took place just a few months after Hitler's accession to power at Archangelsk near Moscow on June 20, 1933. Six lakh working people attended her funeral procession in Moscow from the Hall of the Columns of the House of Trade Unions to Red Square. Among the pall-bearers were Stalin, Molotov, Voroshilov, Ordzhonikidze, Kalinin, Kuibyshev and the members of the Presidium of the Communist International. The funeral orations were delivered by veteran communists such as Sen Katayama, V.M. Molotov and Nadezhda Krupskaya. The ashes of Clara Zetkin were interred in the Red Wall of the Kremlin by the side of Lenin and other great revolutionaries of the world proletariat.

In recent times Clara Zetkin's views on the women's question have been criticised by feminists of different hues and shades. It is maintained by them that Clara Zetkin did not address the question of the sexist division of labour within the household. This criticism is totally misplaced for Clara Zetkin. For the feminists the sexist division of work in the household has an important place in their framework because they seek individualistic solutions to the women's burden of household work. Clara Zetkin was not seeking individualistic solution to the issue of women's 'double burden' which forms the basis of the bourgeois feminist solution for the organisation of household labour. She located the liberation of women within the framework of a society free from exploitation of man by man and, therefore, her understanding of the women's issue was within the larger question of private property which was the initial basis of the subordination of women in society. Her whole understanding of women's liberation was premised on the abolition of private property which could only occur when society is free from exploitation of man by man. That was the reason why she mobilised the working class for their rights with the aim of preparing them for their historic role of demolishing capital. With this understanding of the liberation of women, Clara Zetkin was not looking at any individualistic solution to relieve women of their 'double burden'. There had to be structural communal solutions within the larger societal context, solutions such as community kitchens etc. etc. given by the Soviet state. Only with the support of such communal structural solutions created by the Soviet State, could material conditions be created which facilitated the emancipation of women in the USSR, not just legally but in substantial terms.

Clara Zetkin's ideas have a great relevance for Indian society. With so many forms of oppression from the pre-capitalist era within the overarching framework of capitalism, the need to understand the specificities of those and their underlying relationship to the ever increasing grip of imperialism on India form the crux of the women's question in this country. The increasing dominance of contract labour with lower wages and fewer political rights under the increasing grip of foreign capital, Clara Zetkin's slogan of 'equal wages for equal work' has direct relevance not only for the female labour, but also for the male labour. The dalit question and within that the women's question is staring us in the face. It is not a sheer coincidence that 98% of those who are on death row in the country are dalits. They reflect systemic prejudices and oppression of the dalits. It is also not a sheer coincidence that contract work started first of all with the *safai karamchairs* (sweepers in public institutions and places), and that some women sweepers got these jobs for a pittance through sexual gratification of the contractors and their henchmen. The state organs have been using rape as an adjunct of the state policy to suppress the aspirations of the people of the North-East and Kashmir. It has also come to be used extensively against the tribal women as an instrument of oppression in their struggles against their displacement which follows the handing over of their land with rich resources to the multinationals for loot. Feudal oppression through the use and abuse of the women of the agrarian labouring class, bonded or partly free, is wide spread. Women's wages are still so much lower than the male wages despite legal equality. Dowry deaths and burnings, female-foeticides show the ugly face of the complex social reality in India today. All these newer as well as older forms of women's oppression through a complex intertwining of different forms of oppression are squarely facing us and are crying out for a solution of the type that Clara Zetkin held to be the only solution, the fundamental transformation of society through the demolition of capital.

7th November, 2011

Tripta Wahi
New Delhi

Select Bibliography

1. *Constitution (Fundamental Law) of the Union of Soviet Socialist Republics*, J. Stalin, 'Works', Vol. 14, Red Star Press, London, May 1978, in Stalin Archive, http://revolutionarydemocracy.org/
2. Engels, Frederick, *The Origins of the Family, Private Property and the State*, Foreign Languages Publishing House, Moscow 1978.
3. Evans, Richard, *The Feminists*, London 1977.
4. Field, Alice Withrow, *Protection of Women and Children in Soviet Russia*, London 1932.
5. Hafeez, Amna, 'Marxism and Feminism', *Revolutionary Democracy*, Vol. XVI, No.2, September 2010, New Delhi.
6. Honeycutt, Karen, 'Clara Zetkin: A Left-Wing Socialist and Feminist in Wilhelmine Germany', Ph.D. Thesis, Columbia University 1975.
7. Clara Zetkin : A Socialist Approach to the Problem of Woman's Oppression', *Feminist Studies*, Vol.3, No.3/4 (Spring-Summer 1976), pp. 131-144.
8. Kingsbury, Susan M., *Factory Family and Woman in the Soviet Union*, New York 1934.

9. Lenin, V.I., *Lenin on the Emancipation of Women*, Progress Publishers, Moscow 1965.
10. Newsholme Sir Arthur and John A. Kingsbury, *Red Medicine : Socialized Health in Soviet Russia*, London 1934.
11. Popova, Nina, *Women in the Land of Socialism*, Moscow 1949.
12. Serebrennikov, G.N. *The Position of Women in the USSR*, London 1937.
13. Wilson, Elizabeth with Angela Weir, *Hidden Agendas : Theory, Politics and Experience in the Women's Movement*, London 1986.
14. Zetkin, Clara, 'My Recollections of Lenin', *Lenin on the Emancipation of Women*, Progress Publishers, Moscow 1965, pp.99-126.
15. Zetkin, Clara, *Movements for the Emancipation of Women; Three Essays* translated by Vijay K. Chhabra and Madhu Sahni, edited by Vijay Singh, Kamgar Prakashan, Delhi 1988. In Archival Materials, http:// www.revolutionarydemocracy.org/.

INTRODUCTION BY PHILIP S. FONER

Clara Eissner Zetkin was born on July 15, 1857 in Widerau, a small Saxon village in Germany about ten miles northwest of Chemnitz, and inhabited by weavers in the local textile industry and small farmers. Clara's father, Gottfried Eissner, though raised in a very poor family, had been able to acquire sufficient education to become a teacher and organist. In 1853 he was brought to Widerau as the village school teacher and church organist. Two years after his arrival he married for the second time. His second wife, Josephine Vitale, came from a middle class Leipzig family and was the widow of a Leipzig doctor. Clara was the first of three children of Gottfried Eissner's new marriage.[1]

Josephine Vitale Eissner was an educated woman and a strong believer in the French Revolutionary ideals of liberty, equality, and fraternity. An outspoken supporter of complete economic equality for women, she founded in Widerau a *Frauenverein* in the late 1860s—a women's educational society (modelled on that established in Leipzig by Luise Otto and Auguste Schmidt) to further the education of the female sex. The society established evening courses to provide young women with instruction in handicrafts, languages and office skills.[2]

Gottfried Eissner did not share his wife's liberal political views and, as a devout Protestant, he was often shocked by her criticism of religious institutions. However, in both politics and religion, Clara was to take after her mother. It was Josephine Vitale Eissner who awakened in her daughter a lifelong interest in the cause of women's rights.[3]

Clara Eissner's education in the village school was supplemented by her father's tutoring. (Gottfried Eissner also taught his daughter to play both the piano and organ.) After he retired in 1872, the family moved to Leipzig to enable the children to continue their education. They lived in the city in very straitened circumstances, for their income was limited to the small pension that Clara's father received.[4]

Because of her sex, Clara was unable to study at a *Gymnasium*. Fortunately, Frau Eissner was able to arrange with Auguste Schmidt, who was impressed with Clara's intelligence, for her admission free of charge to the teacher training college of the Van Steyber Institute in Leipzig, the best of its kind in Germany. The four years (1874-78) Clara spent in the school had a profound influence on her intellectual development. She received the finest secondary schooling then available to women in Germany. She deepened her knowledge of literature and history (begun during the long hours she spent in her father's library). Then too, she began learning Italian, French, and English which would prove valuable in her later work. Moreover, she was further indoctrinated with the ideals of the French Revolution; in the Institute, this meant equality for women. She was immersed in discussions of equality for women and established contacts with the Leipzig Women's Educational Society and the National Association of German Women. During frequent visits to Auguste Schmidt's home, where she often met his friend and coworker Luise Otto, Clara strengthened her interest in the women's rights movement.[5]

Although Schmidt was essentially a bourgeois liberal, Clara Eissner's interest in socialism was first aroused in his classes. She read Social-Democratic newspapers and pamphlets, especially the works of Ferdinand Lassalle.[6] In the spring of 1878, shortly after she had graduated from the Steyber Institute at the top of her class and passed with distinction her teaching certificate examination, she made the acquaintance of a group of Russian students and émigrés living in Leipzig. Through them she came into contact with German Social Democrats. With her Russian friends, she attended their meetings and the lectures of Wilhelm Liebknecht, who with August Bebel had founded the German Social-Democratic Party (SPD) in 1869.[7]

Clara's new associates were frowned upon by her liberal teacher and by her mother and sister. But Clara refused to break with them and instead broke off relations with Auguste Schmidt and her own family. She acquired a new teacher—Ossip Zetkin, a Russian émigré from Odessa who lived in Leipzig and divided his time between activities in revolutionary groups and woodworking. Zetkin was a convinced Marxist and within a short time after their meeting, he was lending her books by Marx and Engels and instructing her on the theories of scientific social-

Clara Zetkin as a young teacher, ca. 1880

With sons Kostja and Maxim, 1895

ism. Soon she was accompanying Zetkin to lectures given at the Leipzig Workers' Educational Society. Zetkin also encouraged Clara to live with workers so she could fully understand that the revolutionary movement had to be led by the working class rather than by students.[8]

By the middle of 1878, Clara Eissner had committed herself to the cause of socialism. Although as a woman she was legally barred from becoming a member, she became closely associated with the German Social-Democratic Party (SPD), and identified herself thoroughly with the organization.[9]

On October 21, 1878 Bismarck succeeded in having the Anti-Socialist Law passed. The SPD and its press were immediately declared illegal and its leaders forced into exile. Like many other Social Democrats who remained in Germany, Clara became involved in illegal activities, collecting money for the outlawed party and its exiled leaders. Her relationship with Ossip Zetkin continued, and at the same time she worked as a tutor in a Leipzig suburb. Her first job lasted until the fall of 1880 when Ossip was expelled from Germany as an undesirable alien—a foreigner participating in illegal political activities. Clara decided to follow him in exile and joined Ossip in Austria. Again she worked as a tutor, this time in the home of a wealthy factory owner in Linz. After a year and a half in Linz, she went on to Zürich, Switzerland, planning to continue from there to Paris where Ossip was then living.[10]

Clara Eissner's five-month residence in Zürich brought her closer to the socialist movement. Here she met the principal leaders of the German SPD and worked with Julius Mottler, who was in charge of smuggling *Der Sozialdemokrat,* (the central organ of the exiled party) and other party literature into Germany with the aid of an organization of agents called the "Red Fieldpost."[11]

In November, 1882 Clara left Zürich for Paris to join Ossip Zetkin. Although she shared a flat in Paris with her companion, assumed his last name, and had two sons with him (Maxim and Konstantin) within two years, she chose to remain unmarried so that she would not lose her German citizenship under the patriarchal marriage laws prevailing at the time. They lived together in common-law marriage for nearly a decade.[12]

The Zetkin family lived in great poverty in Paris, for socialists-in-exile had difficulty finding employment. To support themselves the Zetkins wrote for various socialist periodicals,[13] worked as translators and in addition, Clara tutored (on top of being a housewife and mother). What they received for it all was barely enough for subsistence. There was rarely enough money for decent food or housing. In June, 1885 the Zetkins were actually thrown out on the street at dawn for failing to pay the rent, and suffered the confiscation of all their meager possessions except the clothes on their backs.[14]

Despite the hardship and difficulties, the Zetkins were active in political life. With Marx's daughter Laura Lafargue, Clara attended demonstrations, passed out literature and began to recruit Parisian working women for socialism.[15]

The miserable living conditions took their toll on Clara's health. In the spring of 1886 she came down with tuberculosis as a result of inadequate food and overwork. A complete rest was ordered. Clara's mother, learning of her daughter's predicament, offered reconciliation. Clara returned to Leipzig for a few months and moved in with her brother; her mother cared for her two sons.[16]

The visit to Germany proved to be very important. Clara was contacted by her old comrades and again met Wilhelm Liebknecht. It was at a secret meeting in Leipzig that she made her first public speech, speaking on the activities of the German Social-Democrats abroad. She scored such a success that she was besieged with requests to repeat it to other groups, and in the course of her three-month stay, she spoke two or three times every week at illegal gatherings. She wrote enthusiastically about her experience, about illegal party activity, and particularly about women's growing role in the movement:

> The German workers, speaking of the Leipzig comrades, are splendid fellows; as I got to know their life and work so intimately, for the first time in life, I am proud to be German. What gave me the most joy was that women are being drawn more and more into the movement. I met quite a large number of women ... distributing brochures, flyers, and election appeals. Most comrades see participation and activity by women no longer as a nice convenience, but as practical necessity. Quite a transformation in attitudes since I left Germany.[17]

Zetkin's speeches included a discussion of the tremendously popular and influential *Woman and Socialism* by August Bebel. She had had the first chance to study Bebel's significant work shortly after it was published, during her five-month residence in Zürich. While in prison, Bebel had written the book to challenge the existing bourgeois theory that woman's inferior position was an unalterable, natural state of affairs. Bebel answered with the presentation of arguments demonstrating the influence of economic and social conditions in determining women's mental and emotional makeup, her interests, goals, and her achievements.[18]

Bebel's book was of critical importance in shaping Clara Zetkin's views on the question of women's emancipation. His thesis that only through the destruction of bourgeois society would the working class and women be emancipated deeply influenced her own analysis of the woman question. She was influenced, too, by Bebel's argument that in contemporary society it was necessary for women to get out of the home and into industry and the professions, first because economic developments dictated such a step, and second, that by doing so women would reach a higher stage of historical development; in this case one in which they would be closer to the final goal of equality with men. Women's entry into industry, therefore, was a necessary step in that historical process which would terminate in a socialist society. At the same time workingwomen organized by unions and the Socialist party would strengthen the ranks of the proletariat.[19]

For decades Bebel's work comprised the essence of Socialist thinking on the role of woman in society, and set forth the part to be played by the socialist movement in the emancipation of women. Although criticism of Bebel's book grew, especially of those sections in which he relied heavily on Lewis Henry Morgan in developing the evolution of society, his central thesis that economic development was the cause of women's suppression did not lose any of its validity. Nor did Bebel's statement that "there can be no liberation of mankind without independence and equality of the sexes."[20]

Bebel's book was read by working class women in Leipzig at the time Clara Zetkin was lecturing in the city and her discussions of the work were eagerly awaited and well attended. In later years, she noted the theoretical limitations from a Marxist viewpoint of *Woman and Socialism*. But she also noted that the "book must not be judged according to its positive aspects or its shortcomings. Rather, it must be judged within the context of the times in which it was written. It was more than a book, it was an event—a great deed." The book "pointed out for the first time the connection between the women's question and historical development. For the first time, there sounded from this book the appeal: We will only conquer the future if we persuade the women to become our co-fighters."[21]

On her return to Paris, Clara assumed the whole burden of providing for the household and nursed Ossip Zetkin (who was wasting away with spinal tuberculosis) until his death in January, 1889. While recovering from this blow, she was chosen a member of the organization committee to help prepare for the founding congress of the Second International, scheduled to take place in Paris on July 14, 1889, the centennial of the fall of the Bastille. She was also elected by the women associated with the socialist newspaper, the *Berliner Volkstribüne,* to represent the working women of Berlin at the Congress. She was one of eight women among the four hundred delegates from nineteen countries elected to the Congress.[22]

On the sixth day of the Congress, Clara Zetkin spoke on the subject of working women. She explained that large-scale industry and mechanical production had made it possible for women to become part of the labor force of modern industry. She was critical of the Socialists for opposing the entrance of women into industry and for blaming women for the lowering of wages and lengthening of the working day. "The capitalist system alone," she emphasized, "must be blamed for the fact that women's work has the opposite result of its natural tendency.... The pernicious consequences of women's labor, which are so painfully felt today, will only disappear once the capitalist system passes out of existence." The proletarian woman, just like the proletarian man, suffered under long working hours and extremely low wages. Because her fundamental interests were identical with those of the proletarian man, it was clear that she could hope to achieve her liberation only by allying herself with him under the banner of socialism.

Zetkin also spoke out against the special protection of women workers. "Because we do not want to separate our cause from that of the working class in general, we will not formulate any special demands. We demand no other type of protection than that which labor demands in general from the capitalists."[23] But this stand was in sharp contrast with the views of the majority of the delegates at the Paris Congress.[24] Hence while Zetkin's speech was greeted with tremendous applause, the Congress passed a resolution which urged that work for women be forbidden "in all branches of industry where the work is particularly damaging to the female organism," and that "night work for women" also be forbidden. At the same time, the delegates accepted a major recommendation by Zetkin by adopting the following statement:

> The Congress further declares that male workers have a duty to take women into their ranks upon on a basis of equal rights, and demand in principle, equal pay for equal work for the workers of both sexes and without discrimination of nationality.[25]

In supporting Zetkin's position on this issue, the Congress took a major step forward. Another such step was taken when the German delegates set up a Women's Agitation Commission, whose function it was to plan and direct party and trade union agitation among women. It was composed of seven women, and, because its seat was in Berlin, was called the Berlin Agitation Commission. Eventually it became the executive of the socialist women's movement.[26]

In March, 1890 Bismarck was dismissed, and the Reichstag refused to renew the Anti-Socialist Law when it expired in October. Along with other exiled Social-Democrats, Clara Zetkin was permitted to return to Germany. After a bout with tuberculosis, she settled in Stuttgart, the most important center of Social-Democratic publishing activity, where she worked for J.H.W. Dietz's socialist publishing company. During 1891 she wrote and did translations for Dietz, including highly successful translation of Edward Bellamy's *Looking Backward.*[27] At the end of the year, the company took over publication of the Social-Democratic women's journal, *Die Arbeiterin* (Working Woman), changed its name to *Die Gleichheit* (Equality) and made Clara Zetkin its editor, a position she held for almost a quarter of a century.

Die Arbeiterin had been founded, edited and subsidized by Emma Ihrer as a newspaper for working women. The paper was published in Hamburg, and after one year it became clear that it was sustaining a loss which Emma Ihrer could no longer afford. It was then that Dietz stepped in and offered to take it over. Had Ihrer been willing to move to Stuttgart, she could have continued to head the journal. However, she did not want to leave her home in northern Germany, and the editorship was offered to Zetkin, who had been one of the regular contributors to *Die Arbeiterin* as well as an employee of the Dietz firm.[28]

On January 20, 1892 the first issue of *Gleichheit* appeared. In her introductory statement as editor, Zetkin wrote:

> *Gleichheit* proceeds from the conviction that the final cause for the thousand-year-old inferior social position of the female sex is not to be sought in the statutory legislation "made by men," but rather in the property relations determined by economic conditions.[29]

In another article addressed "To the Readers," which was published with few changes at the beginning of each new year throughout the 1890s, Zetkin set forth her conception of *Gleichheit* and its role:

> *Gleichheit* is directed especially to the most progressive proletarians, whether they are slaves to capital with their hands or with their heads. It strives to school these theoretically, to make possible for them a clear understanding of the historical course of development and to make possible for them not only to work consciously in the battle for the liberation of the proletariat, but also to be effective in enlightening and teaching their class comrades and training these as fighters with a clear goal.[30]

"In Zetkin's view," writes Karen Honeycutt, "the chief function of *Gleichheit* was to inform, to instruct, and to guide the enlightened vanguard within the socialist women's movement. . . . The goal of *Gleichheit* was to school 'the female comrades who stand in the forefront of the battle,' in the principles of Marxism and Social-Democracy and to prevent them from becoming infected with bourgeois feminist views."[31]

Zetkin not only edited the paper during its early years but wrote most of the articles that appeared in its pages, as well as editing articles sent in by contributors. She identified the paper with the Social-Democratic Party and the political principles of the Party's left wing. She also made certain that it served as a journal of communication and exchange for the organized working class women, and much space was devoted to descriptions of working conditions in industries in which women were particularly numerous. Strikes and other forms of labor activity among working women in Germany or in other countries were always given prominent coverage and sympathetic support in *Gleichheit*. The paper, moreover, devoted space to the need for women factory inspectors and pushed the Social-Democrats to introduce bills in the national and state parliaments providing for the appointment of women factory inspectors.[32] *Gleichheit* also paid special attention to the problems of domestic servants, the vast majority of whom were women, and published material on the working conditions of sales clerks, many of whom were also women.[33]

Its picture of the working conditions of women employed in German industry was very grim indeed. Many women worked in factories from eleven to fourteen hours per day, six days a week. Their diet consisted largely of black bread and potatoes, supplemented by cabbage of various kinds. Meat was included only occasionally in the noontime meal and then in very small quantities. The result of this inadequate diet was widespread anemia, susceptibility to disease, and stunted growth.[34]

Despite the attention *Gleichheit* paid to the problems, conditions, and organizational activities of working women, criticism of it as an elitist paper soon emerged. A resolution proposed at the 1896 Gotha Conference demanded that "a women's paper which was thoroughly intelligible to all" replace *Gleichheit* and that it should appear as a Sunday supplement to the Party organs. The resolution was defeated but the criticism did not subside, and the charge was added that the paper had failed to produce a large movement of working women. Zetkin responded with the comment that this was the task of "agitation and organization"; that *Gleichheit* could do only one thing and that was "to provide an educational and promotional influence" which it had accomplished. She insisted that the aim of *Gleichheit* was not to win new members, but to serve the needs of the "more advanced women comrades." The paper had "pursued one principal goal, which was to put the woman comrades who were in the forefront of the struggle on the ground of Social-Democracy." This it did every two weeks by differentiating between socialist and bourgeois feminists, socialist and bourgeois goals, and by relating socialist theory to tactics for the advancement of women.[35]

At the first conference of Social-Democratic women of Germany, held in Mainz in September, 1900, an attempt was made by a minority of delegates to get *Gleichheit* to deal with some "popular" women's questions. Zetkin opposed the proposal on the ground that if the magazine changed its character, it would lose its significance for the more advanced women comrades without influencing the masses of women.[36]

Still, the appeals for making the paper more popular were not without effect. At the 1904 Social-Democratic Party Women's Conference, Zetkin announced that beginning the following year a supplement would accompany *Gleichheit,* intended to "serve the education and interests of woman as housewife and mother," as well as providing good reading material for her children. Beginning in January, 1905 every issue of *Gleichheit* was accompanied alternatingly by a supplement, either "For our Housewives and Mothers," or "For Our Children." The supplement designed for housewives and mothers concerned itself with practical problems involved in child-rearing, questions relating to health, cooking and sewing. It emphasized above all the duty of the socialist mother to instill in her offspring unselfishness and feelings of class solidarity, as well as the importance of treating children with respect and developing in them powers of independent thinking.

The supplement "For Our Children" contained articles on science, technology, wildlife and cultural anthropology. Zetkin stressed in particular those viewpoints neglected in the schools attended by working class children, such as the dignity of labor and the economic factors underlying existing political and social conditions.

Both of the *Gleichheit* supplements contained selections from the works of outstanding European writers including Goethe, Schiller, Heine, Balzac, Stendhal, Shelley, Ibsen and Tolstoy; authors associated with the German revolutionary tradition like Freiligrath, Herwegh, Uhland and Gutzkow; those "who dealt with the life and problems of the lower classes" such as Dickens, Zola, Hauptmann, Gogol and Gorky.[37]

Despite poor health, Zetkin continued to edit *Gleichheit* and the supplements alone until October, 1908. By 1903 circulation had attained 11,000 copies. It rose to 67,000 by 1906, 85,000 by 1910 and 125,000 by 1914.[38] In October, 1908, the size of *Gleichheit* was increased from twelve to twenty-four pages, and every issue was henceforth accompanied by a children's supplement *and* a supplement for mothers and housewives. At the same time Zetkin took on Käte Duncher as assistant editor in charge of the supplement for children.[39]

In addition to writing for the socialist press and editing *Gleichheit,* Clara Zetkin also became deeply involved in the rapidly expanding trade union movement. She was one of the most active figures in the Bookbinders' trade union and served on its executive committee. She was also involved in the activities of the Brush Makers' Union, the Garment Workers'

Union, the Woodworkers' Union, the Glovemakers' Union, and a few other South German trade unions. She was particularly active in the Tailors' and Seamstresses' Union, which she served for many years as International Secretary.[40]

In her work with the trade unions, Zetkin wrote and distributed handbills, collected money for workers during layoffs and strikes and helped plan national and international trade union congresses. She used her knowledge of English, French and Italian to establish international connections for a number of German trade unions.[41]

With her knowledge of the conditions of German workers and her familiarity with the operation of trade unions in Germany and abroad, Clara Zetkin quickly developed into one of the most sought after Party speakers for trade unions, women's organizations and Party locals all over Germany. It has been estimated that in some years she delivered over three hundred speeches. Before audiences ranging in size from several hundred to several thousand, she spoke on the role of women in industry, the terrible conditions they were forced to undergo and the burning need for organizing working class women, as well as lectures on a great variety of other subjects.[42]

In her speeches Zetkin now championed the cause of special protection for working women. Previously she had opposed such legislation, but she had been deeply influenced by Engels' view that woman's biological function as mother, together with her relatively defenseless and weak social position, made legal protection an even more pressing necessity for the female than for the male worker.[43] In opposition to middle-class feminists who argued that legal protection of working women degraded women to the status of children, depriving them of their freedom and their right to work, Zetkin insisted that "freedom" and "right" to work oneself to death were no freedom and no right at all.[44]

Zetkin's analysis in general had become increasingly Marxist after she had read Engels' *Origin of the Family, Private Property and the State,* published in 1884. Her early accounts of women's oppression, she now acknowledged, had often reflected a bourgeois feminist analysis by locating the origin in men's physical supremacy. Following in Engels' footsteps, she now traced its origins back to the emergence of private property. In a letter to Kautsky (November 29, 1901) she claimed responsiblity for basing the German working class women's movement on a firm Marxist foundation, and for removing the "rather vulgar feminism" that had plagued the movement in the early 1890s.[45] Most scholars agree that this was a correct self-evaluation, and that she was the key figure determining the early political ideology of the German women's movement.

Despite opposition to her uncompromising stand against bourgeois feminism, Zetkin insisted on maintaining her position that "bourgeois feminism is nothing more than a reform movement [while] the proletarian women's movement is revolutionary and must be revolutionary." On one occasion she declared that disseminating this theme was "the most important task of *Gleichheit*."[46] She had the satisfaction of knowing that Engels supported her views and approved of her conduct.[47]

All this does not mean that Zetkin did not appreciate the ways in which working class women differed from their male comrades and the unique contributions they could make to the socialist cause as women. In fact, not only did she recognize the value of women's special female qualities but she argued for their fullest possible development. Still she made it clear that only the abolition of the capitalist system would make possible the full development of women's potentialities and of the female personality. As she put it in *Gleichheit* in 1901: "The total liberation of the world of proletarian women . . . is only possible in a socialist society. Only in such a society, with the disappearance of the currently dominant economic and property relations, will the social opposition disappear between the haves and the have-nots, between man and woman, and between intellectual and physical work. . . ." The overthrow of capitalism would abolish the contradiction not only between capital and labor but also between the work of women and the work of men. Since woman could develop herself "into a harmonious personality and live out life as a harmonious full nature only in a society of emancipated labor," it followed that "the final battle for the full humanity of the entire female sex" must be waged, not on the field of feminism, but against the rule of capital.[48]

In *Gleichheit* of August 3, 1898, Zetkin declared that "the desire for political rights must be . . . the central point about which any serious women's movement gravitates." She conceded that women's suffrage was not a solution for all problems, since it left private property intact, but it was an essential weapon in the class struggle. The working class would never win its political and economic battles without the help of the women.[49] Zetkin justified women's suffrage only in part because it was a means to greater proletarian strength. In the main she insisted that is was a woman's right—"a social right."

It is not an exaggeration to say that it was largely due to Clara Zetkin that the Social-Democratic Party's official program from 1890 to 1912 included the demand for women's suffrage and that the party demanded the vote for women in state and national legislative bodies.[50]

Zetkin was instrumental in keeping the issue of women's suffrage at all times before the Socialists. She published almost thirty articles on the subject in *Gleichheit,* and she played a leading role in securing passage of resolutions at six Socialist congresses between 1902 and 1910 calling upon all socialists to fight for women's suffrage in all campaigns for suffrage reforms.[51]

The first International Socialist Women's Conference was held in conjunction with the 1907 Stuttgart International Socialist Congress. Fifty-nine women from fifteen countries established the International Women's Bureau to strengthen the organizational ties between socialist women in various countries, elected Clara Zetkin as Secretary, and designated *Gleichheit* as the official organ of the socialist women associated with the Second International. Although Zetkin had long been regarded as leader of international socialist women, the Stuttgart women's conference formalized this status and greatly strengthened her position.[52]

Zetkin also won an important victory at Stuttgart during the controversy over the action of the Austrian socialist party in suppressing even the mention of women's suffrage during its campaigns in 1905 and 1906 for the extension of Austrian suffrage. Zetkin criticized this approach as opportunistic. It was a mistake, moreover, to postpone the struggle for women's suffrage until male suffrage was achieved. She stressed the necessity for Socialist parties to include the demand for women's suffrage as an integral part of all campaigns which they waged for suffrage extension. It was the duty of the proletarian women's movement in all countries to struggle energetically for the greater democratization of society in general, and for women's suffrage in particular.

In their defense, Therese Schlesinger and Adelheid Popp, leaders of Austrian social democracy, argued that their tactics had not harmed or hindered the fight for women's suffrage in Austria, that the special conditions of Austrian society had to be taken into account and that the victory of socialist men would also be a victory for women, for when Socialist deputies were elected to parliament, they would work to achieve women's suffrage.

But Zetkin's position was upheld and it was her universal suffrage motion that was adopted by a vote of 47 to 11. Zetkin's motion read in part:

> The socialist parties of all countries are duty-bound to fight energetically for the implementation of universal women's suffrage . . . which . . . is to be vigorously advocated both by agitation and by parliamentary means. When a battle for suffrage is conducted, it should only be conducted according to socialist principles, and therefore with the demand of universal suffrage for women and men.[53]

A second women's conference of the Second International was held at Copenhagen three years later. Zetkin was reelected by unanimous vote as secretary of the International Socialist Women and *Gleichheit* was retained as their publication.

At Copenhagen in 1910, the battle over women's suffrage centered on the question of restricted female suffrage. The British and Belgian women supported restrictive female suffrage as a positive, if inadequate, reform measure and a first step in the direction of universal women's suffrage. But Zetkin adamantly opposed this view, arguing that not only was it inadequate for the female sex but it was detrimental to the entire working class. Once again her position was upheld and Zetkin's motion on women's suffrage adopted at Stuttgart was reaffirmed at the Copenhagen conference.[54]

It was at Copenhagen that Clara Zetkin introduced a proposal which called for an annual international socialist women's day. March 8 each year would be celebrated in all countries as International Women's Day and would be organized chiefly around the demand for women's suffrage.

The date March 8 was chosen because of an event that had occurred on that day in the United States. Under the leadership of women workers in the New York City needle trades, a number of whom were socialists, a women's demonstration was called on Sunday, March 8, 1908. Hundreds gathered in Rutgers Square in the heart of Manhattan's Lower East Side to demand the vote and to urge the building of a powerful needle trades' union.

So successful was the 1908 demonstration that it came to the attention of socialist women abroad and Clara Zetkin, who had learned of it, made the motion at Copenhagen that the day of the demonstration of American working women become an International Women's Day and that March 8 each year be dedicated to fighting for equal rights for all women in all countries. Her proposal was accepted by the majority of the delegates and the following year, 1911, the first International Women's Day took place.[55]

After May, 1904, Clara Zetkin directed her attention increasingly to the area of public education. Although she had dealt with the question of education on repeated occasions in the 1890s, it was the enactment of legislation aimed at strengthening the influence of religion in the Prussian public schools that led her to devote more attention to the issue. The law which went into effect in July, 1906 required that Catholic children were to be taught henceforth by Catholic teachers and Protestant children by Protestant teachers. Clara Zetkin fought the legislation, calling for the elimination of all religious influences from public institutions of education. At the same time she called for a uniform, tuition-free educational system from kindergarten through college. She also emphasized the importance of developing through education a respect for the dignity and value of labor. Finally, she called for the introduction into the public schools of co-education "to overcome that which is unhealthy, artificially stimulated, and overly excited in the relations of the sexes to one another." This would help assure that children did not grow up ignorant in sexual matters or imbued with prejudices regarding the so-called inferiority of the female sex.[56]

To enable socialist women to participate in the life of the Party, even while prohibited until 1908 from officially joining, provision was made by the Social-Democractic Party in 1890 for the election of women to party congresses in special women's meetings if legal restrictions or male prejudices prevented their election in open public assemblies. Beginning with 1892, Clara Zetkin was elected as a delegate to every Party annual congress as long as she remained a member of the SPD, and participated actively in all. By 1895 she had established herself among the top leaders of the German Social-Democratic Party. That year she was elected to the governing body of the SPD, the first woman to serve in the party executive of German Social-Democracy—in fact, the first woman ever to be elected in Germany to an office of such responsibility "within a sexually integrated organization." Together with Bebel, Mehring, and four other party leaders, she was elected to the SPD's Central Committee on Education which had been created in 1906 for the purpose of supervising and directing the activities of the party's many educational institutions.[57]

In all respects Clara Zetkin was the leading spokeswoman for Germany's socialist women. But Zetkin's relations with the SPD leadership were never entirely harmonious, and they became much less so after 1908. In that year women were granted freedom of association and assembly everywhere in Germany. This was a great victory for German women, who prior to 1908 were prevented by legal restrictions from becoming involved in electoral politics.

After 1908, the SPD leadership ended the autonomy of the socialist women within the party and integrated their organizations fully into the larger, male-dominated party structure. Decisions with regard to socialist women were rendered henceforth by the party executive committee where women were represented by one female member.[58]

The action was a setback for Clara Zetkin. She was the leading advocate of a separate organization for women in the Party, believing that this provided a mechanism whereby socialist women as a minority, could maximize their influence and guarantee representation of their interests. At the same time, autonomy made it possible to maintain the radical nature of the socialist women's movement and its capacity to function effectually as a radical bloc in decisive political situations.[59]

Zetkin was outspoken in her battle against anti-female prejudice among male German Social-Democrats. She was often angered by the tendency of male party leaders to resort to wit (which always provoked the merriment sought from the audience) to put militant socialist women in their place when they charged discrimination was practiced against women in the party.[60] To Zetkin the fact that criticism of the party by socialist women "was made to look ridiculous" was "a break with revolutionary theory."[61]

In the end, Zetkin lost out. It is significant that the woman chosen for the position on the executive committee was not the longtime radical leader Clara Zetkin, but the more moderate, accommodating Luise Zietz. Zietz, the daughter of a Holstein weaver, had emerged during the 1896 Hamburg longshoremen's strike as an effective agitator, organizer and speaker.[62] Zetkin took an active interest in helping Zietz advance in the Party and in 1908 she was elected to the women's bureau and to a seat on the party executive. Immediately thereafter Zietz began to argue in favor of identifying the interests of the socialist women's movement with those of the party establishment, of which she was now a member. She called for the full integration of the socialist women's organizations into the party's bureaucratic apparatus and a union of the two groups on the leadership level.[63]

The SPD leadership's conflict with Clara Zetkin also stemmed from her opposition to revisionism which was making headway in the German SPD. The revisionists were followers of Edward Bernstein who argued that capitalism was evolving in a direction opposite to that foreseen by Marx. According to Bernstein, capitalism had developed a capacity for adjustment which ruled out serious economic crises for the future and insured the possibility of an infinite expansion of the capitalist economic system, accompained by a trend toward more equitable distribution of wealth. The revisionists were systematically abandoning Marxist beliefs, especially that of the class struggle.[64]

To Clara Zetkin as to Karl Liebknecht, militant son of Wilhelm Liebknecht, and to Rosa Luxemburg, the young Polish revolutionary (with whom Clara Zetkin established a long and meaningful friendship), all this was reformism pure and simple and she fought it with all her energy. Zetkin delivered several major speeches and wrote a number of articles criticizing Bernstein and his followers in Germany. She was instrumental as a member of the Central Committee on Education in blocking the appointment of revisionists and for the appointment of radicals to the faculty of the Party school. (Rosa Luxemburg began teaching in the party school as a result of Zetkin's insistence.) Zetkin exerted pressure to include within the curriculum a greater emphasis on Marxist theory.[65]

Zetkin opposed with equal vigor the conservative direction taken by the SPD's leadership, reflected in the ever more exclusive reliance on success at the polls as the basic route to socialism. The SPD leadership viewed with disfavor Zetkin's enthusiasm for the mass strike and for the Russian Revolution of 1905. While the party executive was indifferent, Zetkin campaigned extensively throughout Germany during 1905-06 for the mass strike and in support of the Russian Revolution.[66] In 1907 she wrote to Franz Mehring, "We must abandon the superstitution that the way of the proletariat to victory leads in a straight line over parliamentarianism and that the parliamentary battle is the only true method of class conflict." Zetkin pointed to the "limitations of parliamentarianism" as the chief tactic of a revolutionary party, and demanded that greater emphasis be placed "on the great forces of political life outside parliament," and the organization of mass actions.[67]

Clara Zetkin was also one of the foremost opponents in the SPD of the revisionist interpretation of imperialism and militarism. In two long articles published during 1907 and in a speech at the Essen Party Congress that fall, Zetkin refuted the revisionist argument that the standing army, imperialism and colonial possessions were not evils to be opposed in principle, but mixed blessings amenable to be "reformed." She rejected Gustav Noske's claim that the SPD had every bit as great an interest as bourgeois parties in the preservation and enhancement of German military might. While granting that the working class possessed a love for the fatherland, she emphasized that this was a different sort from that of the ruling classes, "not . . . a difference of degree, but rather a difference of kind." The patriotism of the proletariat, "proceed[ed] from the view that the fatherland [had to] be conquered first from the internal enemy, bourgeois class domination" and could only then "be transformed into a fatherland for all."[68]

Together with Rosa Luxemburg, Clara Zetkin led the struggle against the socialist supporters of German imperialism at the SPD congress at Jena in September, 1911. The Party leadership introduced a vaguely-worded resolution that condemned imperialist rivalries but avoided any specific criticism of German policy in the Moroccan crisis. The opening paragraph declared:

> The congress of German Social-Democracy raises the most emphatic protest against every attempt to bring about a murderous war between civilized peoples, like the French, British, and Germans, and which must necessarily become a world war, ending catastrophically for all.

Led by Luxemburg and Zetkin, the opponents of imperialism

introduced a series of amendments designed to increase greatly the anti-war and anti-imperialist tone of the resolution. The revised resolution affirmed the SPD's rejection of all manifestations of colonialism, denounced the armaments race being conducted by the German bourgeoisie and demanded mass action to obstruct the plans of aggression of German capitalists and militarists. However, the revised resolution was defeated and the Jena Congress indicated its opposition to any actions that might lead to war, but refused to oppose imperialism *per se*, and even hinted that it agreed with certain aspects of German foreign policy.[69]

Up to the outbreak of the First World War in August, 1914, Clara Zetkin conducted a vigorous campaign against militarism and imperialist war. She continued this role even after the war started. When the German Social-Democrats in the Reichstag voted for the August 4, 1914 war credits, Zetkin was one of the first to denounce openly the party position. She was also the first to hail Karl Liebknecht who had initially voted for war credits, (yielding to SPD discipline) but convinced that the war was instigated by imperialist rivalries, refused to vote any additional war credits.[70] Zetkin viewed the socialist vote for war credits this time even worse than that of August 4, "because in the meantime events have destroyed the phony arguments about the necessity to serve the fatherland."[71]

On September 4, 1914 Zetkin noted in *Gleichheit* that martial law had made it "impossible for us to seek a conscientious answer to the question: Did it have to be? It prevents us from showing up plainly the social forces whose inexorable rule has dashed the hopes and desires of the millions in all countries who have now been dragged into the tornado of the war." This did not, however, prevent her from continuing to express her opposition to the war in the pages of the paper. That this increasingly brought *Gleichheit* into conflict with censorship was shown by the amounts of black space in the columns which Zetkin, supported by the editorial board, demonstratively left standing. By now *Gleichheit* was internationally recognized as the organ of women opposed to the war.[72]

The November 7, 1914 issue carried Zetkin's appeal "To the Socialist Women of All Countries." She urged: "When the men kill, it is up to us women to fight for the preservation of life. When the men are silent, it is our duty to raise our voices in behalf of our ideals." The appeal did not have the approval of the Party, but Zetkin refused to be deterred. As president of the International organisation of socialist women, she took the initative in summoning a conference in Bern, Switzerland which also did not have the Party's approval. The "illegal" women's conference met on March 15, 1915 and was attended by 28 delegates from Britain, France, Germany, Italy, Poland, Russia, Holland and Switzerland. This first organized expression of socialist opposition to the war adopted a resolution drawn up by Clara Zetkin which condemned the war,[73] and issued a manifesto also written by Zetkin.

The manifesto, addressed to Women of the Working People, opened with the questions: "Where are your husbands? Where are your sons?" It answered: "For eight months now, they have been at the front. They have been torn from their work and their homes.... Millions are already resting in mass graves, hundreds upon hundreds of thousands lie in military hospitals with torn-up bodies, smashed limbs, blinded eyes, destroyed brains and ravished by epidemics or cast down by exhaustion." Later, the manifesto asked: "Who profits from this war?" It answered:

> Only a tiny minority in each nation: The manufacturers of rifles and cannons, of armor-plate and torpedo boats, the shipyard owners and the suppliers of the armed forces' needs. In the interest of their profits, they have fanned the hatred among the people, thus contributing to the outbreak of the war. This war is beneficial for the capitalists in general. . . .
>
> The workers have nothing to gain from this war, but they stand to lose everything that is dear to them.

The manifesto ended with the ringing call: "Down with War! Break through to Socialism!"[74]

The manifesto was printed in Switzerland and widely distributed in Germany as an underground leaflet. On July 23, 1915 the *New York Times* reported that "criminal proceedings" had been instituted against Clara Zetkin "on account of alleged treasonable articles." Zetkin was described as one of "The most outspoken and active members in the German Socialist party, opposing the continuance of the war and insisting upon an immediate move toward peace negotiations."[75]

Shortly after the women's conference in Bern, Clara Zetkin was arrested for distributing the manifesto drawn up at the meeting. She was held in "protective custody" for four months in Karlsruhe.

In May, 1917 the SPD Executive removed Clara Zetkin as editor of *Gleichheit.* The official explanation was that the articles under Zetkin's editorship "were unpalatable for the great majority of women workers." The real reason was her unwavering criticism of the Majority Socialists' support of the war.[76]

Zetkin responded in "To the Socialist Women of All Countries," published in the *Leipziger Volkzeitung* of June 19, 1917. She insisted that the "real reason" for her expulsion was "the principled stand of this periodical." To have been silent in the face of the war policies of the Majority Socialists "would have been to assume an attitude of undignified cowardice."[77]

Clara Zetkin enthusiastically embraced the Bolshevik Revolution in Russia. She rejected the view of many socialists that because the revolution had occurred in a backward country, it was not a true socialist revolution. Not only was a socialist society being created in Russia, but "from the mere fact that it occurred, new creative impulses will radiate in all directions."[78] Speaking on the occasion of the fifth anniversary of the Bolshevik Revolution, Zetkin described the revolution as a "thunderstorm" in a "stifling atmosphere," and as having "commenced the actual liquidation of Revisionism, of Reformism." Furthermore:

> I venture to say that Soviet Russia is today, notwithstanding its poverty and the disorganization of the economic system, the State with the most advanced labor protection and social welfare legislation and not only on paper.[79]

On New Year's Day, 1916, delegates from around Germany met secretly in the law offices of Karl Liebknecht to establish the *Gruppe Internationale,* which became the Spartacus League in November, 1918 and was the nucleus of the German Communist Party (KPD), founded at the end of December, 1918. Clara Zetkin became a founding member of the KPD. In 1917 she had left the Social-Democratic Party to become a member of the Independent Social-Democratic Party (USPD), newly formed in January, 1917 by a group of anti-war socialists. The Independent Socialists wavered between the SPD and the Spartacus League. Its leadership eventually went back into the SPD after the war, but Clara Zetkin led many of the rank and file into the German Communist Party. Zetkin hailed the KPD as a political organization which "courageously dares to appear what it actually is, a revolutionary, proletarian fighting Party."

After the brutal murders of Karl Liebknecnt and Rosa Luxemburg on January 15, 1919 by the reactionary *Freikorps* working hand-in-glove with right-wing socialist leaders, and the death of Franz Mehring, Clara Zetkin was the most important prewar Socialist leader in the German Communist Party. She was accorded a place of honor in the KPD. She was a member of its central committee from 1919 to 1923, and again in 1927. She sat in the Reichstag for the KPD continuously from the first to the last session of the Weimar Republic.[80]

"The dictatorship of the proletariat can only be achieved and maintained with the intensive and active participation of working class women." So concluded the resolution on women adopted by the founding congress of the Third or Communist International (also called the Comintern) in March, 1919. Clara Zetkin hailed this stand, and immediately gave her endorsement of the new International in the first issue of the KPD women's journal—*Die Komunisten*. By the summer of 1919 her articles were appearing in the *Communist International*, the organ of the Third International.[81]

In the spring of 1920, the executive committee of the Communist International appointed Clara Zetkin, already an active member of the West European secretariat, as International Secretary of Communist Women. She was then sixty-two years old. Thirteen years before she had been chosen secretary of the International Socialist women's movement.[82]

Partly because her work as International Secretary required it and partly because she was often ill and received special medical care, Clara Zetkin lived much of the time in the Soviet Union. She often met with Lenin. "Comrade Lenin frequently spoke to me about the woman question," she began her pamphlet, *Lenin on the Woman Question*. Written after she had held two extended conversations with Lenin in his Kremlin study, Zetkin reported that she had been impressed by Lenin's comments on many aspects of the woman question. She noted his observation that while "a woman communist is a member of the Party just as a man communist, with equal rights and duties," it was still necessary to have special organizations for women in the Communist Party. "We need appropriate bodies to carry on work among them," Lenin emphasized in calling for "methods of agitation and forms of organization" specially geared to deal with the problems of women. "That is not feminism," Lenin insisted, "that is practical, revolutionary expediency."

"I told Lenin," Zetkin wrote, "that his words encouraged me greatly." Recalling her battle with the leadership of the German SPD over special organizations for women, she pointed out to Lenin that many comrades "strongly combatted the idea that the Party should have special bodies for systematic work among women," viewing this as nothing less than "feminism." But Lenin urged her not to yield on this issue. "All that sort of talk breaks down before inexorable necessity. Unless millions of women are with us we cannot exercise the proletarian dictatorship, cannot construct on Communist lines."[83]

Clara Zetkin was so often ill and weak during her years in the Soviet Union that she was confined to bed for long periods, but this did not prevent her from giving whatever help she could to the international working-class movement, to the struggle against racism and war. She headed the International Red Aid organization, known in the Soviet Union as the MOPR, and helped organize international campaigns against persecution of men and women in various countries.[84]

An outstanding example was the campaign to save the Scottsboro Boys from the electric chair. On March 25, 1931, nine Black youths, one barely twelve years old, were accused of raping two white girls while "hobo-ing" out of Alabama and into Tennessee in search of work. They were quickly tried in Scottsboro, Alabama, and found guilty by an all-white jury. Eight of the nine were sentenced to death. A defense campaign was instituted, spearheaded by the International Labor Defense (ILD) and the Communist Party; it grew to international proporations.[85] As head of the International Red Aid, Clara Zetkin issued an appeal in April, 1932 "Save the Scottsboro Black Youths!" addressed to all "who still possess a humane mind and heart! let us save these eight young men from the executioner and the pyre of the electric chair," she appealed. "Their only crime has been that they were born with Black skins."[86]

The Scottsboro youths escaped execution but they remained in prison for years despite the evidence that the rape charge was a hoax. The last of the imprisoned Scottsboro victims was released in 1950.

Despite blindness, illness and Nazi threats on her life, Clara Zetkin returned to Berlin in the summer of 1932. Her last public appearance in Germany was on the occasion of the opening of the Reichstag in which Hitler and the Nazis, with the aid of President Hindenburg, were attempting to assume control although they were still in a minority. In accordance with the tradition that each new Reichstag be convened by its oldest member, Clara Zetkin was entitled to open its first session on August 30, 1932. Although the Nazi terror was already enveloping the country, she came out of hiding and made a dramatic appearance on the rostrum. In her speech, which lasted over an hour, she vehemently denounced fascism, and appealed for "the formation of a United Front of all workers in order to turn back fascism, in order to preserve for the enslaved and exploited the force and power of their organization as well as to maintain their own physical existence." "The United Front of workers," she continued, " . . . must not lack the millions of women, who still bear the chains of sex slavery, and are therefore exposed to the most oppressive class slavery." She closed her final speech in her native land with "the hope that despite my current infirmities, I may yet have the fortune to open as honorary president the first Soviet Congress of a Soviet Germany."[87]

This, of course, was not to be. In January, 1933, Hitler seized power. By that time Clara Zetkin had returned to the Soviet Union. It was there that she died on June 22, 1933.

Clara Zetkin's last work was published shortly before she died. Entitled *The Toilers Against War*,[88] it described the anti-war movement during "the imperialist struggle for power of 1914-18," the bitter fruits of that war for the working class and the people in general, the determination of the capitalist countries to launch a new imperialist war, especially against the Soviet Union, and an analysis of the peace policy of the USSR. "The Soviet Union," she wrote, "is the first and only honestly peaceful state in the world. It has to be so, not from bourgeois-pacifist sentimentality, but in order to fulfill its mighty historical mission, in order to transform through socialism, its far-flung area of rule and to build up therein a new, higher economic and social order."[89]

Clara Zetkin called upon "the workers to throw their whole power into the struggle against imperialist wars without the slightest hesitation or reserve." Echoing the outcry of millions during World War I, she appealed in her last message to the world: "NO MORE WARS!"[90]

In January, 1915, the British journal *Labour Woman* wrote of Clara Zetkin: "She is Socialist in her very fibre, and she is a fighter ready to face death rather than give way in any issue of import in the people's struggle."[91] Clara Zetkin displayed these qualities in leading the largest women's socialist movement in Europe, in editing the most important woman's journal in Europe for over twenty-five years, in organizing working women into trade unions, in battling for women's suffrage and equal rights (in the course of which she established International Women's Day), in the battle against revisionism, and in her militant opposition to militarism, imperialism and the first World War. Through her journal *Gleichheit* (Equality), with a circulation in 1914 of 125,000, and her numerous speeches which she delivered at Party congresses and the Second and Third Internationals, she was able to exert a powerful influence in the formation of socialist and communist policy on the woman question, and on the policy of a number of trade unions toward women workers. In words that have lost none of their meaning, she wrote in *Gleichheit* of November 1, 1893:

> . . . the labor movement will surely commit suicide if, in the efforts to enroll the broad masses of the proletariat, it does not pay the same amount of attention to female workers as it does to male workers.

Clara Zetkin's writings and speeches are still too little known in the United States. With the publication of the present volume, there will finally be available a representative selection of the thoughts of the leading woman of European socialism.

CLARA ZETKIN

Selected Writings

Translated by Kai Schoenhals

1889

FOR THE LIBERATION OF WOMEN

Speech at the International Workers' Congress, Paris, July 19th.

Accompanied by heavy applause, Citizen Zetkin, delegate of the working women of Berlin,[1] now began to speak[2] on the question of women's work.[3] She explained that she had no intention to talk about the situation of female workers because their situation was no different from that of male workers. Instead, with the consent of those that had sent her, she intended to illuminate the general principles of women's work. Since that question was surrounded by a great deal of confusion, it was incumbent upon this workers' congress to address itself clearly to this topic by probing the underlying principles.

She declared that it was not surprising that reactionary elements hold reactionary views about women's work [work outside the home]. What is most surprising, however, is the fact that one encounters the erroneous concept in the Socialist camp, too, that women's work should be abolished. The question of women's emancipation, which in the final analysis is the question of women's work, is an economic question and one is entitled to expect a greater degree of economic understanding from Socialists than the above-mentioned point of view implies.

The Socialists must know that given the present economic development, women's work is a necessity, that the natural tendency of women's work is either to reduce the working hours that every individual must render to society or to augment the wealth of society, that it is not women's work per se which in competition with men's work lowers wages, but rather the exploitation of female labor by the capitalists who appropriate it.

Above all, the Socialists must know that social slavery or freedom rests upon economic dependence or independence.

Those who have proclaimed on their banners the liberation of all those being bearing a human countenance, ought not to condemn half of humanity to political and social slavery through economic dependence. Just as the workers are subjugated by the capitalists, women are subjugated by men and they will continue to be in that position as long as they are not economically independent. The quintessential prerequisite for their economic independence is work. If one wants to transform women into free human beings and into equal members of society just like men, then there is no necessity to abolish or limit women's work except in a few special cases.

Women workers who strive for social equality do not expect to obtain their emancipation from the women's movement of the bourgeoisie which allegedly fights for women's rights. That edifice is built on sand and has no realistic foundation. Women workers are totally convinced that the question of the emancipation of women is not an isolated one but rather constitutes a part of the great social question. They know very clearly that this question in today's society cannot be solved without a basic transformation of society. The question of the emancipation of women is a child of modern times, born by the machine age.

The emancipation of women means the complete transformation of their social position and a revolution in their economic role. The old form of production, with its incomplete means of work, tied women to their families and limited their range of activities to the interior of the home. Within the circle of their families, women comprised an extraordinarily productive force. They produced almost all family commodities. Given the former level of production and trade, it would have been very difficult, if not impossible, to produce these articles outside the family. As long as these ancient ways of production predominated, so long women were economically productive. . . .

Machine production has killed the economic activities of women within their families. Large-scale industry produces all articles cheaper, faster and more massively than small individual workshops which worked with tools of a dwarfish nature. Women must often pay more for the raw materials that they purchase than for the finished product of machine-dominated, large-scale industry. Besides that purchase price (of raw materials), she must contribute her time and labor. As a consequence, productive activity within the family became economic nonsense and a waste of time and effort. Even though a woman involved in production within her family circle might be of use to some individuals, this sort of activity nevertheless constitutes a loss for society as a whole.

That is the reason why the housekeeper of the good old times has all but vanished. Large-scale industry has rendered the production of goods within the home unnecessary and has made the domestic activity of women meaningless. At the same time, it has created the basis for the activity of women within society. Mechanical production, which can do without muscular power and qualified work, has made it possible that women may be employed on a large-scale basis. Women entered industry with the desire to augment the income of their families. With the development of modern industry, female industrial labor became a necessity. Thus with every modern improvement, male labor became superfluous, thousands of workers were thrown out into the street, a reserve army of the poor was created and wages became continuously lower.

In former times, the man's wage along with the productive activity of his wife at home had sufficed to insure the existence of his family. Now it is hardly enough for the survival of a single worker. A married male worker must, by necessity, count upon the salary of his wife.

This factor freed women of their economic dependence upon men. Women who are active in industry cannot possibly remain exclusively at home as the mere economic appendices of men. Thus they became aware of their economic power which made them self-sufficient and independent of men; and, once women have attained their economic independence from men, there is no reason why they should remain socially dependent upon them. At this moment, however, this newly found economic independence does not help women but aids only the capitalists. Due to their monopoly of the means of production, the capitalists have usurped these new economic factors and made them work exclusively to their advantage. Women who had been liberated from the economic dependence upon their husbands merely changed masters and are now subjugated by the capitalists. The slave of the husband became the slave of the employer. Women, nevertheless, gained from this transformation; they are no longer disadvantaged economically vis-a-vis men but have become equals. The capitalists, however, are not content just to exploit women per se; they use female labor to exploit male labor even more thoroughly.

Women's work was, to begin with, cheaper than men's work. A man's wage was originally calculated to cover the expenses of his entire family. A woman's wage from the beginning was designed to cover merely the costs of sustaining a single person and only partially at that because it was assumed that a woman would continue to work at home after finishing her tasks at the factory. Furthermore, the products manufactured with primitive work tools by women domestically represented only a small quantity of the middle-level output by society. This persuaded people to deduce that women produce less than men and consequently ought to obtain less pay for their work. To these reasons for inferior wages must be added the fact that in general women have less requirements than men.

What made women's labor particularly attractive to the capitalists was not only its lower price but also the greater submissiveness of women. The capitalists speculate on the two following factors: the female worker must be paid as poorly as possible and the competition of female labor must be employed to lower the wages of male workers as much as possible. In the same manner the capitalists use child labor to depress women's wages and the work of machines to depress all human labor. The capitalist system alone must be blamed for the fact that women's work has the opposite result of its natural tendency; it results in a longer work day instead of a considerably shorter one. It is not tantamount to an increase in society's wealth, by which is meant a higher standard of living for every individual member of society; it results merely in an increase of profits for a handful of capitalists and, at the same time, in the constantly growing poverty of the masses. The pernicious consequences of women's labor, which are so painfully felt today, will only disappear once the capitalist system of production passes out of existence.

In order not to succumb to his competitors, the capitalist must make the greatest effort to maintain the largest difference between the cost (manufacturing) price and the selling price of his goods. Thus he seeks to produce as cheaply and to sell as expensively as possible. The capitalist, therefore, has every interest to prolong the work day as far as possible and to give to the worker the most ridiculously low pay. This endeavor stands in opposition to the interests of female workers just as much as male workers. Thus there is no real opposition between the interests of male and female workers but there certainly exists an irreconcilable contrast between the interests of the capitalists and of the working class.

Economic reasons speak against the support for the prohibition of female labor. The current economic situation is such that neither the capitalist nor the male citizen can do without women's labor. The capitalist must maintain it in order to remain competitive and the male citizen count on it if he plans to establish a family. The outlawing of women's work by legislation would not improve the wages of men. The capitalists would very soon replace the lack of cheap female labor by the employment of more efficient machinery—and very shortly everything would be just as it was before.

It has been shown that after extensive strikes whose outcome was favorable to the workers, the capitalists destroyed the successes achieved by the workers with the aid of more efficient machinery.

If one demands the abolition or limitation of women's work because of the competition it creates, one might just as well use the same logic and abolish machines in order to demand the recreation of the medieval guild system which determined the exact number of workers that were to be employed in each type of work.

Besides economic reasons, there are reasons of principle which speak out against a prohibition of female labor. Women must base themselves upon principles when they protest with all of their might against such attempts. They must put up the fiercest and, at the same time, most justified resistance because they know that their social and political equality with men rests solely upon their economic independence which enables them to work outside of their families for society.

From the standpoint of principle, we women protest most emphatically against a limitation of women's work. Because we do not want to separate our cause from that of the working class in general, we will not formulate any special demands. We demand no other type of protection than that which labor demands in general from the capitalists.[4]

We will permit only one exception: that of a pregnant woman whose condition requires special protective measures in the interest of the woman herself as well as of her progeny. We do not recognize any special woman's question and we do not recognize any special female worker's question! We do not expect our full emancipation by our admittance into what is called the free enterprise system or equal schooling with men (even though the demand for these two rights is perfectly natural and just) or the granting of political rights. Those countries which allegedly maintain universal, free and direct suffrage show us its relatively insignificant worth. The right to vote which is not accompanied by economic freedom is more or less a change without direction. There would exist no social problem in the countries maintaining universal suffrage if social emancipation would be dependent upon the attainment of political rights. The emancipation of women as well as all of humankind will only occur within the framework of the emancipation of labor from capital. Only within a socialist society will women as well as workers attain their full rights.

In view of these facts, women who are seriously interested in their liberation have really no choice but to join the Social-Democratic Party,[5] which is the only one that fights for the emancipation of labor.

Without the assistance of men, indeed often against their wishes, women stepped under the banner of Socialism. One has to admit that in certain cases they were irresistibly pushed towards this step against their own intentions, simply by their clear realization of the economic situation.

But now they are standing under this banner and they will remain under it! They will fight under it for their emancipation and for their recognition as equal human beings.

By walking hand in hand with the Social-Democratic Party, they are ready to share all burdens and sacrifices that this fight entails but they are also fiercely determined to demand, after the achievement of victory, all of the rights which are rightfully theirs. As far as the sacrifices and duties as well as the rights are concerned, they want no more and no less than those of their male comrades who were accepted under equal circumstances into the ranks of the warriors.

(Loud applause—which is repeated after citizen Aveling[6] has translated this discourse into English and French).

[*Protocol of the International Workingmen's Congress at Paris. Held from July 14th until July 20th, 1889*. Nürnberg 1890, pp. 80-85.] □

1893

WOMEN'S WORK AND THE ORGANIZATION OF TRADE UNIONS

The Party Congress of Cologne will have to address itself to the question of trade union organization, i.e., the relationship between the political and trade union movement. The question will be dealt with because of the urgings of trade union circles. Recently the trade unions have declined; within the trade union movement there is a tendency to blame, among other factors, the attitude of the political movement for this phenomenon. In our opinion, the political labor press correctly rejected the above-mentioned accusations and welcomed the fact that the Cologne Party Congress, by once again addressing this issue, will help to overcome the existing distrust on the part of the unions.

There remains the indubitable fact that in all capitalist countries, women's work in industry plays an ever larger role. The number of industrial branches in which women nowadays toil and drudge from morning till night increases with every year.

Industry	Employed in 1882		Women as % of All Employed
	Men	Women	
Lace Production	5,676	30,204	84.1
Clothing, Linen, Finery	279,978	440,870	61.2
Spinning	69,272	100,459	59.2
Haberdashery Items	13,526	17,478	56.4
Service and Restaurants	172,841	141,407	45.0
Tobacco Production	64,477	48,919	43.1
Embroidery and Weaving	42,819	31,010	42.0
Paper Manufacturing	37,685	20,847	35.6
Textiles	336,400	155,396	31.6
Messenger Service	9,212	3,265	26.2
Commerce	536,221	181,296	25.3
Bookbinding and Carton Making	31,312	10,409	24.9

Factories which have traditionally employed women, employ more and more women workers. It is not only that the number of all industrially employed women is constantly growing, but their number in relation to the men who are working in industry and trade is also on the increase.

Some branches of industry (one has only to think of clothing) are virtually dominated by women's labor which constantly reduces and replaces men's labor.

For understandable reasons, particularly during periods of recession (like the one we are experiencing right now),[1] the number of women workers has increased in both relative and absolute terms whereas the number of employed male laborers has decreased. As we have already reported, during 1892 in Saxony the number of male workers over 16 years of age decreased by 1,633 whereas the number of female workers of similar age increased by 2,466.

According to the Viennese university instructor, J. Singer, five million women were working in Germany's industry during the last few years.[2]

The business survey of 1882 points out that out of 7,340,789 individually employed persons in Germany, 1,509,167 (20.6%) were women. Thus there were 21 women for every 100 persons involved in industrial production.

The extent of women's industrial work is also clearly demonstrated by the most recent annual reports of the factory inspectors. In the factories protected by law, there were employed: in Saxony 241,088 male workers and 123,548 female laborers, in Baden 84,806 male workers and 41,491 female workers, in Hessen 41,778 male workers and 12,210 female workers, in Saxony-Altenburg 9,553 male laborers and 4,043 female workers etc. In Württemberg there were 27,719 adult female workers and in Prussia over 250,000 (this number does not include all those women working as domestic servants and in the mining industry).

These statistics give only an approximate idea of the extent to which female labor is being used since the myriad of women who work in factories which are not "under the protection of the law" and do not, therefore, come under factory inspection, have not been included. How extensive is just the number of women who slave away as domestic servants!

The reasons for the constantly growing use of female laborers have been repeatedly pointed out: their cheapness and the improvement of the mechanical means and methods of production. The automatic machine, which in many cases does not even stand in need of having to be regulated, works with the powers of a giant, possesses unbelievable skill, speed and exactness and renders muscle power and acquired skills superfluous. The capitalist entrepreneur can employ only female labor at those places where he previously had to use male employees. And he just loves to hire women because female labor is cheap, much cheaper than male labor.

Even though the productive capacity of female workers does not lag behind that of male workers, the difference between men's and women's wages is very significant. The latter is often only half of the former and often only a third.

According to the Leipzig Chamber of Commerce, the following weekly wages were paid:

	Men (Marks)	Women (Marks)
Fabrication of Lace	20-35	7-15
Factory for Paper Lanterns	16-22	7.50-10
Woolen Industry	15-27	7.20-10.20
Cloth Glove Factory	12-30	6-15
Fabrication of Leather and Leather Goods	12-28	7-18
Linen and Jute Factory	12-27	5-10
Sugar Factory	10.50-31	7.50-10
Rubber Factory	9-27	6-17

In 1892, the Leipzig Health Insurance Office made a statistical analysis of wages which determined that 60% of the women workers have weekly earnings of below or up to 9 marks, 32% up to 12 marks and only 7% up to 15 or 19 to 21 marks. As far as earnings are concerned, men, too, do not fare well but they do better than their female counterparts; 37% of the men earn up to 15 marks, 30% up to 19 marks and 33% up to 21 marks.

The women laborers of Berlin's chemical industry earn highly unfavorable wages; 74% of them have a weekly wage of only up to 10 marks and 50 pfennigs. Of the remaining 26%, only 2% have a weekly salary of up to 24 marks.

From Hessen, Bavaria, Saxony, Thuringia, Württemberg, i.e., from all of God's little German fatherlands, the factory inspectors report that the wages of women workers are far below those of male laborers. Factory Inspector Worrishoffer of Baden undertook a very thorough investigation of the social situation of factory workers. It, too, demonstrates very clearly the miserable earnings of women who work in industry. Worrishoffer divided male and female workers according to their earnings into three wage groups: a low one with a weekly salary of less than 15 marks, a medium one whose weekly wages amount to 15 to 24 marks and a high one whose weekly salary is more than 24 marks. Of the female workers of Mannheim, 99.2% belong to the low category, 0.7% to the medium and 0.1% to the higher wage group. In other words, of 100 women workers in Mannheim, 99 have a weekly salary of below 15 marks and 27 [of these] have a salary of up to 10 marks. These statistics amply illustrate the fact that the living conditions of these female workers correspond to their miserable earnings. It is easily understandable that these customary starvation wages for female laborers push thousands of them from the proletariat into the lumpenproletariat. Their dire straits force some of them to take up part-time or temporary prostitution so that by selling their bodies, they may earn the piece of bread that they cannot secure by the sale of their labor.

But it is not just the women workers who suffer because of the miserable payment of their labor. The male workers, too, suffer because of it. As a consequence of their low wages, the women are transformed from mere competitors into unfair competitors who push down the wages of men. Cheap women's labor eliminates the work of men and if the men want to continue to earn their daily bread, they must put up with low wages. Thus women's work is not only a cheap form of labor, it also cheapens the work of men and for that reason it is doubly appreciated by the capitalist, who craves profits. An entire branch of industry—the textile business—is living proof of how women's work is used to depress wages. The low salaries paid to textile workers is in part the result of the extensive use of female labor in that industry. The wool and cotton barons have used the cheap work of women in order to lower the working and living conditions of an entire category of the proletariat to a level that defies culture.

The transfer of hundreds of thousands of female laborers to the modernized means of production that increase productivity ten or even a hundredfold should have resulted (and did result in some cases) in a higher standard of living for the proletariat, given a rationally organized society. But as far as the proletariat is concerned, capitalism has changed blessing into curse and wealth into bitter proverty. The economic advantages of the industrial activity of proletarian women only aid the tiny minority of the sacrosanct guild of coupon clippers and extortionists of profit.

Frightened by the economic consequences of women's work and the abuses connected with it, organized labor demanded for a while the prohibition of female labor. It was viewing this question merely from the narrow viewpoint of the wage question. Thanks to Socialist propaganda, the class-conscious proletariat has learned to view this question from another angle, from the angle of its historical importance for the liberation of women and the liberation of the proletariat. It understands now how impossible it is to abolish the industrial labor of women. Thus it has dropped its former demand and it attempts to lessen the bad economic consequences of women's work within capitalist society (and only within it!) by two other means; by the legal protection of female workers and by their inclusion in trade union organizations. We have already mentioned above the necessity and the advantageous effects of the legal protection of women workers. The above-listed statistics concerning the extent of women's industrial labor and the low wages paid to the female labor force as well as the universally known fact of the wage-depressing influence of female work all speak clearly for the necessity and the significance of organizing working women into trade unions.

Given the fact that many thousands of female workers are active in industry, it is vital for the trade unions to incorporate them into their movement. In individual industries where female labor plays an important role, any movement advocating better wages, shorter working hours, etc., would be doomed from the start because of the attitude of those women workers who are not organized. Battles which began propitiously enough, ended up in failure because the employers were able to play off non-union female workers against those that are organized in unions. These non-union workers continued to work (or took up work) under any conditions, which transformed them from competitors in dirty work to scabs.

It is not only because of the successful economic battles of trade unions that women should be included in them. The improvement of the starvation wages of female workers and the limitation of competition among them requires their organization into unions.

The fact that the pay for female labor is so much lower than that of male labor has a variety of causes. Certainly one of the reasons for these poor wages for women is the circumstance that female workers are practically unorganized. They lack the strength which comes with unity. They lack the courage, the feeling of power, the spirit of resistance and the ability to resist which is produced by the strength of an organization in which the individual fights for everybody and everybody fights for the individual. Furthermore, they lack the enlightenment and the training which an organization provides. Without an understanding of modern economic life in whose machinery they are inextricably caught up, they will neither be able to take advantage of periods of boom through conscious, calculating and unified conduct nor will they be able to protect themselves against the disadvantages occurring during periods of economic recession. If, under the pressure of unbearable conditions they finally fight back, they usually do so at an inopportune moment and in a disorganized fashion.

This situation exercises a great influence upon the miserable state of women's work and is further reflected by the bitterness that male workers feel about women's competition. Thus in the interest of both men and women workers, it is urgently recommended that the latter be included in the trade unions. The larger the number of organized female workers who fight shoulder to shoulder with their comrades from the factory or workshop for better working conditions, the sooner and the greater will women's wages rise so that soon there may be the realization of the principle: Equal pay for equal work regardless of the difference in sex. The organized female worker who has become the equal of the male worker ceases to be his scab competitor.

The unionized male workers realize more and more just how important it is that the female workers are accepted into the ranks of their organization. During these past few years, there was no lack of effort on the part of the unions in regard to this endeavor. And yet how little has been accomplished and how incredibly much remains to be done in this respect.

According to the Report of the General Commission of the Trade Unions of Germany, out of fifty-two organizations, there are only fourteen that have a membership of both male and female workers. Then there are two organizations that consist only of women and girls. What does all this mean given the large and steadily growing number of industries which employ women?

Even in those industrial branches in which the trade union organization of women began, these organizations are still in their infancy:

Trade Union Organization	Number of all Members	Number of Female Members	Percentage of Female Members
Tobacco Workers	11,079	2,560	23.1
Textile Workers	6,515	620	9.5
Book Binders	2,752	210	7.6
Brushmakers	858	59	6.9
Cigar Sorters	480	30	6.2
Woodworkers	608	28	4.6
Gold and Silver Workers	1,934	83	4.3
Pastry Makers	395	14	3.5
Gilders	555	16	2.9
Tailors	6,272	131	2.1
Shoemakers	10,150	150	1.5
Metal Workers	26,121	152	0.6
Turners	2,288	1	
Saddle Makers	1,102	1	
Ironers	100	1	
Central League of the Women and Girls	200	200	

NOTE: Female workers who might be organized in local unions have not been included. There are no statistics about their number, which is insignificant anyway.

As far as the percentage of female membership is concerned, the Tobacco Workers rank first, and yet these women workers do not even constitute a fourth of its entire membership. In 1882, 43.1% of all tobacco industry workers were women. In the other four trade unions which come next, as far as the percentage of women that work in the industries they represent are concerned, women workers do not even constitute 10% of the membership. The Organization of Gold and Silver Workers does not have a female membership of even 5% even though there are large numbers of women workers who are employed by the gold and silver industry. In 1882, 60% of all laborers in spinning mills and 30% of all laborers in weaving mills happened to be women, yet the percentage of them who were unionized amounted to only 9½%. These numbers, in conjunction with the slave wages which generally prevail in the textile industry, speak whole volumes about the necessity of unionizing women.

In recognition of this necessity, the trade unions should use all of their energies to work for the inclusion of women in their organizations.

We certainly do not fail to recognize the difficulties raised by women workers which are detrimental to the solution of this problem. Stupid resignation, lack of a feeling of solidarity, shyness, prejudices of all kinds and fear of the factory tyrant keep many women from joining unions.[3] Even more than the just mentioned factors, the lack of time on the part of female workers represents a major obstacle against their mass organization because women are house as well as factory slaves and are forced to bear a double workload. The economic developments, however, as well as the increasing acuteness of the class struggle, educate both male and female laborers and force them to overcome the above-mentioned difficulties.

We certainly recognize the fact that during the past few years, the trade unions have made a serious effort to enroll female workers alongside their male colleagues. But what has been accomplished and aimed for does not come up to the urgency and the importance of the task. Theoretically, most male union members admit that the common unionization of both male and female workers of the same trade has become an unavoidable necessity. In practice, however, many of them do not make the effort that they could be making. Rather there are only a few unions and within them only certain individuals who pursue with energy and perseverance the organization of female workers. The majority of trade union members give them precious little support. They treat such endeavors as a hobby which should be tolerated but not supported "as long as there are still so many indifferent non-union male workers." This point of view is totally wrong.

The unionization of women workers will make significant progress only when it is no longer merely aided by the few, but by every single union member making every effort to enlist their female colleagues from factory and workshop. In order to fulfill this task, two things are necessary. The male workers must stop viewing the female worker primarily as a woman to be courted if she is young, beautiful, pleasant and cheerful (or not). They must stop (depending on their degree of culture or lack of it) molesting them with crude and fresh sexual advances. The workers must rather get accustomed to treat female laborers primarily as female proletarians, as working-class comrades fighting class slavery and as equal and indispensable co-fighters in the class struggle. The unions make such a big thing out of having all of the members and followers of the political party become members of the unions. It seems to us that it would be much more important to put the emphasis on enrolling the broad, amorphous masses in the labor movement. In our opinion, the main task of the unions is the enlightenment, disciplining and education [of all workers] for the class struggle. In view of the increasing use of female labor and the subsequent results, the labor movement will surely commit suicide if, in its effort to enroll the broad masses of the proletariat, it does not pay the same amount of attention to female workers as it does to male ones.

[*Die Gleichheit*[4] Stuttgart, November 1, 1893] □

Clara Zetkin (1.) with Frederick Engels at her side and August Bebel during the International Socialist Workers' Congress, Zurich, 1893.

1895

CONCERNING THE WOMEN'S RIGHTS PETITION

*Last summer, twenty-two women's rights organizations joined in a Rutli League and "most humbly" implored in a petition to the Kaiser, his cabinet council and his allied princes, the legal prohibition of prostitution and the severe punishment of prostitutes, pimps, etc. The obsequiousness of this petition was a reflection of the sociopolitical ignorance that suffused this "plea" and the arrogance of these organizations which "dared" to plead, assuming that they would be regarded as "experts on women's questions."[1]

Now an actual total of three women have been dug up who plead in a petition for the female sex to have the right to form associations and hold meetings. A total of three women took the initiative on behalf of the bourgeois women's world to advocate the gaining of a basic right, the lack of which happens to be one of the major signs of the social inferiority of the female sex in Germany!

The petition appeals to the women "of all parties and all classes." Hence, the signatures of the proletarians, the female Social Democrats, are also welcomed.

I do not want to inquire whether it is necessary for proletarian

*The Editors of *Vorwarts:* We offer space for the following article without agreeing with all of its aspects. We want to emphasize that we are just as loyal to the principles of our party as Comrade Zetkin and the *Gleichheit*. The live ammunition that Comrade Zetkin expends is out of all proportion to the significance of this battle and should be saved for more important objects of attack. The petition that is being assaulted here did not emanate from women's leagues and a women's rights organization, but from three women who happen to be members of our party. By the way, before the *Vorwärts* took a position on this petition, it was signed by the women of our party.

women to sign a petition for the right to form associations and to hold meetings at the same time the party which represents their interests as much as those of the male proletariat, has submitted a bill concerning this matter in the Reichstag (Imperial Diet). As is well known, the Social-Democratic faction in the Reichstag demands the substitution of the individual state laws concerning the right of forming associations and assemblages by new uniform legislation for the entire empire. This new legislation calls for equal rights of both sexes and, at the same time, the legal guarantee for the unrestricted exercise of the freedom to form coalitions. Thus it does not only request what the petition demands, but even more.

It might seem "expedient" to some people, perhaps even to many (expediency seems to come before principle for quite a few people within our party, too), that the petition obtain the support of unionized male workers and the signatures of proletarian women. A petition which is thus supported by massive signatures seems to them an appropriate demonstration in favor of the Social-Democratic Bill and as proof that all strata of women feel the urgent desire to possess the right of forming associations and of holding assemblies.

In my opinion such a demonstration is permanently extant even without the petition, and the proof of that is rendered constantly and most emphatically by the tough and bitter fight which the closely allied police and legal shysters have been waging for years against the proletarian women's right to form associations and hold meetings.

In this fight the police, by displaying splendid bravery and utter obedience so characteristic of German officialdom, have truly deserved the highest honors bestowed upon them by those that own the means of production. The jurists, on their part, practice such a brilliant interpretation of the law that common sense at times does not appreciate them fully. One dissolution of a proletarian women's organization follows another, prohibition after prohibition of women's assemblies takes place, the expulsion of women from public meetings are a daily occurrence and penalties for women for violating the Law for the Formation of Associations, inundate the courts. During the period from October 1, 1893 until August 31, 1894, proletarian women had to pay the sum of 681 marks for such crimes and this figure is based merely on the cases which came to my personal attention.

But in spite of it all, new unions regularly take the place of those that have been smashed. Again and again women rush to new assemblies and organize yet others.

The proletarian woman who lives in indigence, if not bitter poverty, this proletarian female that is overburdened with chores, constantly makes new sacrifices involving her precious time and her material goods which are needed for the continued existence of unions and organizations. She courageously puts up with official persecution and she bears the penalties which are "legally" imposed upon her. According to my opinion, this fact is unambiguous proof that it is their vital interest and not any frivolity or addiction to found organizations that drives proletarian women to espouse the right to form coalitions. If the Reichstag and the government are unable to comprehend the powerful and penetrating message of this fact, they will be even less susceptible to show consideration for a petition.

Perhaps at this point, the following objection will be raised: "Oh well, even if the petition is of little use, it cannot really do any harm. It deals with the extension of the limited rights of the female sex, ergo by signing it, we will support women's rights." My reply to this is: This is all very well, but if this point of view has any validity, then the petition's content must reflect proletarian concepts or at least (I want to remain modest) it must not stand in sharp contrast to our concepts. But this is not the case at all; on the contrary, the petition originated in bourgeois circles and literally exudes a bourgeois spirit, yes, one may even call it (in reference to some of the details) a narrow-minded bourgeois spirit.

That is why we do not understand at all why Social-Democratic newspapers have gone all out to support this petition, recommending quasi-officially that unionized male workers ought to support it and proletarian women to sign it. Since when is it the custom of the Social-Democratic Party to support petitions which emanate from bourgeois circles and bear the bourgeois trade mark only because they support something positive, something that Social-Democracy has also advocated for a long time? Let us assume that bourgeois democrats had initiated another petition whose purpose and character would be similar to the present women's petition. The Social-Democratic press would have criticized the petition and would have never supported the idea that class conscious workers appear as having been taken in tow by bourgeois elements. Why should we alter our basic position vis-a-vis the policy of the bourgeois world only because, as chance would have it, one action of this policy has been originated by women who do not demand a reform for the entire population but only for the female sex? If we abandon our principles because of it, then we relinquish our fundamental concept that we will only consider and further the women question within the context of the general social question.*

In Issue 7 of January 9th, the *Vorwärts* assumed an entirely correct attitude towards this petition. It registered it, criticized it and pointed out that it simply took up an ancient Socialist demand. Unfortunately, to my amazement, the *Vorwärts* changed its attitude overnight. And why? Because it was informed that the petition did not deserve any criticism due to the manner in which it evolved. I regret very much that this explanation as well as the reference to an "appendix" persuaded the *Vorwärts* to change its position. Besides, in spite of the "appendix," all the criticism that had been initially raised remains valid. The "appendix" has nothing to do with the petition and the manner in which it came about. It is merely an accompanying letter, a circular addressed to the persons whose support is requested; i.e., signatures for the petition. It reads: "The women's 'own interests' (especially their job situation), which could not be listed in the petition because of its brevity, demand that a law be passed that reflects the spirit of this petition."**

Is this paragraph supposed to be a lecture about the value of the right of women to form associations and hold meetings? If

*__The Editors of__ *Vorwarts*. We cannot accept the serious transgression which Comrade Zetkin has fabricated here. Unfortunately, the position of women within the state is still totally different from that of men: they are totally without rights. As far as bourgeois women are concerned, they are without any political training so that any step towards independence must be viewed as progress. Let us recall the manner in which Herr von Koller last week labeled the here-criticized petition as a sign of "growing subversive activities." All of this must demonstrate to Comrade Zetkin that there is a difference whether even a petition like this emanates from women or men.

**__The Editors of__ *Vorwärts*. It was proven to us that the petitioners did not carry out the error in the manner that we subjected to criticism. We did not urge people to sign the petition but merely commented that there were no objections to signing such a document. We already knew at that time that a number of women who belong to our party had signed the petition.

so, we express our gratitude for this lecture, but we do not need it. The proletariat has recognized the value of the freedom to form coalitions for all of its members, regardless of sex, at a much earlier time than the authors of this petition. And, in recognition of this fact; the proletariat fights for the obtainment of the debated right. Is this paragraph supposed to be an asseveration that the originators of this petition are aware of the significance of this right and its basis? We politely acknowledge this sign of sociopolitical enlightenment which is usually lacking among German suffragettes. This paragraph, however, has no significance for the petition. As far as the petition and its possible adoption are concerned, it matters little what its authors and signers thought when they drew it up. What matters are their reasons for advocating it now. The petition contains not a word that it is in the vital interest of women employees to possess the right to form associations and to hold meetings, which have become an irrefutable necessity for them. The petition fails to state the reason why the proletariat backs this demand. It lacks the reason why such a legal reform is so essential, given the fact that newspaper articles (which have not been contradicted) report that Bavarian Center Party delegates intend, during the next session of their Landtag (Provincial Diet) to submit a bill which calls for the right of the female sex to form associations and hold meetings in order to further the livelihood chances of women.

It sounds like a lame excuse when it is asserted in the "appendix" that this reason cannot be divulged because of the brevity of the petition. Why did this consideration for preserving brevity not prevent the appendix from pointing out that the obtainment of the right to form associations was urgently needed because of the mediating influence of women in regard to legislation dealing with "questions of morality."* What the bourgeois women want from the legislature in regard to the "questions of morality" has been sufficiently illuminated by the previously mentioned supplication to the Kaiser.

According to my views, no proletarian women, least of all,

*The Editors of *Vorwärts*. We, too, were critical of that, but we found an ameliorating (if not sufficient) excuse in the circumstance that the originator of the petition, for tactical reasons, did not want to forego the signatures of bourgeois women. She would have had to relinquish these signatures if the underlying principles of the petition had been published.

however, the resolute women comrades, can sign a sign a petition which out of consideration for "brevity" skips in silence over the most important reason for its issuance—a reason which supports from a proletarian standpoint the requested reforms. This petition, however, apparently unharmed by "brevity," cites a reason that must evoke ridicule from anybody who possesses a halfway clear and enlightened sociopolitical concept, as an effluence of naive ignorance about social conditions. Proletarian circles have no reason whatsoever to display solidarity with a petition of such a nature whose content is unworthy of their sociopolitical knowledge.

There is an additional reason which makes it impossible for the Socialist movement to support this petition. The petition does not ask the Reichstag or one of its political parties to submit a bill dealing with this reform. It merely asks it to plead with the associated governments to submit such a bill. Thus the petition ignores the competence of the Reichstag in respect to initiating bills and looks at it merely as a messenger boy that opens the gates for the petitioners approaching the exalted government. Such a process cannot be supported by Social-Democracy, which will not participate. Social-Democracy has always fought against the dualism of the legislative powers, a dualism which exists in Germany because our bourgeoisie did not break the power of absolutism but, on the contrary, is cooperating with it in a cowardly fashion. Social-Democracy must put up with the fact that this dualism exists and that the legislative powers—the people's representative body and the government—do not even face each other on equal terms since the former has to submit to the latter. Social-Democracy, however, has always fought with all of the legal means at its disposal to transform the people's representative body into the organ it ought to be. One of the few rights and prerogatives which parliament possesses in this splendid German Empire is the right to submit bills and to make demands in the name of the people instead of begging from the government. This petition, however, avoids the only correct way which leads to the Reichstag.*

***The Editors of** *Vorwärts*. Comrade Zetkin completely forgets that the workers in extraordinarily many cases have turned directly to the Bundesrat (Federal Council) and the Imperial Chancellor. We certainly do not advocate such a path, but we cannot criticize a way of proceeding that has often been employed by our comrades. Furthermore, the party has not yet taken a position in regard to the question of the petition

Proletarian women cannot and do not want to participate in this process. They do not want to participate at any time, but particularly not at a time when the governments are waging the most bitter battles against the right of the female proletarians to form associations and hold meetings and at a time when the associated governments have submitted the bill on subversion. Proletarian women who expect from their governments a favorable reform of the laws concerning the formation of unions and the holding of meetings would hardly expect to reap figs from thorns and grapes from thistles.

If, in pursuance of a common goal in regard to the petition, the bourgeois women had really intended to achieve a temporary cooperation with the proletarian women, they would naturally have drawn up the petition in such a way that the women workers could have signed it without betraying their cause. Such a draft would have required as an antecedent the agreement of the representatives of the class-conscious female proletarians. As the originators of the petition well know, there exists in Berlin a Women's Agitation Commission.[2] Why did not the originators of the petition approach this commission with two questions: 1) Would you perhaps agree to support the planned petition and 2) How must the petition read in order to obtain the support and the signatures of the proletarian women without them having to sacrifice any of their principles?

Such behavior, displaying intelligence and courtesy, should have been natural in any effort to aquire the signatures of the proletarian women. The actual draft of the petition as well as the behavior of its authors is characteristic of the concepts of bourgeois women and their relationship to the world of proletarian women. One is enough of a humanitarian under certain circumstances to do something for the "poorer sisters," one is clever enough under all circumstances to accept their manual labor, but to cooperate with them on an equal basis, no Sir!, that is something totally different.

The originators of the petition will point to their good "intentions" and claim that they were not at all conscious of holding views that are opposite to those held by the proletarian women. But this admission will not change our minds as far as their actions are concerned. Not only the greatest crimes but also the greatest stupidities have been committed in the name of good intentions. And that the thought processes of the authors of the petition ran diametrically opposed to proletarian concepts is characteristic of the abyss which separates us from them.

I am convinced that I do not only speak in my name but in that of the majority of class-conscious women when I declare:

Not a single proletarian signature for this petition!

Stuttgart, January 12th, 1895.

[*Vorwärts*[3] Central Organ of the Social-Democratic Party of Germany, January 24, 1895] □

A REPLY

In regard to the comments of the *Vorwärts* concerning my article about the Women's Rights Petition, I want to reply as follows:* I did not at all assert that the critical petition was the labor of women's rights organizations. On the contrary, I stressed that it was the work of three bourgeois women. I emphasized this fact at the very beginning of my article, alluding furthermore to the petition to the Kaiser concerning the prohibition of prostitution by order of the cabinet, a petition which had received the massive support of bourgeois suffragettes. I did all this with the purpose of illuminating the bourgeois women's movement in its entirety, to show its half-heartedness and the comparatively more decisive conduct of the three female authors of the petition.

The fact that the petition was co-authored by a member of our party and signed by a few women comrades does not make it any better nor any more immune from criticism. Whatever confronts the public and especially our party, must not be judged according to the persons involved or their intentions, but whether it corresponds to our fundamental principles or not. I can well understand that some women comrades signed the petition.

The special law-less position [without legal rights] of the female sex which, given her social subjugation as a member of the proletariat, affects the proletarian woman particularly hard, makes it understandable that brave women comrades at times

*__The Editors of__ *Vorwärts*. Unfortunately, the plethora of material that we had to print made it impossible until now to publish the following reply of Comrade Zetkin at an earlier time.

let the fact that they are females supersede their positions as class-conscious women proletarians and Social-Democrats. Far be it from me to throw stones at them because of this, but be it also far from me to approve of this conduct. And farthest be it for me to use their conduct in order to view any criticism of the petition as inappropriate. Let the male and female comrades draw their own general conclusions from the different standpoints that I and the *Vorwärts* represent on this controversy over the petition.

Certainly any step towards the independence of bourgeois women must be regarded as progress. But I believe that the recognition of this fact must not lead to the phenomenon that the politically mature proletarian women's movement participates in the uncertain, clumsy and groping steps of the bourgeois suffragettes or to overestimate them. If Herr von Koller views the petition as evidence of a growing subversive movement and lends great importance to it, then we must attribute his opinion to his utterly desperate attempts to scrape together official proof about "subversive tendencies," proof that he hunts out with sweat running down his face. If his judgment of and his enmity towards the petition are taken as the criteria for our judgment and attitude, then we must also render great importance to the police bugbear of the Anarchists and the Anarchists must be taboo for us, along with everything else against which the reaction is turning its momentary wrath.*

I am sure that both male and female comrades will agree with me that a criticism of the petition is fully justified because it is not only deficient but stands in stark contrast to our concepts. The "suggestion" that the petitioners did not make the mistakes that were criticized by the *Vorwärts* in the manner that we denounced them does not change anything. Because the petition itself is not touched by the "suggestion," i.e., the circular, it becomes neither more nor less meaningful.

I understand that the authors of the petition maintained "tactical considerations" for the bourgeois women. Why, however, did they not maintain the same "tactical considerations" for the proletarian women? Why did they make all concessions to the

*The Editors of *Vorwärts*. Comrade Zetkin forgets that on the one hand, we will never let external circumstances change our tactics but, on the other hand, our tone vis-a-vis our opponents will have to change if they are attacked by enemies that also happen to be ours.

prejudices of bourgeois women and demand from the proletarian women the sacrifice of their concepts? If one wanted their support, one should have known that what is good for the goose is also good for the gander.*

I know very well that workers, too, have turned in many cases to the Bundesrat (Federal Council) and the Imperial Chancellor. But what reason is there for the petitioners to request the reform of the Union and Assemblage Laws from, of all places, the government rather than the Reichstag? And can one expect the female proletarians to go along with this petition at the very moment when the government is getting ready for the total suppression of the working class? And can such a petition be recommended quasi-officially by the Socialists?

The *Vorwärts* comments that it did not call for the signing of the petition but that it had merely stated that it had no objections to those who wanted to sign it. I believe that I have amply demonstrated that from our standpoint, everything speaks out against the signing of this document. Many female comrades have entirely failed to detect the fine nuances of the *Vorwärts'* attitude towards the petition. I obtained proof of this in black and white when I received literally dozens of inquiries; in fact, so many of them that I expressed my attitude towards this problem in several party papers which expressed their thorough agreement with me.

I had good reason to use the harsh tone that was criticized by the *Vorwärts*. The phenomenon of the latest direction of the bourgeois suffragette fad, which I would like to label "ethical,"**

***The Editors of** *Vorwärts*. It is exactly these "tactical considerations" which explain the action of the three women. That the proletarian women want the right to form unions was clear to them since our program and innumerable resolutions of ours say as much. Thus the female comrades needed these tactical considerations much less than the much more politically retarded women of the bourgeoisie. If the authors of the petition had acted according to the plan of Comrade Zetkin, the tactical considerations would have cancelled each other out and the petition would not have been co-signed by the women of the bourgeoisie. So much for our explanation. We, too, consider common action by the bourgeoisie and the proletariat normally as impossible. If, however, such an attempt is made in good faith, one should intelligently weigh the pros and cons before energetically condemning it.

****The Editors of** *Vorwärts*. No other newspaper of the party has more energetically drawn the line between the Ethical Movement and Social Democracy which is firmly based on the class struggle.

has here and there caused confusion in the ranks of our female comrades.[1] This new direction of the women's rights movement demands more than previous efforts. It is a step above the previous variety because of its recognition of social problems, its recognition and criticism of social harm and its advocacy of certain social reforms. And that is why illusions arose in the Socialist camp about the nature of its direction and the significance of it to our proletarian women's movement. Only recently, somebody belonging to our party wrote to me "that these women basically advocate the same things we do"!* In view of the prevailing uncertainty in judgments of the above-mentioned bourgeois course, it seemed to me appropriate to use such a harsh tone. I hope that by now all such illusions have once and for all been laid to rest by Frau von Gizycki's emphatic denial that she had declared her support for the Social-Democratic Women's Movement (*Vorwärts* 23 December 1894).

Since none of the comments of the *Vorwärts* dealt with the basic and objective parts of my article but, on the contrary, addressed minor matters, I may assume that this paper agrees with the nucleus of my observations.** Yet in view of this situation, it would be most appropriate if it would state succinctly whether or not it is recommending to the women comrades to sign this petition.***

Finally, I would like to make a few important personal observations. My statements solely addressed themselves to the turnabout of the *Vorwärts* in the matter of the petition and my expression of regret concerning that. There was no sharp attack. The only somewhat harsh passage against the *Vorwärts* that my article originally contained was expunged by the editors. In the course of my exposition, I have neither referred to *Gleichheit* nor cited it in any way. Nowhere and never have I upheld the *Gleichheit* as truer to principles than the *Vorwärts*. Then what was it that possessed the *Vorwärts* to start talking about the

*The Editors of *Vorwärts*.[2] Surely the *Vorwärts* cannot be held responsible for the political obscurantism of this or that woman.

**The Editors of *Vorwärts*. We do not hesitate to agree with Comrade Zetkin by and large but we do believe that she is making much too much ado about nothing.

***The Editors of *Vorwärts*. It is natural, that after having published the declaration of the Women's Agitation Commission, the *Vorwärts* sees no reason to recommend the signing of the petition.

Gleichheit? When and where have I copied the *Vorwärts* by praising my own adherence to principles? I have duly registered the self-praise which the *Vorwärts* displayed since it is my duty and obligation to peruse all comments of that paper.

Whether this registration had changed anything regarding my judgment of the *Vorwärts* is written on another page which must not be consulted at this most inappropriate time and with the *Vorwärts* representing a most inappropriate location.*

*The Editors of *Vorwärts*. That we will calmly leave up to Comrade Zetkin.

Stuttgart, 25 January 1895

[*Vorwärts* Central Organ of the Social-Democratic Party of Germany, February 7, 1895] □

1896

ONLY IN CONJUNCTION WITH THE PROLETARIAN WOMAN WILL SOCIALISM BE VICTORIOUS

Speech at the Party Congress of the Social Democratic Party of Germany, Gotha, October 16th[1]

The investigations of Bachofen,[2] Morgan[3] and others seem to prove that the social suppression of women coincided with the creation of private property. The contrast within the family between the husband as proprietor and the wife as non-proprietor became the basis for the economic dependence and the social illegality of the female sex. This social illegality represents, according to Engels,[4] one of the first and oldest forms of class rule. He states: "Within the family, the husband constitutes the bourgeoisie and the wife the proletariat." Nonetheless, a women's question in the modern sense of the word did not exist. It was only the capitalist mode of production which created the societal transformation that brought forth the modern women's question by destroying the old family economic system which provided both livelihood and life's meaning for the great mass of women during the pre-capitalistic period. We must, however, not transfer to the ancient economic activities of women those concepts (the concepts of futility and pettiness), that we connect with the activities of women in our times. As long as the old type of family still existed, a woman found a meaningful life by productive activity. Thus she was not conscious of her social illegality even though the development of her potentials as an individual was strictly limited.

The period of the Renaissance is the storm and stress period of the awakening of modern individuality that was able to develop fully and completely in the most diverse directions. We encounter individuals who are giants in both good and evil, who spurn the commandments of both religion and morals and despise equally both heaven and hell. We discover women at the center of the social, artistic and political life. And yet there is not a trace of a women's movement. This is all the more characteristic because at that time the old family economic system began to crumble under the impact of the division of labor. Thousands upon thousands of women no longer found their livelihood and their lives' meaning within the family. But this women's question, as far as one can designate it as such, was solved at that time by convents, charitable institutions and religious orders.

The machines, the modern mode of production, slowly undermined domestic production and not just for thousands but for millions of women the question arose: Where do we now find our livelihood? Where do we find a meaningful life as well as a job that gives us mental satisfaction? Millions were now forced to find their livelihood and their meaningful lives outside of their families and within society as a whole. At that moment they became aware of the fact that their social illegality stood in opposition to their most basic interests. It was from this moment on that there existed the modern women's question. Here are a few statistics to demonstrate how the modern mode of production works to make the women's question even more acute. During 1882, 5½ million out of 23 million women and girls in Germany were fully employed; i.e., a quarter of the female population could no longer find its livelihood within the family. According to the Census of 1895, the number of employed women in agriculture, in the broadest meaning of this term, has increased since 1882 by more than 8%, in the narrow sense by 6%, while at the same time the number of men employed in agriculture has decreased by 3%, i.e., to 11%. In the area of industry and mining, the number of employed women workers has increased by 35%, that of men by only 28%. In the retail trade, the number of women employed has increased by more than 94%, that of men by only 38%. These dry numbers stress much more the urgency of solving the women's question than any highfalutin declamations.

The women's question, however, is only present within those classes of society who are themselves the products of the capitalist mode of production. Thus it is that we find no women's question in peasant circles that possess a natural (although severely curtailed and punctured) economy. But we certainly find a women's question within those classes of society who are the very children of the modern mode of production. There is a women's question for the women of the proletariat, the bourgeoisie, the intelligentsia and the Upper Ten Thousand. It assumes a different form according to the class situation of each one of these strata.

How does the women's question shape up as far as the Upper Ten Thousand are concerned? The woman of the Upper Ten Thousand, thanks to her property, may freely develop her individuality and live as she pleases. In her role as wife, however, she is still dependent upon her husband. The guardianship of the weaker sex has survived in the family law which still states: And he shall be your master. And how is the family of the Upper Ten Thousand constituted in which the wife is legally subjugated by the husband? At its very founding, such a family lacks the moral prerequisites. Not individuality but money decides the matrimony. Its motto is: What capital joins, sentimental morality must not part. (Bravo!) Thus in this marriage, two prostitutions are taken for one virtue. The eventual family life develops accordingly. Wherever a woman is no longer forced to fulfill her duties, she devolves her duties as spouse, mother and housewife upon paid servants. If the women of these circles have the desire to give their lives a serious purpose, they must, first of all, raise the demand to dispose of their property in an independent and free manner. This demand, therefore, represents the core of the demands raised by the women's movement of the Upper Ten Thousand. These women, in their fight for the realization of their demand vis-a-vis the masculine world of their class, fight exactly the same battle that the bourgeoisie fought against all of the privileged estates; i.e., a battle to remove all social differences based upon the possession of property. The fact that this demand does not deal with the rights of the individual is proven by Herr von Stumm's advocacy of it in the Reichstag. Just when would Herr von Stumm ever advocate the rights of a person? This man in Germany signifies more than a personality, he is capital itself turned into flesh and blood (How accurate!) and if this man has put in an appearance in a cheap masquerade for women's rights, then it only happened because he was forced to dance before capitalism's Ark of the Covenant. This is the Herr von Stumm who is always ready to put his workers on short rations if they do not dance to his tune and he would certainly welcome it with a satisfied smile if the state as employer would also put those professors and scholars who meddle in social politics on short rations.[5] Herr von Stumm endeavors nothing more than instituting the entail for movable female property in case of female inheritance because there are fathers who have acquired property but were not careful in the choice of their children, leaving only daughters as heirs. Capitalism honors even lowly womanhood and permits it to dispose of its fortunes. That is the final phase of the emancipation of private property.

How does the women's question appear in the circles of the petit-bourgeoisie, the middle class and the bourgeois intelligentsia? Here it is not property which dissolves the family, but mainly the concomitant symptoms of capitalist production. To the degree this production completes its triumphal march, the middle class and the petit-bourgeoisie are hurtling further and further towards their destruction. Within the bourgeois intelligentsia, another circumstance leads to the worsening of the living conditions: capitalism needs the intelligent and scientifically trained work force. It therefore favored an overproduction of mental-work proletarians and contributed to the phenomenon that the formerly respected and profitable societal positions of members of the professional class are more and more eroding. To the same degree, however, the number of marriages is decreasing; although on the one hand the material basis is worsening, on the other hand the individual's expectations of life are increasing, so that a man of that background will think twice or even thrice before he enters into a marriage. The age limit for the founding of a family is raised higher and higher and a man is under no pressure to marry since there exist in our time enough societal institutions which offer to an old bachelor a comfortable life without a legitimate wife. The capitalist exploitation of the proletarian work force through its starvation wages, sees to it that there is a large supply of prostitutes which corresponds to the demand by the men. Thus within the bourgeois circles, the number of unmarried women increases all the time. The wives and daughters of these circles are pushed out into society so that they may establish for themselves their own livelihood which is not only supposed to provide them with bread but also with mental satisfaction. In these circles women are not equal to men in the form of possessors of private property as they are in the upper circles. The women of these circles have yet to achieve their economic equality with men and they can only do so by making two demands: The demand for equal professional training and the demand for equal job opportunities for both sexes. In economic terms, this means nothing less than the realization of free access to all jobs and the untrammeled competition between men and women. The realization of this demand unleashes a conflict of interest between the men and women of the bourgeoisie and the intelligentsia. The competition of the women in the professional world is the driving force for the resistance of men against the demands of bourgeois women's rights advocates. It is, pure and simple, the fear of competition. All other reasons which are listed against the mental work of women, such as the smaller brain of women or their allegedly natural avocation to be a mother are only pretexts. This battle of competition pushes the women of these social strata towards demanding their political rights so that they may, by fighting politically, tear down all barriers which have been created against their economic activity.

So far I have addressed myself only to the basic and purely economic substructure. We would, however, perform an injustice to the bourgeois women's rights movement if we would regard it as solely motivated by economics. No, this movement also contains a more profound spiritual and moral aspect. The bourgeois woman not only demands her own bread but she also requests spiritual nourishment and wants to develop her individuality. It is exactly among these strata that we find these tragic, yet psychologically interesting *Nora* figures, women who are tired of living like dolls in doll houses and who want to share in the development of modern culture. The economic as well as the intellectual and moral endeavors of bourgeois women's rights advocates are completely justified.

As far as the proletarian woman is concerned, it is capitalism's need to exploit and to search incessantly for a cheap labor force that has created the women's question. It is for this reason, too, that the proletarian woman has become enmeshed in the mechanism of the economic life of our period and has been driven into the workshop and to the machines. She went out into the economic life in order to aid her husband in making a living, but the capitalist mode of production transformed her into an unfair competitor. She wanted to bring prosperity to her family, but instead misery descended upon it. The proletarian woman obtained her own employment because she wanted to create a more sunny and pleasant life for her children, but instead she became almost entirely separated from them. She became an equal of the man as a worker; the machine rendered muscular force superfluous and everywhere women's work showed the same results in production as men's work. And since women constitute a cheap labor force and above all a submissive one that only in the rarest of cases dares to kick against the thorns of capitalist exploitation, the capitalists multiply the possibilities of women's work in industry. As a result of all this, the proletarian woman has achieved her independence. But verily, the price was very high and for the moment they have gained very little. If during the Age of the Family, a man had the right (just think of the law of Electoral Bavaria!) to tame his wife occasionally with a whip, capitalism is now taming her with scorpions. In former times, the rule of a man over his wife was ameliorated by their personal relationship. Between an employer and his worker, however, exists only a cash nexus. The proletarian woman has gained her economic independence, but neither as a human being nor as a woman or wife has she had the possibility to develop her individuality. For her task as a wife and a mother, there remain only the breadcrumbs which the capitalist production drops from the table.

Therefore the liberation struggle of the proletarian woman cannot be similar to the struggle that the bourgeois woman wages against the male of her class. On the contrary, it must be a joint struggle with the male of her class against the entire class of capitalists. She does not need to fight against the men of her class in order to tear down the barriers which have been raised against her participation in the free competition of the market place. Capitalism's need to exploit and the development of the modern mode of production totally relieves her of having to fight such a struggle. On the contrary, new barriers need to be erected against the exploitation of the proletarian woman. Her rights as wife and mother need to be restored and permanently secured. Her final aim is not the free competition with the man, but the achievement of the political rule of the proletariat. The proletarian woman fights hand in hand with the man of her class against capitalist society. To be sure, she also agrees with the demands of the bourgeois women's movement, but she regards the fulfillment of these demands simply as a means to enable that movement to enter the battle, equipped with the same weapons, alongside the proletariat.

Bourgeois society is not fundamentally opposed to the bourgeois women's movement, which is proven by the fact that in various states reforms of private and public laws concerning women have been initiated. There are two reasons why the accomplishment of these reforms seems to take an exceptionally long time in Germany: First of all, men fear the battle of competition in the liberal professions and secondly, one has to take into account the very slow and weak development of bourgeois democracy in Germany which does not live up to its historical task because of its class fear of the proletariat. It fears that the realization of such reforms will only bring advantages to Social-Democracy. The less a bourgeois democracy allows itself to be hypnotized by such a fear, the more it is prepared to undertake reforms. England is a good example. England is the only country that still possesses a truly powerful bourgeoisie, whereas the German bourgeoisie, shaking in fear of the proletariat, shies away from carrying out political and social reforms. As far as Germany is concerned, there is the additional factor of widespread Philistine views. The Philistine braid of prejudice reaches far down the back of the German bourgeoisie. To be sure, this fear of the bourgeois democracy is very shortsighted. The granting of political equality to women does not change the actual balance of power. The proletarian woman ends up in the proletarian, the bourgeois woman in the bourgeois camp. We must not let ourselves be fooled by Socialist trends in the bourgeois women's movement which last only as long as bourgeois women feel oppressed.

The less bourgeois democracy comprehends its task, the more important it is for Social-Democracy to advocate the political equality of women. We do not want to make us out to be better than we are. We are not making this demand for the sake of a principle, but in the interests of the proletarian class. The more women's work exercises its detrimental influence upon the standard of living of men, the more urgent becomes the necessity to include them in the economic battle. The more the political struggle affects the existence of each individual, the more urgent becomes the necessity of women's participation in this political struggle. It was the Anti-Socialist Law [6] which for the first time made clear to women what is meant by the terms class justice, class state and class rule. It was this law which taught women the need to learn about the force which so brutally intervened in their family lives. The Anti-Socialist Law has done successful work which could never have been done by hundreds of women agitators and, indeed, we are deeply grateful to the father of the Anti-Socialist Law as well as to all organs of the state (from the minister to the local cop) who have participated in its enforcement and rendered such marvelous involuntary propaganda services. How then can one accuse us Social-Democrats of ingratitude? (Amusement).

Yet another event must be taken into consideration. I am referring to the publication of August Bebel's book *Woman and Socialism*.[7] This book must not be judged according to its positive aspects or its shortcomings. Rather, it must be judged within the context of the times in which it was written. It was more than a book, it was an event—a great deed. (Very accurate!) The book pointed out for the first time the connection between the women's question and historical development. For the first time, there sounded from this book the appeal: We will only conquer the future if we persuade the women to become our co-fighters. In recognizing this, I am not speaking as a woman but as a party comrade.

What practical conclusions may we now draw for our propaganda work among women? The task of this Party Congress must not be to issue detailed practical suggestions, but to draw up general directions for the proletarian women's movement.

Our guiding thought must be: We must not conduct special women's propaganda, but Socialist agitation among women. The petty, momentary interests of the female world must not be allowed to take up the stage. Our task must be to incorporate the modern proletarian woman in our class battle! (Very true!) We have no special tasks for the agitation among women. Those reforms for women which must be accomplished within the framework of today's society are already demanded within the minimal program of our party.

Women's propaganda must touch upon all those questions which are of great importance to the general proletarian movement. The main task is, indeed, to awaken the women's class consciousness and to incorporate them into the class struggle.

The unionization of female workers is made extremely difficult. During the years 1892 until 1895, the number of female laborers organized in central trade unions grew to around 7,000. If we add to this number the female workers organized in local unions and realize that there are at least 700,000 female workers actively involved in large industrial enterprises, then we begin to realize the magnitude of the organizing work that still lies ahead of us. Our work is made more burdensome by the fact that many women are active in the cottage industry and can, therefore, be organized only with great difficulty. Then we also have to deal with the widely held belief among young girls that their industrial labor is only transitory and will be terminated by their marriage. For many women there is the double obligation to be active in both the factory and the home. All the more necessary is it for female workers to obtain a legally fixed workday. Whereas in England everybody agrees that the elimination of the cottage industry, the establishment of a legal workday and the achievement of higher wages are important prerequisites for the unionization of female workers—in Germany, in addition to these obstacles there is also the enforcement of our unionization and assemblage laws. The complete freedom to form coalitions, which has been legally guaranteed to the female workers by the Empire's legislation, has been rendered illusory by the laws of individual federal states. I do not even want to discuss the manner in which the right to form unions is handled in Saxony (as far as one can even speak of a right there). But in the two largest federal states, in Bavaria and Prussia, the union laws are handled in such a way that women's participation in trade union organizations is becoming more and more of an impossibility. Most recently in Prussia, the district of the "liberal," eternal candidate for minister, Herr von Bennigsen has achieved everything humanly possible in the interpretation of the Law of Unionization and Assemblage. In Bavaria all women are excluded from public meetings. In the Chamber there, Herr von Freilitzsch declared very openly that in the handling of the law of unionization not only the text but also the intention of the legislators should be taken into account. Herr von Freilitzsch is in the most fortunate position to know exactly what were the intentions of the legislators, all of whom have since died, before Bavaria became more lucky than anybody could have imagined in their wildest dreams, by appointing Herr von Freilitzsch as her minister of police. That does not surprise me at all, because whoever receives an office from God also receives concomitantly intelligence, and in our Age of Spiritualism, Herr von Freilitzsch has thus obtained his official intelligence and by way of the fourth dimension has discovered the intentions of the long deceased legislators. (Amusement).

This situation, however, does not make it possible for the proletarian women to organize themselves together with men. Until now they had to wage a fight against police power and juridical stratagems and on the surface they seemed to have been defeated, In reality, however, they emerged as victors because all those measures which were employed to smash the organization of the proletarian woman only served to arouse her class consciousness. If we want to obtain a powerful women's organization in both the economic and political realms, then we must, first of all, take care of the possibility of women's freedom of movement by fighting against the cottage industry, for shorter working hours and, above all, against what the ruling classes like to call the right to organize.

We cannot determine at this party congress what form our propaganda among women should take. We must, first of all, learn how we ought to do our work among women. In the resolution which has been submitted to you, it is proposed to elect shop stewards among the women whose task it will be to stimulate the union and economic organization of women and to consolidate it in a uniform and planned manner. This proposal is not new; it was adopted in principle at the Party Congress of Frankfurt, and in a few regions it has been enacted most successfully. Time will tell whether this proposal, when introduced on a larger scale, is suited to draw proletarian women to a greater extent into the proletarian movement.

Our propaganda must not be carried out solely in an oral fashion. A large number of passive people do not even come to our meetings and countless wives and mothers cannot come to our meetings. Indeed, it must certainly not be the task of Socialist propaganda among Socialist women to alienate the proletarian woman from her duties as mother and wife. On the contrary, she must be encouraged to carry out these tasks better than ever in the interests of the liberation of the proletariat. The better the conditions within her family, the better her effectiveness at home, the more she will be capable of fighting. The more she can serve as the educator and molder of her children, the better she will be able to enlighten them so that they may continue to fight on like we did, with the same enthusiasm and willingness to sacrifice for the liberation of the proletariat. When a proletarian then exclaims: "My wife!" he will add mentally, "Comrade of my ideals, companion of my battles, mother of my children for future battles." Many a mother and many a wife who fills her husband and children with class consciousness accomplishes just as much as the female comrades that we see at our meetings. (Vivid agreement).

Thus if the mountain does not come to Mohammed, Mohammed must go to the mountain: We must take Socialism to the women by a planned written propaganda campaign. For such a campaign, I suggest the distribution of pamphlets and I do not mean the traditional pamphlet on which the entire Socialist program and the entire scientific knowledge of our century are condensed on one quarto page. No, we must use small pamphlets which discuss a single practical question from one angle of vision, especially from the point of view of the class struggle, which is the main task. And we must not assume a nonchalant attitude toward the technical production of pamphlets. We must not use, as is our tradition, the worst paper and the worst type of printing. Such a miserable pamphlet will be crumpled up and thrown away by the proletarian woman who does not have the same respect for the printed word that the male proletarian possesses. We must imitate the American and English teetotallers who put out pretty little booklets of four to six pages. Because even a female proletarian is enough of a woman to say to herself: "This little thing is just charming. I will have to pick it up and keep it!" (Much amusement and many cheers.) The sentences which really count must be printed in great big letters. Then the proletarian woman will not be frightened away from reading and her mental attention will be stimulated.

Because of my personal experiences, I cannot advocate the plan of founding a special newspaper for women. My personal experiences are not based upon my position as the editor of *Gleichheit* (which is not designed for the mass of women, but rather their progressive avant-guard), but as a distributor of literature among female workers. Stimulated by the actions of Frau Gnauck-Kühne, I distributed newspapers for weeks at a certain factory. I became convinced that the women there did not acquire from these papers what is enlightening, but solely what is entertaining and amusing. Therefore, the big sacrifices which are necessary in order to publish a cheap newspaper would not be worth it.

But we also have to create a series of brochures which bring Socialism closer to the woman in her capacity as female proletarian, wife and mother. Except for the powerful brochure of Frau Popp,[8] we do not have a single one that comes up to the requirements we need. Our daily press, too, must do more than it has done heretofore. Some daily newspapers have made the attempt to enlighten women by the addition of special supplements for women. The *Magdeburger Volksstimme* set an example in this endeavor and Comrade Goldstein at Zwickau has skillfully and successfully emulated it. But until now the daily press has regarded the proletarian woman as a subscriber, flattering her ignorance, her bad and unformed taste, rather than trying to enlighten her.

I repeat that I am only throwing out suggestions for your consideration. Propaganda among women is difficult and burdensome and requires great devotion and great sacrifice, but these sacrifices will be rewarded and must be brought forth. The proletariat will be able to attain its liberation only if it fights together without the difference of nationality and profession. In the same way it can attain its liberation only if it stands together without the distinction of sex. The incorporation of the great masses of proletarian women in the liberation struggle of the proletariat is one of the prerequisites for the victory of the Socialist idea and for the construction of a Socialist society.

Only a Socialist society will solve the conflict that is nowadays produced by the professional activity of women. Once the family as an economic unit will vanish and its place will be taken by the family as a moral unit, the woman will become an equally entitled, equally creative, equally goal-oriented, forward-stepping companion of her husband; her individuality will flourish while at the same time, she will fulfill her task as wife and mother to the highest degree possible.

[*Protocol Concerning the Proceedings of the Party Congress of the Social-Democratic Party of Germany Held at Gotha from October 11 to October 16, 1896. Berlin, 1896.* pp. 160-168] □

1902

PROTECT OUR CHILDREN

Among the many serious crimes of capitalism about which history will one day sit in judgment, none is more brutal, horrible, disastrous, insane, in one word—outrageous—than the exploitation of proletarian children. Exploitation of proletarian children by capitalism means the deprivation of health, vitality, childhood and education as well as the destruction of the body and the soul of future generations. It is deprivation and destruction committed against the weakest, most defenseless and most helpless of all the members of society. Capitalism pounces upon the proletarian child that is already threatened and damaged prenatally by the ruthless exploitation of its father and mother. Capitalism, aided by the poverty or ignorance of the parents, drives the child into the factory, the workshop, the brick kiln, street peddling, beet planting, animal care, pinsetting in bowling alleys, deliveries and the murderous cottage industry. Wherever the child goes, capitalism puts it through the profit mill to squeeze out every ounce of muscular and mental strength, which is converted into gold. What remains is a deplorable creature that has been physically and mentally ground up. The exodus of the rural population to the industrial centers and the opening of underdeveloped regions and countries by the modern means of transportation relieve the capitalistic entrepreneurs of the necessity to spare today's proletarian child in order to obtain the indispensable adult worker of tomorrow. Thus, the capitalistic exploitation of child labor has condemned, crippled and mowed down generation upon future generation. Thus way beyond the present time period, it has committed unscrupulous crimes which will affect the future, and far beyond the proletariat, will prove to be detrimental to the entire nation.

How it smashes and withers the body, spirit and morality of proletarian children is amply illustrated by a plethora of facts. It is shown by the frighteningly large numbers of weak, sickly, senescent children in the elementary schools. It is proven by the teachers' well-founded complaints about the lack of attention, mental alertness, power of comprehension and inferior performance of pupils who, having to work early in the morning and late at night, sit tired, weak and apathetic over their schoolbooks both in school and at home. It takes on horrible forms in the shape of increasing gangs of youthful degenerates and criminals. It must even frighten the "loyal" admirers and beneficiaries of militarism because every new levy of recruits demonstrates a large, and in some cases alarming, increase of unfit men who cannot be trained [for use] against both the external and the internal enemy.[1]

The path of capitalism and its proper realm are littered with the innumerable corpses of children who were slaughtered because of their tender fingers, as is written in *Das Kapital.* The path of capitalism is covered with spiritual and moral powers that have been destroyed and ground into the dust. It was not "propagandistic exaggeration," but scientific research into the horrors of the capitalistic exploitation of children which made Engels exclaim in protest in his 1845 *Conditions of the Working Class in England:* I accuse the bourgeoisie "literally of social murder"! And verily, just as "all the scents of Araby" could not clean the bloodstained hand of Lady Macbeth, the miraculous works of capitalism will be unable to make up for the horrible capital crime of its "Bethlehemite infanticide." It constitutes an indestructible monument of shame on the capitalistic system, its brutalizing influence which drowns human feelings and thoughts "in the ice-cold waters" of lust for profit and narrow-minded egoism, so that until this very day society is impelled to issue only ridiculously inconsequential measures for the protection of the proletarian child against the strangling exploitation of its labor power.

What has been done in Germany about this problem until now? The disastrous results of the capitalists' exploitation of children already appeared during the first decades of the nineteenth century. Because the factory regions could not satisfy his levies of recruits, Frederick William III issued a decree in 1827 calling for the protection of children employed in factories.[2] Yet, in disregard of all the proven horror, the Trade Regulations of 1869 did not even completely outlaw factory work for children under twelve years of age. The few ameliorations of child labor in factories which these regulations did contain remained a dead letter. The very robust "public conscience" awakened only when Social-Democracy[3] (which had conquered its first strongholds in Saxony where capitalism was exploiting children in a criminal manner) appeared with its accusations, calling for reforms. In 1873 the Reichstag asked the Imperial Chancellor to look into the matter of women's work, child labor, work on Sundays, etc. As a consequence the Federal Council was asked to make an investigation which was published in 1877. Thus the government mechanism, reflecting the class state it represents, worked with that culpable slowness which is so characteristic of its conduct when it comes to reforms affecting the exploited masses. As deficient as the investigation had been, it neverthelss revealed the corroding damage wrought by the exploitation of child labor. And yet the government did not hesitate to present a bill in 1878 which, although advocating the absolute prohibition of factory labor for children under twelve, respected in every other way the exploitative power of the entrepreneurs much more than the need for child protection. The Reichstag on its part improved little upon this reformist bungling job of the lowest sort. It was only fear of the victoriously advancing Social-Democracy which pressured the ruling class to pass the amendment to the Trade Regulations of 1890/91 which represented a small step forward toward the protection of the exploited children. Permission for them to perform factory work was not to be granted until they had concluded their elementary education which meant not before they had reached twelve years of age. On the other hand, the workday of the child wage slaves remained fixed at six hours (including a one-hour break). Not even these weakly-diluted laws protected the child laborers who were working in the most diverse fields outside the factories from the capitalists' werewolf hunger. The protective legislation did not even cover the entire industrial realm. The modern cottage industry had created a hell where, as the comprehensive literature on the subject incontestably proved, children from their most tender ages are subjected to the most horrible physical and mental torture as well as inescapable sacrifice. The capitalist desire to exploit these victims was hypocritically disguised by the alleged "respect for the family rights." This phrase was to save their El Dorado from being invaded by this legislation.

In vain did Social-Democracy at every opportunity, then or earlier,.tear away the deceiving cover from the festering wounds of the cottage industry. In vain did it prove that the untouched exploitation by the cottage industry lessened, if not destroyed, the value of the legal protection of child labor in the factories. Unrestricted freedom for the cottage industry to exploit—and the clever entrepreneur is able to scorn all the legal decrees in prolonging the work day for his children factory slaves by having them take their work home with them! Unrestricted cottage industry exploitation—and the greedy capitalist decentralizes his factory into the cottage industry with all of the horrors of its exploitation. The laws of the capitatlistic economic life must not be scoffed at! The facts have confirmed, in an uncanny way, the Social-Democractic prophecies. This is clearly shown by the reports of factory inspectors, the research of the cottage industry by scholars, and the investigations and material collections of the elementary school teachers. Besides the indescribable, miserable conditions of children in the cottage industry, there is the no less destructive sucking out of the children's marrow by the other industrial activities and the work in the forests and in agriculture, not to speak of their employment as servants in private homes. The highest eternal merit must be accredited to the German teachers (above all the brave, warmhearted Agahd) who have shone a light into the darkest corners of child exploitation in a dark Germany.

The numerous factual proofs tower as high as mountains concerning the culture-ravishing despoliation which the Junkers[4] of industry and the clod-hopping squires of agriculture, the knights of the shops and saloons are practicing against the most valuable treasure of the nation—the life force of the upcoming generations. Since 1891 the legislative authorities have kept a deaf ear towards the screams of many hundreds of thousands of tortured human beings. Their eyes have been blind to the twitching pain of the mangled bodies and spirits. Their hands have been empty of reforms. The Federal Council has not even made the fullest use of its right to give a little more protection by extending the decrees of the labor code to proletarian children in other non-factory industrial workshops. Its law of 1896, which placed the workshops of the clothing industry under the appropriate legal decrees, was hardly an ameliorating droplet of water upon the red-hot stone of child exploitation. The legislators of the individual federal states kept their hands idly in their laps. In some counties and districts, police decrees were issued which were supposed to curb the excesses of child exploitation among street vendors, goods and newspaper carriers, pinsetters, etc. Not only did the decrees remain behind even the most modest demands, in addition they were often declared to be null and void by the courts. It was not until 1897 that the Imperial Office of the Interior allowed itself to be prodded into taking the tiniest step forward. By a circular in 1898, it called for an investigation of industrial child labor outside the factories. From the very beginning, the investigation did not encompass the large extent of school-age children that work in forests, agriculture and homes. The investigation was carried out differently in the various states but in a uniformly deficient manner. Its results were published in the third issue of the *Periodical for the Statistics of the German Empire* for 1900. They led to the proposed Bill Concerning the Protection of Children Involved in Industrial Labor whose most important features were reported in our last issue. This bill has already been read for the first time in the Reichstag. We are now in 1902! The highest imperial office for social reform has thus once again not worked with the same feverish energy that it is prone to display when it comes to passing special favors for the Barons of the Smoke Stacks and the Counts of the Oxen or when it has to deal with penal and tariff legislation. Perhaps the German working class, in imitation "of famous precedents", ought to have used a 12,000-mark Propaganda Fund in order to speed up the preparations for reform? But only the gods know how many times more the sun will have to set over the unutterable horror of the exploited children before the introduced reform bill will become a reality. No daily allowance for attendance of the Child Protection Commission will be available to further the consultations of the twenty-one "strongmen" who have been entrusted by the Reichstag to study the governmental draft. And what meager improvements will the law finally bestow upon the child of the German proletarian?

What had previously been foreshadowed by the investigation concerning the industrial activities outside of the factories of school-age children has been fully confirmed by the rough draft of the Child Protection Law. The willingness of the government to reform collapses meekly and sadly before the exploitative power of the Junker parasites. Just as the government initially did not even dare to illuminate with the torch of official inquiry the immense extent of the bloody crime of children's exploitation in agriculture and domestic service, so it also ignores in its rough draft, with the disgraceful indifference of the well-known priest and Levite, all the piled-up misery of physical and mental ruin. Not even the slightest legal protection is to be given to the children who slave away as farm hands and domestic servants.

This means more or less that the large majority of industrially employed, school-age children will be totally exposed to the worst exploitative desires. . . . The Social-Democratic Deputy Wurm estimates the number of school children who work in forestry, agriculture and domestic service to be almost two million strong . . . This fact alone suffices to label the draft of the pro-Junker government as "weighed and found to be too light."

And this judgment is surely not eliminated by the degree of protection which the draft offers to the children who are employed outside of the factories . . .

Disregarding the narrowly defined Paragraph 4, the draft surrenders the extraneous child already at the age of twelve to the exploitation of the industrial world. One's own child—one is ashamed to put this down on paper—may be handed over to industrial exploitation at the age of ten. According to the Census of 1898, 75% of all children in Prussia were more than ten years of age and 46% were over twelve years old! Given these facts, it becomes obvious that the draft leaves in the future, too, the overwhelming majority of industrially employed children to their fate. . . .

The draft contains only a single regulation which applies to all working school children. This regulation is concerned with the most shameful and disastrous abuse of child labor, that of nocturnal work. Children are not permitted to work in industrial enterprises between 8 p.m. and 8 a.m. But the government does not even dare to enforce this most natural and necessary control of exploitation for all children in the near future. As a matter of fact, the lower administrative authorities are empowered, during the first five years after the enactment of this law, to permit that children over twelve years may deliver goods or perform messenger services beginning at 6:30 a.m., before their morning classes. The already limited value of the other measures for the protection of the exploited child is even further limited and diminished by a serious, inexcusable, major flaw. The draft distinguished throughout its text between the industrial labor of other children and one's own. In employing the revolting, hypocritical argument that one must have tender consideration for the rights of parents and the family, it decreases the protection for one's own child which it grants fully to the extraneous one....

Not even on Sunday does the draft of this Bible-touting, pious government liberate one's own child, to even the smallest degree, from the all-embracing, ruthless crunch of labor. Not even one day out of seven does it grant for the "Sabbath," as the day of sun, full relaxation, rest and enjoyment. Not even the extraneous child is assured the full observation of the status of Sunday as a day of rest. If it is involved in obtaining meager wages by delivering goods and performing messenger services, it may be subjected to the yoke of labor on Sundays for two hours. Before or after the child has moved its weak limbs it may "pray," because the period of the main church service as well as the afternoon must remain free. What a deceitful and miserable respect for the commandment of the Most Highest in the heavenly realm of the future: "Thou shalt keep the Sabbath holy!" The state as the political trustee of the possessing classes raises, as far as the proletarian child is concerned, the command of the omnipotent of the earthly class state, the command of capitalism: "Thou shalt let yourself be exploited!" above this commandment (which it still allows to be taught in school)....

The totally inadequate supervision of the protective regulations is an egregious flaw of the draft.... Disregarding the experiences with factory inspection, the government is apparently counting on the sociopolitical inexperience of the country as a whole. Either it fools itself or it tries to fool others by assuming that the police will pursue violations of child protection regulations with the same fervor and intensity with which it pursues violations by workers of the laws concerning assemblages, strikes and especially the brutal Nuisance and Blackmail Clause....

In short, the inadequate guarantees concerning the observance of the law complement the inadequate regulations. The rule—the protection of the exploited children—becomes the exception, and the exception—the unrestricted exploitation of child labor—becomes the rule.

What the government has concocted, however, will hardly be improved upon by the bourgeois majority of the Reichstag. The first reading of the draft in parliament shows this clarly. The speakers of all of the bourgeois parties, from the Center Party's Hitze to the Liberals Pachnicke, Zwick and Müller, wasted so much of their brain power and breath in lauding and thanking the reformist government, that they had no words left for the necessary critique of the defective draft. . . . It is true that the Liberal Pachnicke declared that the horrendous misery of children's exploitation was "very regrettable," but he stated at the same time that "one has to proceed with caution" against it, which means that children in the future, too, will be exposed to ruthless exploitation. He concluded with a eulogy for "the golden means" between exploitation and indulgence which the omniscient government had discovered. And the equally Liberal Müller ended a heart-rending description of the children's misery in the toy industry of Sonneberg with the cowardly observation that the prohibition of work for school-age children was "a leap into the dark" which he hesitated to take. Conservative loyalists, Guelph, Polish and Alsatian enemies of Reich, as well as Stöcker,[5] "the newly retired Luther," all joined in a ravishing chorus under the direction of the Junker-fearing Posadowsky to praise the poetic charms of herding cattle, harvesting beets, gathering potatoes, etc. Only the bourgeois maverick Rösicke joined the Social-Democracy that raised its old battle cry of: "Let us be done with all child labor!" Its three speakers, Wurm, Reisshaus and Herzfeld, based this demand upon factual and objective arguments which blasted the devastating abuse of child labor by the Junkers, among other targets.

Now it is up to the proletarian masses to speak. With sound knowledge and strong willpower, they must back up the loyal activities of their parliamentary leaders. You proletarian fathers and, above all, you proletarian mothers who have desperately witnessed the destruction of your own flesh and blood, join the battle for a genuine Child Protection Law! Do you want to go on being the guardians for the interests of capitalism? Should you continue, for the benefit of other people's wealth, to let yourselves be transformed from being the protectors and educators of your children to being their slavemasters and tormentors? Should the spirit of capitalism be allowed to distort the holy instinct of your parental love so that you serve up your child as a sacrifice to exploitation, rather than to fight with the grimness of an indomitable natural instinct agains this exploitation? That must not happen!

Shout in a chorus of millions of voices the slogan: Fight exploitation, protect our children!

[*Die Gleichheit* Stuttgart, May 21, 1902 and June 4, 1902] □

1903

WHAT THE WOMEN OWE TO KARL MARX

On March 14th is the twentieth anniversary of Karl Marx's death in London. Engels, whose life for forty years in both struggle and work was intimately linked to Marx's life,[1] wrote at that time to their mutual friend Comrade Sorge in New York:

> Humankind has been shortened by one head, which also happens to be the most significant head of our times.[2]

His evaluation hit the bull's eye.

It cannot be our task within the framework of this article to discuss what Karl Marx has bestowed upon the proletariat in his role as a man of science, as a revolutionary fighter and what he means today to the proletariat. If we would do this, we would only repeat what is written during these days in the Socialist press of Marx's immensely fertile and profoundly scholarly and practical life's work as well as his gigantic, homogeneous personality which stood so totally devoted in the service of the proletariat. Instead we prefer to indicate what the proletarian, or better yet, the entire women's movement owes to him.

To be sure, Marx never dealt with the women's question "per se" or "as such." Yet he created the most irreplaceable and important weapons for the women's fight to obtain all of their rights. His materialist concept of history has not supplied us with any ready-made formulas concerning the women's question, yet it has done something much more important: It has given us the correct, unerring method to explore and comprehend that question. It was only the materialist concept of history which enabled us to understand the women's question within the flux of universal historical development and the light of universally applicable social relationships and their historical necessity and justification. Only thus did we perceive its driving forces and the aims pursued by them as well as the conditions which are essential to a solution of these problems.

The old superstition that the position of women in the family and in society was forever unchangeable because it was created on moral precepts or by divine revelation was smashed. Marx revealed that the family, like all other institutions and forms of existence, is subjected to a constant process of ebb and flow which changes with the economic conditions and the property relationships which result from them. It is the development of the productive forces of the economy which push this transformation by changing the mode of production and by coming into conflict with the prevailing economic and property system. On the basis of the revolutionized economic conditions, human thought is revolutionized and it becomes the endeavor of people to adjust their societal superstructure to the changes that have taken place in the economic substructure. Petrified forms of property and personal relationships must then be removed. These changes are wrought by means of the class struggle.

We know from Engels' foreword to his illuminating study, *The Origin of the Family, Private Property and the State,* that the theories and viewpoints developed in this book are derived in good measure from Marx's unpublished work, which his incomparably loyal and brilliant friend watched over as testamentary executor.

Whatever parts of it can be (and ought to be) dismissed as hypotheses, one thing is for sure: Taken as a whole, this work contains a dazzling number of clear theoretical insights into the complex conditions which gave rise to the present forms of the family and marriage and the influence of economic and property relationships which are connected with it. It teaches us not merely to judge correctly the position of women in the past, but it enables us to comprehend the social, legal and constitutional positions of the female sex today.

Das Kapital shows most convincingly that there are incessant and irresistible historical forces at work in today's society which are revolutionizing this situation from the bottom up and will bring about the equality of women. By masterfully examining the development and nature of capitalist production down to the most refined details, and by discovering its law of motion, i.e., the Theory of Surplus Value, he has conclusively proven in his discussions of women and child labor that capitalism has destroyed the basis for the ancient domestic activity of women, thereby dissolving the anachronistic form of the family. This has made women economically independent outside of the family and created a firm ground for their equality as wives, mothers and citizens. But something else is clearly illustrated by Marx's works: The proletariat is the only revolutionary class which by establishing Socialism, is able to and must create the indispensable prerequisites for the complete solution of the women's question. Besides the fact that the bourgeois suffragettes neither want nor are able to achieve the social liberation of women proletarians, they are incapable of solving the serious new conflicts which will be fought over the social and legal equality of the sexes within the capitalist order. These conflicts will not vanish until the exploitation of man by man and the contradictions arising therefrom are abolished.

Marx and Engels' common work *The Communist Manifesto* concisely summarizes what *Das Kapital* teaches us in scholarly fashion about the disintegration of the family and its causes:

> The less the skill and exertion of strength implied in manual labor, in other words, the more modern industry becomes developed, the more is the labor of men superseded by that of women. Differences of age and sex have no longer any distinctive social validity for the working class. All are instruments of labor, more or less expensive to use according to their age and sex. . . .
>
> The bourgeoisie has torn away from the family its sentimental veil and has reduced the family relation to a mere money relation. . . .
>
> In the conditions of the proletariat, those of old society at large are already virtually swamped. The proletarian is without property; his relation to his wife and children has no longer anything in common with the bourgeois family relations. . . .
>
> On what foundation is the present family, the bourgeois family, based? On capital, on private gain. In its completely developed form this family exists only among the bourgeoisie. But this state of things finds its complement in the practical absence of the family among the proletarians, and in public prostitution. . . .
>
> The bourgeois claptrap about the family and education, about the hallowed co-relation of parent and child, becomes all the more disgusting as by the action of modern industry all family ties among the proletarians are torn asunder, and their children transformed into simple articles of commerce and instruments of labor. . . .

Marx, however, does not only show us that historical development demolishes, but he also fills us with the victorious conviction that it constructs a newer, better and more perfect world.

Das Kapital states:

> As horrendous and disgusting as the disintegration of the old family system within capitalism appears to be, modern industry, by involv-

ing women and young people of both sexes in the socially organized production processes outside of the domestic sphere, has, nevertheless, created the economic basis for a higher form of the family and the relationship between the two sexes.

Proud and with superior scorn, Marx and Engels in *The Communist Manifesto* counter the dirty suspicions cast upon this future ideal by this merciless characterization of present conditions:

> The bourgeois sees in his wife a mere instrument of production. He hears that the instruments of production are to be exploited in common and, naturally, can come to no other conclusion than that the lot of being common to all will likewise fall to the women.
>
> He has not even a suspicion that the real point aimed at is to do away with the status of women as mere instruments of production.
>
> For the rest, nothing is more ridiculous than the virtuous indignation of our bourgeois at the community of women which, they pretend, is to be openly and officially established by the Communists. The Communists have no need to introduce community of women; it has existed almost from time immemorial.
>
> Our bourgeois, not content with having the wives and daughters of their proletarians at their disposal, not to speak of common prostitutes, take the greatest pleasure in seducing each other's wives.
>
> Bourgeois marriage is in reality a system of wives in common and thus, at the most, what the Communists might possibly be reproached with is that they desire to introduce, in substitution for what is hypocritically concealed, an openly legalized community of women. For the rest, it is self-evident that the abolition of the present system of production must bring with it the abolition of women springing from that system, i.e., of prostitution both public and private.

The women's movement, however, owes much more to Marx than just the fact that he, as no other person before him, shed bright light upon the painful path of the development that leads the female sex from social servitude to freedom and from atrophy to a strong, harmonious existence. By his profound, penetrating analysis of the class contradictions in today's society and its roots, he opened up our eyes to the differences of interest that separate the women of the different classes. In the atmosphere of the materialist concept of history, the "love drivel" about a "sisterhood" which supposedly wraps a unifying ribbon around bourgeois ladies and female proletarians, burst like so many scintillating soap bubbles.[3] Marx has forged and taught us to use the sword which has severed the connection between the proletarian and the bourgeois women's movement. But he has also forged the chain of discernment by which the former is inextricably tied to the Socialist labor movement and the revolutionary class struggle of the proletariat. Thus he has given our struggle the clarity, grandeur and sublimity of its final goal.

Das Kapital is filled with an immeasurable wealth of facts, perceptions and stimuli concerning women's work, the situation of the female workers and the legal protection of women. It is an inexhaustible spiritual armory for the struggle of our immediate demands as well as the exalted future Socialist goal. Marx teaches us to recognize the small, everyday tasks which are so necessary in raising the fighting ability of the female proletarians. At the same time, he lifts us up to the firm, farseeing recognition of the great revolutionary struggle by the proletariat to conquer political power without the attainment of which, a Socialist society and the liberation of the female sex will remain empty dreams. Above all, he fills us with the conviction that it is this exalted aim that lends value and significance to our daily work. Thus he saves us from losing sight of the great fundamental meaning of our movement when we are beset by a plethora of individual phenomena, tasks and successes and stand in danger of losing our ability, during the enervating daily toil, to view the wide historical horizon which reflects the dawn of a new age. Just as he is the master of revolutionary thought, so he remains the leader of the revolutionary struggle in whose battles it is the duty and the glory of the proletarian women's movement to fight.

[*Die Gleichheit* Stuttgart, March 25, 1903] □

1907

WOMEN'S RIGHT TO VOTE

A Resolution Introduced at the International Socialist Congress

The International Socialist Congress welcomes joyfully the fact that for the first time an International Socialist Women's Conference has congregated at Stuttgart and it expresses solidarity with the demands made at that Conference.[1] The Socialist parties of all countries are obligated to fight energetically for the introduction of the universal suffrage for women. Their battles waged on behalf of the proletariat's suffrage leading to the democratization of the legislative state and county governing bodies must be simultaneously waged as battles for women's suffrage, which is to be demanded energetically in the propaganda campaigns as well as in the parliaments. In countries where the democratization of men's suffrage has already progressed very far or has been accomplished, the Socialist parties must take up the battle for the introduction of universal women's suffrage. They must, of course, at the same time support all demands which are still made in the interests of full civil rights for the male proletariat. It is the duty of the Socialist women's movements of all countries to participate with all of their energy in all battles waged by the Socialist parties for the democratization of the suffrage, but also to employ the same amount of energy to take part in all battles in which the demand for universal women's suffrage is seriously raised on the basis of its fundamental importance and practical significance. The International Congress recognizes the inappropriateness for every country to announce a timetable for the commencement of the voting rights campaign but, at the same time, it declares that wherever a struggle is to be waged for the right to vote, it must be conducted only according to Socialist principles, i.e., with the demand for universal suffrage for both women and men.

In Support of the Resolution On Women's Right to Vote

I must report to you about the deliberations of the Commission on Women's Suffrage and the resolution before you which was also adopted by the First International Socialist Conference by a vote of 47 to 11. The Socialist women do not consider the women's right to vote as the most significant question, whose solution will remove all social obstacles which exist in the path of the free and harmonious development and activity of the female sex. That is because it does not touch upon the deepest cause: Private property in which is rooted the exploitation and suppression of one human being by another. This is clearly illustrated by the situation of the politically emancipated, yet socially suppressed and exploited male proletariat. The granting of suffrage to the female sex does not eliminate the class differences between the exploiters and the exploited from which are derived the most serious social obstacles to the free and harmonious development of the female proletarian. It also does not eliminate the conflicts which are created for women as members of their sex from the social contradictions that occur between men and women within the capitalist system. On the contrary: The complete political equality of the female sex prepares the ground on which the conflicts will be fought with the greatest intensity. These conflicts are varied, but the most serious and painful one is the conflict between professional work and motherhood. For us Socialists, therefore, women's suffrage cannot be the "final goal" as it is for bourgeois women. However, we yearn most fervently for its acquisition as one phase of the battle towards our final goal. The obtainment of suffrage aids the bourgeois women to tear down the barriers in the form of male prerogatives which tend to limit their educative and professional opportunities. It arms the female proletarians in their battle against class exploitation and class rule, in their effort to acquire their full humanity. It enables them to participate to a higher degree than heretofore in the attainment of political power by the proletariat, for the purpose of erecting a Socialist order which alone will solve the women's question.

We Socialists do not demand women's suffrage as a natural right with which women are born. We demand it as a social right which is anchored in the revolutionized economic activity and in the revolutionized social state and personal consciousness of women. Capitalist production has sent the domestically employed housewife of the good old days to an old-age home. The professional woman, especially the salaried woman who stands right at the center of the economic life of society, has taken her place and become the typical form which female economic activity represents in its most essential social capacity. The professional and trade statistics of all capitalist countries reflect this change. That which women at an earlier time produced within their four walls served the consumption and the welfare of their family. Today, whatever streams out of her industrious hands, whatever her brain thinks of that is useful, acceptable and pleasant, appear as goods on the social market. Millions of women themselves appear as sellers of their labor, the most important social good on society's labor market. Thus a revolution is wrought in her position within the family and society. The woman is detached from the household as the source of her livelihood and she gains her independence from her family and her husband. In many case, too, the family no longer offers her a satisfactory meaning of life. Just like the man under equally hard conditions (and at times under even more difficult ones), she has to take up the fight for the vital necessities against a hostile environment. She needs for this, just like the man, her full political rights because such rights are weapons with which she can and must defend her interests. Together with her social being, her world of perception and thought is being revolutionized. The political impotence which the female sex accepted as natural for so many centuries is [now] viewed by her as an outrageous injustice. By a slow, painful developmental process, women are emerging from the narrowness of family life to the forum of political activity. They are demanding their full political equality as it is symbolized by suffrage as a vital social necessity and a social emancipation. The obtainment of suffrage is the necessary corollary to the economic independence of women.

One would assume that in view of this situation, the entire politically disenfranchised female sex would form one phalanx to fight for universal women's suffrage. But that is not the case at all. The bourgeois women do not even stand united and determined behind the principle of the full political equality of the female sex. They are even more reluctant to fight energetically, as one united force, for universal women's suffrage. In the final analysis, this is not due to the ignorance and shortsighted tactics of the leaders of the suffragettes' camp, even though they can be correctly blamed for a number of deficiencies. It is the inevitable consequence of the diverse social strata to which women belong. The value of enfranchisement stands in a reverse relationship to the size of the estate. It is of least importance to the women of the Upper Ten Thousand and it means the most to the female proletarians. Thus the struggle for women's suffrage, too, is dominated by class contradictions and class struggle. There cannot be a unified struggle for the entire sex, particularly when this battle does not relate to a bloodless principle, but rather to the concrete and vital question of the women's right to vote. We cannot expect bourgeois women to proceed against their very nature. The female proletarians in their struggle for civil rights cannot, therefore, count on the support of the bourgeois women because the class contradictions preclude that female proletarians will join the bourgeois suffragette movement. All of this does not mean that they should reject the bourgeois suffragettes who want to march behind them or at their side in the battle for the women's right to vote. They may march separately but fight together. But the female proletarians must know that they cannot acquire the right to vote in a struggle of the female sex without class distinctions against the male sex. No, it must be a class struggle of all the exploited without differences of sex against all exploiters no matter what sex they belong to.

In their fight for the attainment of universal women's suffrage, the proletarian women find strong allies in the Socialist parties of all countries. The advocacy of universal women's suffrage by the Socialist parties is not based on ideological and ethical considerations. It is dictated by historical perception but, above all, by an understanding of the class situation as well as the practical battle needs of the proletariat. This proletariat cannot fight its economic and political battles without the participation of its women who, awakened to class consciousness, organized and trained, have been equipped with social rights. Due to the increased employment of women in industry, movements that fight for increased wages can be successful only if they include female workers who have become trained and organized class fighters. But political work, the political work of the proletariat, must also be shared by women. The intensification of the class struggle between the exploiters and the exploited increases the significance of the awakening of class consciousness in women and their participation in the proletarian movement of emancipation. Contrary to the expectations of bourgeois fools, the strengthening of trade union organizations has not resulted in social peace but in an era of gigantic lockouts and strikes. The resolute involvement of the proletariat in the political life has led to the sharpest intensification of the political battle, an intensification which has led to new methods and means of combat. In Belgium and Holland, the proletariat had to complement its parliamentary struggle by the political mass strike. In Russia it tried the same weapon during the revolution with the greatest success.[2] In order to grasp the suffrage reform from its enemies, the Austrian proletariat had to keep the revolutionary weapon of the mass strike in readiness. Gigantic strikes and gigantic lockouts, especially, however, revolutionary mass strikes, call for the greatest sacrifices on the part of the proletariat. It cannot, like the possessing classes, devolve these sacrifices upon hirelings and it cannot pay for them out of a well-filled purse. These are sacrifices that every member of this class must personally bear. That is why these sacrifices can only be made if the proletarian women, too, are filled with historical insight into the necessity and the significance of them. Just how significant and indispensable it is that the female proletariat be imbued with Socialist convictions from which a willingness to sacrifice and heroism flow, has just been demonstrated by the brilliant Austrian suffrage battle.[3] It would not have ended victoriously without the active participation of the proletarian women. It must be emphasized that the success of our Austrian brothers was to a considerable extent the result of the loyalty, hard work, willingness to sacrifice and courage displayed by our Austrian women comrades. (*Bravo!*)

This brief sketch shows that the proletariat has a vital stake in the political equality of the female sex and that it must fight for the full civil rights for women. This battle arouses the women masses and helps them to acquire a sense of class consciousness. The granting of women's suffrage is the prerequisite for the resolute participation of women proletarians in the proletarian class struggle. At the same time, it creates the strongest incentive to awaken, gather and train the female proletariat with the same fervor as the enlightenment and organization of the male proletariat is being pursued. As long as women are politically disenfranchised, they are frequently viewed as powerless and the influence which they exercise upon political life is underestimated. At the stock exchange of parliamentary life, only the ballot possesses an exchange value. The shortsighted individuals who view the political struggle only within the framework of ballots and mandates view the efforts to arouse the female proletariat to a class-conscious life merely as a kind of amusement and luxury which Social-Democracy should only indulge in if it possesses an excess of time, energy and money. They overlook the proletariat's compelling class interest in seeing to it that the class struggle also develops within the women's world so that the female proletarians will fight resolutely alongside their brothers. From the moment when women will be emancipated and capable of casting their votes, this interest will become clear to even the most shortsighted individual in our ranks. A race will begin by all parties to obtain the votes of the female proletarians since they constitue the majority of the female sex. The Socialist parties then must make sure that their enlightenment campaign will keep away all the bourgeois parties and their fight for the attainment of civil rights by women must work in that direction. This has been proven by the history of the suffrage battle in Finland and by the first suffrage campaign there which was conducted in a situation in which both men and women had the right to vote. Women's suffrage is an excellent means to push forward into the last, and perhaps the strongest, bulwark of the ignorant masses: The political indifference and backwardness of broad segments of the female proletariat. This fortress aggravates and hurts our current proletarian struggle and threatens the future of our class. That is why we have to do away with it. (*Bravo!*)

In these days of intensified class struggle, the question arises: For what kind of women's suffrage should the Socialist parties fight? Years ago, this question would hardly have mattered. One would have answered: For women's suffrage, period. Then too, limited women's suffrage was regarded as an imperfection and insufficient progress, but still it was viewed as the first phase of the political emancipation of the female sex.[4] Today this naive concept is no longer justified. Today the Socialist parties must emphatically declare that they can only fight for universal women's suffrage and that they decisively reject limited women's suffrage as a falsification and mockery of the principle of the equality of women. What was previously done instinctively—by the introduction of limited women's rights in order to strengthen the position of property—is now done consciously. Two tendencies are at work within the bourgeois parties that will break the fundamental resistance against the women's suffrage: The rising external and internal difficulties of large circles of the bourgeois women's world that have to fight for their civil rights and the growing fear of the political advances of the fighting proletariat. In such a situation, the introduction of limited women's suffrage appears as a saving alternative. The proletariat is slated to pay for the costs of maintaining the peace between the men and women of the possessing classes. The possessing classes consider the introduction of limited women's suffrage because they view it as a protective wall against the increasing power of the fighting proletariat. This was first demonstrated by the events in Norway. When universal suffrage in respect to local elections could no longer be denied to the attacking proletariat which was fighting under the leadship of Social-Democracy, this reform was vitiated by the introduction of limited women's suffrage. Bourgeois politicians declared candidly that the limited suffrage for women is designed as a counterweight to the universal suffrage for men. . . .

We regard the limited women's suffrage not so much as the first step towards the emancipation of the female sex, [but] as the final step towards the political emancipation of property. It is a privilege of property and not a universal right. It does not emancipate the female because she is a woman, but rather in spite of the fact that she is a woman. It does not not raise her to full citizenship because of her personality but because of her wealth and income. Thus it leaves the great majority of the female sex disenfranchised and it simply credits this disenfranchisement to another account. But beyond the disenfranchised female proletarians, it hits their entire class. It represents a plural vote for the propertied class and strengthens its political power. That is why it is not accurate to view limited women's suffrage as a practical step towards the eventual political emancipation of female proletarians by universal suffrage. On the contrary, by increasing the political power of the proprietary class, it strengthens the reactionary forces which oppose the further democratization of the suffrage in favor of the proletariat and without distinction of sex. One more thing: It allows the pacified bourgeois women to drop out of the battle for political equality of the entire female sex. There is not one country in which the administrative and legislative bodies have been elected by limited women's suffrage where the politically emancipated women have fought with all of their strength for the civil rights of their poor sisters and for universal women's suffrage. The more the tendency of reaction grows to use the introduction of limited women's suffrage as a bulwark against the rising power of the proletariat, the more necessary it becomes to enlighten the female proletarians about this phenomenon. It must be prevented that the female proletarians allow themselves to be abused for a crime against themselves and their class under the motto: Justice for the female sex so that it may perform as servants and serfs.

Our demand for the women's right to vote is no suffragettes' request, but a mass and class demand of the proletariat. It is theoretically and practically the important organic part of the entire Social-Democratic suffrage program. Therefore, there must not only be constant propaganda for this demand but the demand must become the centerpiece of all suffrage battles which the Socialist parties are conducting on behalf of political democracy. A majority of the Commission shared this opinion and decided that every voting rights battle must also be fought as a battle for women's suffrage. Proletarian women and proletarian men will be the winners of this common fight. This was proven above all by the suffrage campaign in Finland. The majority of the Commission could not share the opinion that the demand for women's suffrage should under certain circumstances be withdrawn, for tactical reasons and without a fight, from the voting rights campaigns of the proletariat. The proprietary classes assume a twilight of the gods attitude towards any suffrage demand by the proletariat. They view even the most modest democratization of suffrage as the beginning of the end of their class' splendor and put up the fiercest resistance. It is not the character and the extent of the Socialist suffrage demands which will decide the outcome of the battle, but the power relationship between the exploiting and the exploited classes. It is not our clever modesty and restraint which will assure us victories, but the power of the proletariat which stands behind our demands.

In consequence, the question arises: Is the broaching of our entire suffrage program, especially the demand for women's suffrage, suited to strengthen the power of the Socialist party and the proletariat? In all seriousness and with great emphasis, we answer this question in the affirmative. The more principled [that] Social-Democracy conducts its suffrage battles, the more thoroughly it will stir up and revolutionize broad strata of the population and fill them with confidence in the earnestness and faithfulness of its actions, which will lead to enthusiasm for its fighting goals. What will be repeated will be the old fable of the rods which cannot be broken because they are tied together in a bundle. The more numerous the politically disenfranchised whose interest Social-Democracy represents in its suffrage battle, the more numerous the disinherited who expect the obtainment of their rights from its victory, the more swells the army of female and male combatants who will help to fight our Socialist battles. And must not a demand have this effect when it concerns itself with the civil rights of one-half of the entire nation's proletariat, the half that the citizens are supposed to educate but from whose council they have been excluded while they are pounding on the gates of parliament? The suffrage battle that Social-Democracy also wages on behalf of women's rights gains a broader basis, a more comprehensive aim and a greater thrust and drive. It forces people to take issue with ancient, deep-rooted prejudices and it therefore shakes up the masses. Finally, it carries uncertainty, confusion and disunion into the camp of the enemy. It causes the social contradiction between the men and women of the proprietary classes to come to the fore.

We are convinced, therefore, that it lies in the very class interest of the proletariat that the Socialist parties must go beyond the mere recognition of the principle of women's suffrage and that they must take up the battle to change principle into practice. Which is not to say that the Social-Democracy of whatever country should commence an electoral battle for women's suffrage at an inappropriate moment. Nor ought it be the case that women's suffrage should constitute the leading issue in every electoral campaign or that electoral campaigns must be conducted with the motto: Women's suffrage or bust! The role which women's suffrage ought to play depends upon the entire historical background of each country. As far as the suffrage is concerned, the Socialist parties must fight for all demands that they raise on principle in the interest of the proletariat. They will carry home as loot as much as they are able to wrest from the enemy. What is important is that women's suffrage must be emphatically demanded in the course of agitation among the masses or in parliament, and the intensity of the demand must correspond to the importance of the subject. We are aware of the fact that in most countries the conquest of women's suffrage will not occur from one day to the next because of such action. On the other hand, we also know that it is just such an action which will make preparations for a future victory.

In the proletarian battle for the civil rights of the female sex, the Socialist women must be the driving force, not only by participating with all of their energy in the proletarian suffrage battles but also by persuading the mass of female proletarians to become their co-fighters. By incorporating the masses of female proletarians into the ranks of the fighting brothers, they prove two things, i.e., that the masses of women themselves desire the right to vote and that the female proletarians are mature enough to use the suffrage correctly. Let us step forward without hesitation to battle for women's suffrage. It serves to arouse the female proletariat to a class-conscious political life which is of the highest significance for the present and future of the proletariat and its war of liberation. Not the patient bearer of crosses, not the dull slave, but the resolute fighting woman will raise a generation of strong male and female fighters. With every reason, the woman can state that avengers will rise from her bones, children who were nourished by the bold thoughts of her brain and the passionate wishes of her heart, male and female fighters who will not only replace her one day, but even surpass her as far as their battle virtues are concerned.

[*The International Socialist Congress at Stuttgart, August 18, 1907,* Berlin 1907, pp. 40-47.] □

1910

INTERNATIONAL WOMEN'S DAY

In agreement with the class-conscious, political and trade union organizations of the proletariat of their respective countries, the Socialist women of all countries will hold each year a Women's Day, whose foremost purpose it must be to aid the attainment of women's suffrage. This demand must be handled in conjunction with the entire women's question according to Socialist precepts. The Women's Day must have an international character and is to be prepared carefully.

Clara Zetkin, Käthe Duncker and Comrades,[21] August 27, 1910.

[From a proposal to the Second International Women's Conference at Copenhagen, August 27, 1910. *Die Gleicheit* Stuttgart, August 29, 1910.] □

Clara Zetkin (1). and Rosa Luxemburg during the Congress of the Social Democratic Party, Magdeburg, 1910.

1914

PROLETARIAN WOMEN BE PREPARED

The horrible specter before which the people of Europe tremble has become reality. The war is ready to crush human bodies, dwelling places and fields. Austria has used the senseless outrage of a twenty-year-old Serbian lad against the Successor to the Throne, as a pretext for a criminal outrage against the sovereignty and independence of the Serbian people and in the final analysis, against the peace of Europe.[1] She wants to use this opportune moment because Serbia can hardly hope to obtain help from Russian Tsarism. France at the present moment can hardly support Russian despotism's bellicose plans of conquest. Sessions in the Senate have revealed grave shortcomings in the army, and the reintroduction of the three-year draft has shaken military morale and created bitter dissatisfaction. England is so preoccupied with the situation in Ulster and other tasks of a similar nature that she does not have any great desire to participate in the horrors and crimes of a world war. Thus Austrian imperialism is calculating that it can violate international law in its dealings with Serbia without being challenged by the Triple Entente.[2] She believes that Serbia's defeat will block Tsarism's push towards the Mediterranean Sea.

The proletarian women know that the expansion of Russian Knout Tsarism would mean the worst type of slavery for all of the people concerned. Yet they also understand that Austro-Hungarian imperialism does not protect the rights and the liberties of people. It merely fights for the interests of the reactionary Hapsburg Dynasty and for the gold and power hunger of the insensitive, unscrupulous magnates and capitalists. Within its own realm, the Austro-Hungarian Monarchy has smashed the rights of the different nationalities and even more so the rights of the exploited working-class masses. In spite of the raging crisis, it has for years increased the price of even the barest necessities and it has used brutality and tricks to hinder the fight against exploitation and misery. Now it crowns its work by forcing the sons of workers to murder and to let themselves be murdered. It does not constitute a vanguard for the welfare and liberty of the people. Its war must never become a murder of the people.

In Germany, the profit- and laurel-seeking warmongers try to deceive the people in respect to this simple truth. They claim that Austria's war, in the final analysis, is directed against the threatening barbarism of Russia; that it represents a Germanic crusade against "arrogantly advancing Slavdom." In an unscrupulous manner, they scream about duty and about the preservation of "German Nibelung Loyalty." They want to see to it that Germany, as a member of the Triple Alliance, will adopt Austria's war as her own and that she will waste the blood and wealth of her people.

The sacrilege of such an activity is as great as the crime of Austrian imperialism. It wants to ignite a world conflagration in the course of which the peoples of Europe will slaughter each other while a handful of powerful and prescient people smilingly reap their profits. This must never be allowed to happen. The proletarians of Germany, men and women, must prove by deeds that they have been enlightened and that they are ready to assume a life in freedom. Their will to maintain peace, alongside the desire for peace on the part of the workers of other countries, especially of France, is the only guarantee that the war of the clerical Hapsburgs will not turn into a general European holocaust. It is true that the Government of the German Empire assures us that it has done and is doing everything in its power to keep the war localized. But the people have already found out that the tongues of the government's representatives are forked like the tongues of snakes. It is also familiar with the ineptitude of the diplomatic agents of the German Empire. And it certainly has no illusions about this unique fact: The international situation is so intricately enmeshed and entangled that one coincidence can destroy all of the good intentions of the governments. One coincidence could very well decide whether the thin thread from which the sword of world war is suspended over humankind will break.

The proprietors and rulers, too, swear solemnly that they

detest the horrible barbarism of war. Yes, they too tremble before its hellish horrors. And yet it is they who constantly prepare and agitate for war. One has only to listen to the left liberal press which, in the name of all kinds of cultural values, urges Germany to join Austria, thereby challenging Russia and France to join the bloody fray. And yet, the pages of this press are still wet from the maudlin tears which it shed over the psalms of peace heard at the Reconciliation Conference of German-French Parliamentarians at Bern.[3] How shamelessly pious Christian newspapers are calling for horrible bloodshed and mass murder while they are daily reciting the commandment of their Almighty: "Thou shalt not kill!" All masks are dropping from the vampire of capitalism which is nourished by the blood and marrow of the popular masses. How could it be otherwise? The killing among nations will never be condemned as fratricide by those who find it perfectly natural that every year hundreds of thousands of people's comrades are slaughtered for profit upon the altars of capitalism.

Only the proletariat uses its broad chest to stem the approaching disaster of a world war. The horrors of this war would already have been upon us if one of the most unscrupulous murderers of people, Tsarism, had not been prevented from plunging upon the craved-for battlefield by the political mass strikes of the Russian proletariat. It has only been the revolutionary struggle of our Russian brothers and sisters which in these fateful days has, until now, preserved world peace. Let us not be more fainthearted than they are. Their glorious battle, waged without guaranteed political rights and in the face of dungeons, exile and death, shows us by deeds what a determined, bold and unified working class is able to accomplish.

Let us not waste a minute. War is standing before the gate. Let us drive it back into the night before its ferocity will strip the unenlightened masses of their last ounce of rationalism and humanity. Leave your factories and workshops, your huts and attics to join the mass protest! Let the rulers and proprietors have no doubt about our serious determination to fight for peace to our last breath.

The exploited masses are strong enough to carry on their shoulders the entire edifice of the new society. They are used to living in poverty while the wealth that they create is being wasted in riotous living by idlers. Every day, while eking out a living, they face death. And these types of people are supposed to shun deprivations, dangers and death when it comes to fighting for peace and freedom? They are supposed to give way before a military cabal which has just been publicly flogged for the brutal mistreatment of their sons and brothers?[4] The mighty peace force of the working-class masses must silence the jingoist screaming in the streets. And wherever two or three exploited men or women are assembled, they must express their detestation of war and their support for peace.

For the working class, the brotherhood among peoples is no utopia, and world peace is more than an empty word. A concrete fact supports it; the firm solidarity of all the exploited and suppressed of all nations. This solidarity must not allow proletarians to fire upon proletarians. It must make the masses determined, during a war, to use all available weapons against the war. The might with which the proletarian masses will oppose the fury of war will constitute a victorious battle in their war of liberation. The revolutionary energy and passion of their struggle will expose them to dangers and demand sacrifices. What of it? There comes a moment in the life of each individual and people when everything can be won if one risks everything. Such a moment has come. Proletarian women, be prepared!

[*Die Gleichheit* Stuttgart, August 5, 1914] □

1914

TO THE SOCIALIST WOMEN OF ALL COUNTRIES

Comrades! Sisters![1] Week after week, there is an increase in the chorus of women's voices in the belligerent as well as in the neutral countries that protests against the terrible conflict which originated from the drive of the capitalist countries for world power and world domination. This battle between the Dual Alliance and the Triple Entente, which has lasted for almost four months now, is pulling ever more people and regions of this earth into its bloody maelstrom.

The best physical, spiritual and moral forces of the people, the riches of their economy, marvelous cooperative organizations, valuable accomplishments of science and wonders of technology, all have been roped into serving the war effort. Heaps of ruins and mountains of dead and maimed people are piling up to an extent that history has not seen heretofore in spite of all the streams of blood and tears that cross her path. This war grinds the welfare and the happiness of millions underfoot. It tears up international treaties, philosophizes with the sword over venerable concepts and institutions and orders people to pray to what they burned yesterday and burn what they prayed to until now. It besmirches all ideals which uncounted generations of all nations and races, under the pains and joys of belonging to humankind, created on the developmental ascent from the animal kingdom to the realm of genuine human freedom. What has happened to the commandments of the Christian God: "Thou shalt not kill!" and "Love thine enemies!"? What has happened to the cosmopolitan ideology which the greatest and noblest spirits of all modern civilized nations praised to high heaven? What has happened to the international Socialist brotherhood of the proletarians of all countries of which we so proudly dreamt?

The longer this war lasts, the more the glittering phrases and thoughts which were supposed to disguise its capitalist nature before the eyes of the people are fading and are being torn to shreds. The masks, the beautifully decorated covers that fooled so many, are dropping. Before us stands a war of conquest and world power in all of its naked ugliness. . . .

World Peace as a symbol and a guarantee of the international brotherhood of the proletarians of all countries has been especially sacred to us Socialist women because that brotherhood alone will be able to open up the gate to the future Socialist system that we women desire with all of our hearts. And because that is the case, the world war with all of its horrors does not constitute a barrier between us. Unperturbed by the thunder of battle, sabre-rattling speeches and uncritical mass moods, we shall preserve in all countries the old ideals of Socialism, even in these times. From everywhere we stretch our sisterly hands across streams of blood and piles of ruins, united in the old realization and the unshakable determination: We must break through to Socialism!

Our last great common project, the planned conference at Vienna, was supposed to meet in an aura of peace. The iron fist of the world war has prevented it. Now this determination for peace must dictate to us our first great common task. We women Socialists must call upon the women of all countries to oppose the prolongation of this insane genocide. From a million voices our irresistible cry must arise: Enough of killing, enough destruction! No total war until our people bleed to death! Peace! Permanent peace!

Therefore there must be no violation of the independence and dignity of any nation! There must be no annexations and no humiliating demands which would not constitute any guarantee for the security of neighboring states. On the contrary, they would only serve to set off a new burdensome armament race which would in turn lead to renewed world conflict! There must be ample space for peaceful work! Open the way for the fraternization of all people and their cooperation in making international culture bloom!

It is true that we women have only limited political rights in practically all countries, but we are not without social power. Let us make use of every tiny bit of this power. Let us use our words and actions in order to influence the narrow circle of our family and friends as well as the broad public. Let us use every means of oratory and writing. Let us use individuals as well as masses as they become available in the different countries. We will not be confused or frightened by the roaring of the chauvinistic stream upon which are bouncing the profiteering percentage patriots, the power-hungry imperialist politicians and the unscrupulous demagogues. It is exactly in the face of this stream's roaring that we loudly talk about the cultural values which all nations have contributed to a common human heritage and about the necessity of a large international community of nations. Let us proudly unfurl the banner of Socialism and Socialist peace demands! In all countries, we will be calumniated and persecuted as traitors without a fatherland, who lack intelligence and the sense of altruism. So be it! We know that we help our homeland much more by our efforts towards peace than by the denunciations and belittling of foreign countries or by sabre-rattling warmongering. When the men kill, it is up to us women to fight for the preservation of life. When the men are silent, it is our duty to raise our voices on behalf of our ideals.

Female comrades, sisters! Fulfill the promise which your representative at the memorable Peace Congress of the Socialist International made at Basel: "It is for this reason that even during a war we will be among those advancing, attacking units that fight against war!"

[*Die Gleichheit* Stuttgart, November 7, 1914 but blanked-out by the censors.] See also pp. 36-37, p. 191 n.1. □

1914

LETTER TO HELEEN ANKERSMIT

Wilhelmshöhe, December 3, 1914

Dear Comrade Ankersmit:[1]

First of all, I want to send you once again the reassuring message that I apparently received all of your communications. I can only write "apparently." Why this is so, my subsequent lines will tell you. I received the "message" of our English comrades, the equally nice letter of my friend Longman and your own long nice letter as well as a card. I have previously confirmed the receipt of all of these items. But did you receive my confirmation? That is the question. I have twice sent you my Appeal (issued in my capacity as Secretary of the International)[2] in which I call upon the women comrades of all countries to work for peace.[3] I placed one copy of this Appeal between the pages of old issues of the *Gleichheit*. I informed you of this fact on an open post card and asked for an acknowledgement. Although fourteen days have passed, I have yet to receive one. I am herewith enclosing two more copies of the Appeal and I must ask you to publish them as soon as possible in the Dutch party press. Please see to it that a copy of the German text will safely reach our English comrades. Mary Longman will translate it well and most willingly.

Please do not be surprised if I write to you infrequently and in a noncommital way. It cannot be any other way as long as the mail which leaves Germany must be sent in unsealed envelopes. In addition to the general situation, there is the additional factor that the authorities keep "a special eye" on me because of my views and opinions. There is no doubt that, at least from time to time, I am being shadowed and my correspondence is being "carefully" controlled. Even though such a control is superfluous and ridiculous, it is nonetheless most bothersome. It is not only a symbol of the general situation but also (and that is most depressing and humiliating) of the political and moral bankruptcy of German Social-Democracy. When I talk to you about all of this, I do it not only to make you understand what difficulties I have to deal with which obstruct my functions as Secretary of the International, but also in order to acquaint you with developments within German Social-Democracy and thus the milieu in which we live. I am making use of this favorable opportunity to write to you. What I am writing to you is designed for your information as well as for the enlightenment of the leading women comrades who work with you. It is not to be published. By that I am not implying that you should not spread the information that I am supplying. But given the current situation, you must not publish this information in the form of a letter from me. Otherwise all of my national and international work in Germany would be totally suspended.

The most disastrous phenomenon of the current situation is the factor that imperialism is employing for its own ends all the powers of the proletariat, all of its institutions and weapons, which its fighting vanguard has created for its war of liberation. Social-Democracy bears the main guilt and responsibility for this phenomenon before both the International and history. The granting of the war credits was the harbinger for the equally comprehensive and revolting process of capitulation of German Social-Democracy.[4] This majority nowadays no longer constitutes a proletarian Socialist party of class battles, but a nationalist social reforming party which waxes enthusiastic over annexations and conquests of colonies. One part of it does so with eloquence, the other sans phrase. This metamorphosis occurs all the more rapidly as the war has created a greenhouse atmosphere for this development with the greatest percentage of our young, trained and energetic comrades stationed at the front. Our organizations are more than decimated. Our treasuries are being emptied by the support contributions; membership meetings may only take up what the authorities approve of. Some of the party leaders and party bureaucrats go even further than the authorities and use the organizational apparatus to prevent a discussion of the causes and the character of this war, which could lead to a criticism of our party's attitude and the demand: Peace, no annexations, etc. Of the 91 organs of our party press, of the many trade union journals, the overwhelming majority is nationalistic, even chauvinistic, through and through and not a few even surpass the jingoist sentiments of the more decent and reasonable bourgeois papers. Social-Democratic and trade union organs have approved of the illegal invasion of Belgium,[5] of the massacre of suspected guerrillas, as well as their wives and children, as well as the destruction of their homes in various towns and districts. Social-Democratic and trade union organs demanded the annexation of all of the countryside between Antwerp and Calais, of all of Lorraine etc. The Executive Committee of the Social-Democratic Party of Germany has repeatedly rejected the suggestion to issue a manifesto in which the Party as a whole would denounce the hidden annexationist plans and come out for peace. This rejection was based on the following grounds: 1) Such a manifesto would be superfluous because it is generally known how the Party views annexations and peace. Its position was solemnly confirmed by the Reichstag Declaration of the Socialist Delegates on August 4th. 2) It would be an impossibility anyway because the authorities will not permit anybody to speak or write for or against annexations and peace. Needless to say, in spite of the authorities' declarations, they do not hear and see anything when it comes to demands *for* annexations and colonial conquests. The demand for a prompt peace, however, is scorned and fought. Summa summarum: A defeat suffered while pursuing its aims would not have weakened, confused and disoriented the German proletariat as much, nor would it have caused such sacrifices in property and blood as the betrayal by the Party has done.

It is true my dear Comrade Ankersmit, that there exists both within the Social-Democracy and outside of it within the proletarian masses, a resolute and decisive opposition against this state of affairs and its further development. You know, of course, that fourteen Social-Democratic Reichstag deputies were opposed to the approval of war credits on August 4th.[6] Three other deputies would have joined them had they taken part at that session. In all large cities dissatisfaction and ferment exist. But the opposition is tied up and gagged. The state of siege has made it impossible for it to speak up at meetings or in the press. The "revisionists" (to use an expression which has become much more comprehensive nowadays and includes the majority of the party comrades and trade unionists) make use of this state of siege systematically and unscrupulosuly in order to persuade the masses of their point of view and in order to silence the opposition completely. They are able to do this all the more easily because they enjoy the disguised or undisguised favor of the authorities and because they control the major part of the working class press and the organizations. Within the organizations, the "revisionists" meet with only weak resistance because the younger and more resolute comrades are performing their military duty outside of the country.

Thus the opposition against the denial of the Socialist principles is existent but it cannot speak out and be counted on. All it can do is to limit itself to closely following the course of events, to evaluate it within the framework of our Socialist beliefs, to counter the disintegration wherever and whenever that is possible and to gather and prepare the resolute and decisive elements for the inevitable and fundamental battle. I am speaking of an inevitable fight which the resolute Left will have to wage in spite of its desire to preserve party unity. This fight has been forced upon it by the Right Wing who ever more rapidly and completely are throwing overboard everything that has survived of the proud past and tradition of German Social-Democracy. Once peace is reestablished, the German proletariat will confront the gigantic task of clearing away the rubble and reconstructing a new society.

Thus it will be the task of the opposition to gather all forces and to make them resolute, strong-willed and ready to sacrifice. Just how large this opposition is, what strength it possesses, how influential it is among the masses, cannot be determined exactly for the above-mentioned reasons. But it would not be smart to deceive oneself over its present smallness. It would also not be smart to overlook or to underestimate the fact that this minority will inexorably grow as the duration of the war keeps increasing. Many enlightened proletarians have envisioned "the danger to preservation and the culture of the fatherland" and the character, the effects and the sacrifices of this war in an entirely different fashion than is now revealed by the facts.

Do I have to explain to you, my dear Friend Ankersmit, why I belong to the minority oppositon? I believe that my life's work will tell you enough concerning the reasons. I am sure that you have read the declaration which I had published with Rosa Luxemburg and Comrades Liebknecht and Mehring.[7] From the very beginning, I considered it to be my honor-bound duty to preserve the *Gleichheit* as a Socialist periodical, untarnished by chauvinistic tendencies so that it may continue to represent the banner of progressive womanhood which it has constituted for almost a quarter of a century. This belief comes to me all the more naturally since the *Gleichheit* was also the international organ of our women comrades. You know, of course, from my previous dispatches, how extremely difficult it is for me to do just what is natural to me. I know, of course, the situation well enough to realize that it is impossible to present the situation according to my views, which represent the Socialist point of view and the duties of the proletariat. Thus I refrain from the very start to express what I cannot and may not express because the authorities have the legal right and the power to force me to leave it unexpressed. Yet I resolutely refused from the very beginning to express that which, as an international Socialist woman, I could not and must not state. I tried not to make any concessions to the dizzy chauvinism and totally bourgeois patriotism which has nothing in common with true love of one's fatherland. On the contrary, I tried to counter this insanity and suicidal activity of Social-Democracy as effectively and resolutely as possible. I have the satisfaction that the attitude of the *Gleichheit* was understood and appreciated. During the almost twenty-four years that I have edited the *Gleichheit*, there has never been a period during its embattled existence during which I have received so many signs of approval. They have come from all regions of the Empire, from women and men and from those enrolled in political organizations and trade unions.

But my dear Comrade, due to its content, the *Gleichheit* is subjected to the most arbitrary harassment by the censors and the military command. You have to remember that we are much worse off under the state of siege than we were under the Anti-Socialist Legislation. The latter required the authorities to abide by certain rules. They could be fought through the whole hierarchy of courts and in the Reichstag. This state of siege is not bound by any rules. The Supreme Army Command and its district representatives may act in an entirely sovereign manner. They do not have to list any reasons and their measures may not be fought in the courts. Within the Reichstag, however, Social-Democracy allowed itself to be gagged voluntarily. No debates take place there in order to prevent the weakening "of the unity of the entire German people." A muzzle for the opposition has never been a sign of strength but rather of fear. Now the enlarged

Budget Commission is supposed to deal secretly with important questions including press and censorship matters. I did what was humanly possible in order to make use of this diminutive possibility to act by sending to Comrade Haase (he is the Chairman of the SPD and the SPD Reichstag Delegation and a lawyer)[8] all of the collected material concerning the harassment of the *Gleichheit*. But I acted only in order to fulfill my duty, without having the least illusion that I could obtain any results if only for the reason that the main element of criticism was lacking: The public.

Mais revenons à nos moutons:[9] The situation of the *Gleichheit*. The authorities observe with displeasure that the periodical does not join the Teutonic choir of the party press. What makes their displeasure even greater is the reputation and fame of the *Gleichheit*. They use and abuse their power in order to tame the periodical "because it stubbornly refuses to conform to the great movement of this period and its people." They do this all the more resolutely and ruthlessly because they know how isolated our periodical stands vis-a-vis the Party, because a large part of the other working-class papers disapprove of this attitude and because a number of comrades and trade unionists even openly or secretly applaud every blow that is bestowed upon the *Gleichheit*. There is no lack of people who would like nothing better than to see this "radical rag" totally prohibited. It is a shame, my dear Comrade Ankersmit, but that is the way it is: One does not even need the fingers of both hands to list those of the 91 organs of the Party (the trade unions journals are not included here) that courageously and unerringly follow the same line as the *Gleichheit*. If all of our papers, or at least most of them, would do that, no civilian or military authority would dare to use the kind of censorship that it employs now to stifle the free expression of opinion. The authorities need the working class press, they cannot dispense with it. They could not risk to annoy and embitter the proletarian masses and they would, therefore, leave the press alone if, yes, if the Party and most working-class papers had not placed themselves voluntarily in the service of imperialism. As things stand now, the revolting conduct of the majority of our papers is not only a betrayal of our Socialist principles but it represents a constant encouragement to the authorities to demand from the minority of Socialist opposition journals the same kind of betrayal and to suspend freedom of expression if they continue to write in a Socialist manner. Their actions towards the *Gleichheit* prove that.

Issue 23 of the *Gleichheit* was confiscated even though it was written and printed before the war and even though it had to be released after a few weeks. Once the periodical was allowed to reappear, we had to be extremely careful, reconnoitering the terrain in the attempt to restore at least some of the connections which had been torn asunder because the authorities had seized all of the books and addresses of the publishing house. They watched with Argus-eyes over every word that we wrote. So I was forced to maneuver my thoughts around all sorts of rocks and sandbanks and to be quite apocalyptical in style in order to be able to publish Issue 24 at all. To suspend publication from the beginning would have meant to give up the fight right away. The appearance of every single issue caused objections on the part of the authorities. The preventive censorship expunged whatever aroused its displeasure, often in the most petty and ludicrous manner. In the first few issues after its reappearance, I attempted "to patch up" the eliminated passages by substitutions which would not prove to be "offensive" to the authorities. It was a difficult task during which I tried not to do violence to my convictions and yet was forced to compromise. After the appearance of a few issues, it became clear to me that it would be better for the cause to follow a different path. The "patched-up" passages were often ambiguous and contained the potential danger of sowing confusion, particularly among the female comrades who were untrained or who lived abroad and were unfamiliar with the situation. The greater the confusion within the Party, the more necessary it became that the *Gleichheit* avoided every uncertainty and possibility of being misunderstood. That is why I now categorically refused to make any changes, leaving the passages that were eliminated by the censors simply blank. I hope that the majority of my female comrades will use the logical entirety of any article in order to fill in what is missing and that they are able to tie together the ruptured passages. Besides the blank spaces speak their own language. They are an unambiguous illustration of the nature of the famous "cessation of party strife" which is nothing more than the disarming of the proletariat in its struggle for its interests and ideals.

When it came to Issue 5, the authorities really went crazy. The entire issue was prohibited by the General Command upon the urgings of the censorship authorities that "wanted to make an example" of this issue. The censors not only objected to individual passages but to almost all articles, even rather harmless ones such as an article concerning the care of soldiers' families by their communities. At first the censorship authorities assumed the responsibility to permit the issuance of a new issue which was to consist of the few articles that had not been purged. The new issue was put together. At the beginning of this expurgated issue there was to be a notice, dutifully informing the female readers that this issue contained only four pages instead of eight, because the General Command, by threatening to seize the issue had prohibited certain articles (their titles were then listed) and the column "For Peace". Apparently even this matter-of-fact information aroused the ire of the censorship authorities. They now declared that the decision of the General Command must be carried out in its entirety by prohibiting the whole issue. Among the contributions which were singled out for special criticism was not only the "Appeal" but also the "Message To Our English Women Comrades," even though a large part of that message had been previously printed in the Social-Democratic dailies and in the Viennese *Arbeiterinnen-Zeitung,* which brings me to our international relations and our common international work.

Dear Comrade Ankersmit, when the war broke out and all communications with foreign countries and the female comrades of individual nations were interrupted, I said to myself immediately: Now more than ever! It was clear to me that in my position as Secretary of the International, I had to attempt to restore the disrupted communications as soon as possible and to reorganize the ranks of the women comrades for a common task. I also had no doubt what this common task had to involve. It was to be a fight for peace, a peace based on Socialist principles for which we women Socialists of all countries could work by using all available means. According to my opinion, it is the proud privilege and the honorable duty of the Socialist Women's International to lead the battle for peace and to arouse and lead the women of all classes and countries. I am also convinced that we would not only be able to enroll in our ranks a good portion of the suffragettes in all countries but women in general, except for those who have been rendered blind and deaf towards their interests and duties as personalities and mothers by the imperialist poison. These concepts are reflected in the *Gleichheit's* lead article: "We Mothers." I intended to inititate the international peace work as soon as I could be sure that the women comrades of several countries had answered my appeal and as soon as I would have the opportunity to come into contact with at least a part of my dear former women correspondents. During the second half of October I was sure that these two prerequisites had been met. When I was in Berlin around October 21st and 22nd, I informed Comrade Zietz[10] of my intentions. She counseled against its immediate implementation and felt that it would be more effective if, to start out with, she and I would direct a peace appeal to our German women comrades. I was basically in agreement with such an appeal which would occur either before or simultaneously with an international appeal. But now I must mention why until now nothing has come of it. Comrade Zietz was of the opinion that our appeal must appear contemporaneously with a peace manifesto by the Executive Committee of the SPD and not before it. Comrade Zietz informed me, however, that the Party's Executive Committee was holding back with the publication of its peace manifesto until the German army in the West had achieved its decisive victory. This victory is supposed to occur yet in October (!!) which means "next week." I told Comrade Zietz that I would join her at any time in signing a peace declaration but I stated at the same time, that I would also have to act as the Secretary of the International. The proposed common manifesto ought to be directed from a group of advanced German women comrades to all German women comrades. Such a manifesto would certainly have a great significance. I would rather sign today than tomorrow and with both of my hands. I have promised Comrade Zietz to work on an outline for such an appeal. However, my dear Comrade Ankersmit, you will understand, that after much soul-searching, I have become convinced that whatever I can and must do as the leading German woman comrade must not prevent me from acting as the Secretary of the International. Since then, I have only been confirmed in this conviction by your dispatches, dear Friend, by the letters from female comrades of other countries and also by discussions with Swiss friends and with Angelica Balabanov.[11] As Secretary of the International—what am I saying, I must go further: As an international woman Socialist I must not and I cannot view the situation from a narrow and specifically German point of view. I must not and I cannot make the initiation of a peace action by the women of all countries dependent on a preceding decisive victory of German arms. The English, Belgian, French and Russian women could demand equal consideration for the triumph of their flags. By taking into account each individual country, the entire internationality would go to hell. That is very obvious and one does not really have to waste any words over it.

Thus at the beginning of November, I composed the international appeal. In order to make it acceptable to the women comrades of all countries and to bring them together, I had to keep it very general, so general indeed, that it seemed colorless to me. I would have loved to raise my voice and to have chided, believe me! In composing this very general and pale version, I had to take special care because of the conditions in Germany, not because I was afraid, but because I thought its publication in Germany would be very important. Since the official Social-Democracy was silent about peace in all of its variations, it seemed to me all the more important to talk about it. Not just as an international, but as a German female Social-Democrat, it was my heart's desire to raise my voice for peace and international Socialist brotherhood in the midst of this din of battle and the chauvinistic screaming. That is why I wanted to write a version which would make the publication and the propagation of the appeal also possible in Germany. But it did not do any good. I expected the censoring of a few sentences, but the censorship authorities objected to the entire appeal. I still hope that there will be a possibility to spread it at a later time. In the meantime, I am relying upon you, my dear Comrade, to forward the appeal to the International Secretariat so that it will become known among the female comrades of the different countries, particularly the English and Belgian ones. I hope to convey the appeal to the French women comrades by another route.

I received the "message" of the English sisters almost simultaneously through you and the Norwegians and yesterday once again via Sweden. Without the brutal interference of the censorship, it would already have been published during the middle of November. For the time being, I will have to abide by the prohibition. After some time has passed, however, I will try to present a "purified" version or an extensive excerpt. The same goes for the article from *Proletarische Vrouw* which I received in translation from our friend A.F. at L. Because of the prohibition of Issue 5, it was dropped along with all other contributions to the column entitled "For Peace." Yet I hope that I will eventually be able to print it after making the necessary changes and adding meaningful hyphens. At least I will try to do so since I do not give up so easily. I received the verbatim text of the Austrian women comrades' answer to the English message from our friend Popp. What applies to the other two manifestations of international attitude, applies to it also. In Issue 6, I could not irritate the lions of censorship with international material. Issue 7 will present a longish report of Comrade Popp. Perhaps I will then be able to publish all of this international material.

Now let me mention a manifestation of international solidarity from Germany. I am enclosing a personal letter for Mary L. as well as an answer for the English sisters. The content may also suit the French, Russian and Belgian women. For the time being, it has only been signed by me in my capacity as Secretary of the International but I hope that I will be able to report to you in a few days that Comrade Zietz had expressed her solidarity with it. The situation is as follows: Comrade Zietz had authorized me to place her name, too, under my answer to the English women comrades. However, she is not familiar with the text so far and I am not sure that she will approve of certain passages. That is why I first want to send her the text. If Comrade Zietz declares her agreement with it (I tried to make that possible for her to do by the version of the answer) I will send you directly a card with the message: Luise will sing in the concert. This message will authorize you to add Comrade Zietz's name. So that you may not misunderstand all of this, let me add the following: I am convinced that Comrade Zietz feels and thinks in an international manner. She has proved often enough that she is no coward. However, she feels a constraint because of her position as a member of the Executive Committee of the SPD. She wants to avoid any personal act for which the entire Executive Committee can be held responsible. The famous German discipline has its two sides, of which the one can become very questionable. That is shown once again by the "Liebknecht Case" in the Reichstag.[12] I just hope that as far as his case is concerned, the International will honor what the narrow-minded party discipline condemned. Liebknecht showed much more courage, and a better type of courage, than the wrongly celebrated Frank, who, accompanied by the frenetic applause of all Super Germans went to battle for imperialism and was killed.

But to go back to what I was writing about. Of course, it would not only be a good thing, but a necessity, that the peace campaign be carried out by meetings. Here in Germany, however, this is for the moment an impossibility. The Stuttgart comrades attempted to hold a meeting with Liebknecht as speaker on the topic of: "Against the Campaign for Annexations!" It was prohibited. At Berlin and environs, Liebknecht and Comrade Luxemburg wanted to talk about similar topics. The meetings were prevented by the local party organizations. Shortly before Christmas, however, I will try to organize a women's assembly which could be turned into a peace rally. As far as the meetings are concerned, it is the same as with the press: If the Executive Committee of the SPD would seize the initiative and select a day to call for peace rallies in the entire Empire, the authorities would think twice before issuing an interdict. Individual meetings, of course, they crush with an iron fist without giving it a second thought. It is all the more important that the female and male comrades in the neutral countries go ahead with peace demonstrations. Thus they will exercise moral pressure upon Social-Democracy in the belligerent countries and (wherever that is applicable) make it feel ashamed and ready to change. They can also influence their native governments into launching energetic, common peace campaigns of all neutral countries. Dear Comrade Ankersmit, I know that I do not even have to ask you and the Dutch comrades to work with all of your might in that direction. There is only one thing that I would like to say to you: If it seems possible and useful that I should participate at such a peace rally, I am happy to come. But we have to arrange matters at an early time, so that I can organize everything here. We can write about many matters by referring to the International as "the large family," to the parties of individual countries as "close relatives," of meetings as "concerts, weddings, etc." I am sure that we will be able to guess what we mean to convey to each other. It would be great if you could locate somebody reliable near the German border who could mail important letters for me on German soil so that they would not be opened. In this case, you would have to use the following address: Miss Marie Plettner, c/o Fink, Altenbergstrasse 1 at Stuttgart. The letter for me should be placed in a separate envelope and addressed: For Clara.

Even the longest letter must eventually come to an end and thus it is with this tapeworm. I felt, however, that I owe it to you and the comrades to render a frank and unvarnished description of the situation here. . . .

I am just now reading the telegraphic confirmation that our party delegation has approved for the second time five billion marks for the war effort. It has rejected the last opportunity to find its way back to Socialism.[13] The vote of December 2nd is even worse than the vote of August 4th because in the meantime events have destroyed the phony arguments about the necessity to serve the fatherland.

I hope that you understand that I have spoken in this endless letter only with the dry objectivity of my mind. If I would have let my heart speak, there would have been an endless outpouring of the suffering, disappointment, bitterness and despair of these last few months. I have not gotten over all of this, but I had to repress and tame it by my determination to do my duty to the end. When the collapse of the International came, I thought that I would either go crazy or kill myself. I was very sick for a month and I am still not feeling well. My oldest son is serving as a doctor in Belgium, a country which was drawn into the horrors of this war by the shameful violation of international law. He might even be in Russia by now. I am almost without news from him. How often do we get the news that one of our most loyal and modest ones has been killed! But what does all of this mean, considering the historical fact that the International has collapsed! The rest is silence. Your letters are rays of hope. I understand the feelings of your Dutch comrades and I share them. Do whatever you can. I gratefully accept your faithful help and I feel closer to you and the others than ever before.

At least mentally, I shake your hand, dear Friend Ankersmit, as well as the hands of the other women comrades, most heartily.

Clara Zetkin

[Archive of the Institute of Marxism-Leninism at the Central Committee of the Communist Party of the Soviet Union, Moscow; File: Clara Zetkin.] □

1915

WOMEN OF THE WORKING PEOPLE

Where are your husbands?
Where are your sons?

For eight months now, they have been at the front. They have been torn from their work and their homes. Adolescents, the support and hope of their parents, men at the prime of their lives, men with greying hair, the supporters of their families: All of them are wearing military uniforms, are vegetating in trenches and are ordered to destroy what diligent labor created.

Millions are already resting in mass graves, hundreds upon hundreds of thousands lie in military hospitals with torn-up bodies, smashed limbs, blinded eyes, destroyed brains and ravished by epidemics or cast down by exhaustion.

Burnt villages and towns, wrecked bridges, devastated forests and ruined fields are the traces of their deeds.

Proletarian Women! One has told you that your husbands and sons left for the war in order to protect their weak women and children and to guard home and hearth.

But what is the reality?

The shoulders of the weak women now have to bear a double burden. Bereft of protection, you are exposed to grief and hardships. Your children are hungry and cold. One threatens to take away the roof over your head. Your hearth is cold and empty.

One has talked to you about a grand brother and sisterhood between the high and the low, of a cessation of strife between poor and rich. Well, the cessation of strife meant that the entrepreneur lowered your wages, the tradesman and unscrupulous speculator raised prices and the landlord threatens to evict you. The state claims impoverishment and the bourgeois welfare authorities cook a meager soup for you and urge you to be thrifty.

What is the purpose of this war which has caused you such terrible suffering?

One tells you, the well-being and the defense of the fatherland. Of what does the well-being of the fatherland consist?

Should it not mean the well-being of its millions, those millions who are being changed to corpses, cripples, unemployed beggars and orphans by this war?

Who endangers the well-being of the fatherland? Is it the men who, clad in other uniforms, stand beyond the frontier, men who did not want this war any more than your men did and who do not know why they should have to murder their brothers? No! The fatherland is endangered by those that reap profit from the hardships of the broad masses and who want to build their domination upon suppression.

Who profits from this war?

Only a tiny minority in each nation.

The manufacturers of rifles and cannons, of armor plate and torpedo boats, the shipyard owners and the suppliers of the armed forces' needs. In the interest of their profits they have fanned the hatred among the people, thus contributing to the outbreak of the war. This war is beneficial for the capitalists in general. Did not the labor of the dispossessed and the exploited masses accumulate goods that those who created them are not allowed to use? They are too poor to pay for them! Labor's sweat has created these goods and labor's blood is supposed to create new foreign markets to dispose of them. Colonies are supposed to be conquered where the capitalists want to rob the natural resources and exploit the cheapest labor force.

Not the defense of the fatherland but its augmentation is the purpose of this war. The capitalist system wants it that way, and without the exploitation and suppression of man by man, that system cannot exist.

The workers have nothing to gain from this war but they stand to lose everything that is dear to them.

Wives of Workers, Women Workers! The men of the belligerent countries have been silenced. The war has dimmed their conscience, paralyzed their will and disfigured their entire being.

But you women who besides your gnawing concern for your dear ones at the front have to bear deprivations and misery, what are you waiting for in expressing your desire for peace and your protest against this war?

What is holding you back?

Until now you have been patient for your loved ones. Now you must act for your husbands and sons.

Enough of murdering!

This call resounds in many tongues, millions of women raise it. It finds its echo in the trenches where the consciences of the people's sons are stirred up against this murder.

Working Women of the People! In these difficult days, Socialist women from Germany, England, France and Russia have gathered. Your hardships and sufferings have moved their hearts. For your own sake and the sake of your loved ones, they are asking you to work for peace. Just like their minds met across the battlefields, so you must get together from all countries in order to raise the cry: Peace! Peace!

The world war has demanded the greatest sacrifices from you. The sons that you bore in suffering and pain, the men who were your companions during your difficult struggles, have been torn away from you. In comparison with these sacrifices, all other sacrifices must seem small and insignificant.

All humankind is looking upon you women proletarians of the belligerent countries. You are destined to be the heroines and redeemers!

Unify as one will and one deed!

What your husbands and sons cannot yet aver, announce with a million voices:

The laboring people of all countries are a people of brothers. Only the united will of this people can stop the killing.

Socialism alone will assure the future peace of humankind.

Down with capitalism which sacrifices hecatombs of people to the wealth and the power of the possessing class!

Down with War! Break through to Socialism![1]

[Bern, March 1915, the International Socialist Women's Conference. *Berner Tagwacht* 3 April 1915] □

1917

TO THE SOCIALIST WOMEN OF ALL COUNTRIES

The inevitable clarification process within the German Social-Democracy, among other bad and painful concomitant symptoms, has resulted in my expulsion by the Executive Committee of the Social-Democratic Party from the editorship of the *Gleichheit* which I directed for 27 years.[1] The real reason for this punishment is the principled stand of this periodical. To adjust it to the concepts of the Majority Socialists, to the approval of war credits and the Cessation of Party Strife Policy of the Government and to praise all of the above-mentioned aberrations as historical feats, seemed to me a betrayal of the requirements of international Socialism. To be silent in the face of such policies would have been to assume an attitude of undignified cowardice.

For the task and the very justification of the existence of the *Gleichheit* was to serve the aims of international Socialism. It was designed to make the working women of the population realize that only Socialism is the savior, the world historical deliverer that guarantees everybody full human rights. It was supposed to make available to Socialism the rich streams of spiritual and moral values which today, unrecognized and unused, roar subterraneously among the broad women masses. Thus the obligation was created to measure all emerging questions as well as moot points with the ideas and ideals of international Socialism, regardless of current opinions, undesirous of applause, without fear of criticism and fearless and loyal in the face of hatred and danger. I have done my best to fulfill these obligations of the *Gleichheit* even during the difficult times which were produced for Social-Democracy and the proletariat by the world war. Yes, especially in these times when imperialism has had the effect of the Tower of Babel upon the Socialists and proletarians of all countries. My punishment is the consequence of my beliefs.

The transformation of the *Gleichheit* is not only of concern to the German women Socialists but affects the interests of the Socialist women of all counties. The *Gleichheit* was the leading intellectual and unifying organ of the Socialist Women's International. This was decided upon by the International Socialist Women's Conferences of Stuttgart and Copenhagen. That decision was not at all based upon the fact that the *Gleichheit* also happened to be an organ (one among many) of the Social-Democratic Party of Germany and that, according to bourgeois law, the executive committee of that party, in its capacity as representative and business agent, was the owner (and according to party statutes, supervisor) of said periodical. What was important was the international dissemination and the international reputation of the *Gleichheit* as well as the trust which the women comrades of all countries placed in it because, loyal to the above-mentioned principles, it discussed the various aspects of the women's question and its universal social and historical application within the framework of Scientific Socialism. What was important was the fact that the *Gleichheit* was directed by me, who in my capacity as Secretary of the International, edited the periodical in agreement with the directives and decisions of our International Women's Conferences and the general International Socialist Congresses. By many years of work and cooperation with the leading women comrades of all countries, I had gained an overview of the entire Socialist women's movement. In my hands, its connecting threads ran together, and enlightened reports as well as positive suggestions were deposited.

The objective and personal prerequisites of the international organ of Socialist women cannot be simply transferred from one editorial board to another just because the Social-Democratic Executive Committee orders it, no more that the name *Gleichheit* may be bestowed upon another periodical which is alien to its nature. The "purged" *Gleichheit* cannot be the organ of the Socialist Women's International. It will merely become one more paper of the Social-Democratic Party of Germany, one among many. The women comrades of all countries will have the same relationship to it that they have to all of the other people of the Party. They will certainly not feel any longer a special relationship of trust. This will be even less the case since the *Gleichheit* will be edited in complete contradistinction to the basic views of its previous editor.

In view of this situation, all reports, contributions etc. of the women comrades of individual countries are to be sent, as before, to me in my capacity as Secretary of the International. It will be, as before, my obvious duty to disseminate and publish these items. In spite of my disciplinary punishment, the Socialist Women's International has not become homeless. A substitute for the "old *Gleichheit*" will shortly make its appearance.[2] Preparations for that event are practically finished. In addition, the daily newspapers of the Independent Socialist Party[3] will regard it as their natural duty and honor to publish whatever the Secretary of the International will send them. I will see to it that these publications will reach the corresponding female comrades of all countries on a regular basis. Special circulars, informational bulletins etc. on my part will reproduce reports and suggestions and thus keep alive the exchange of ideas and the relationships between the various female comrades.

I hope that our foreign female comrades agree with this temporary solution of a problem which will be taken up and resolved permanently at the next International Women's Conference. I trust that they will reciprocate loyalty with loyalty and that they will unanimously uphold those principles for which the *Gleichheit* perished. We women who found in Socialism the country of our souls' longing and humankind's fatherland for future generations, we women must not make deals with unprincipled half-measures and weaknesses. Our place is where the pure red banner waves. The "old" *Gleichheit* has perished. Long live international Socialism. In that spirit, I greet the Socialist women of all countries!

Clara Zetkin
Secretary of the International

[*Leipziger Volkszeitung* June 19, 1917] □

1917

THE BATTLE FOR POWER AND PEACE IN RUSSIA

Once again the eyes of the peace-seeking peoples of Europe are turned towards Russia, and with more passionate longing than ever before. The duration and intensification of this ghastly world war has increased in all countries the desire for peace and the powerful revolutionary event in Russia brings peace within striking distance, provided that the belligerents want peace because they are compelled to desire it.

Just as in March, the Revolution has risen again with all of its terrifying and magnificent strength. Its nature is the same and yet not the same. Once again the upheaval is spearheaded by the Socialist-led proletariat of the great industrial centers and by a considerable part of the peasantry, the petit-bourgeoisie and the army. But as far as its aims are concerned, and the paths it is taking to reach those aims, this Revolution is far more decisive than the February Revolution.[1] The latter forced the Russian bourgeoisie (including the liberalized Zemstvo Aristocracy) to let go of its ideal of a dressed-up bourgeois coup d'etat which merely placed the reins of government into other hands and with a bittersweet mien began to smash Tsardom which had proved to be such an excellent patron of capitalism. It remained, however, a bourgeois-political revolution. . . .

Politically speaking, the February Revolution resulted in constantly changing provisional governments. No matter how the different parties and personalities coalesced, two characteristics remained constant. Its domestic policy was determined by a coalition of revolutionary democracy and the bourgeoisie, and by Socialists of the most diverse factions and the Cadets. The foreign policy was determined by the alliance of Russia with tho Western Powers. Thus international imperialism, in revolutionary Russia, too, united nationally what should have been divided by irreconcilable class contradictions and divided internationally what should have been fused by indestructible class solidarity.

Class contradictions, however, are not to be scoffed at. They cannot be argued away by the most refined periwigs nor can they be coaxed away by the most cunning *Realpolitiker*. They cannot be tamed by brutal jailers and hoodlums, nor can they be talked away by democratic eulogies. As long as the means of production are not taken out of private hands, they will make their appearance in history again and again and insist upon their prerogatives. Strikes, hunger riots, Jacqueries, the restriction and abolition of just proclaimed political freedom, abrogation of just promulgated progressive measures: All of this clearly indicates that in spite of all the lip service rendered to revolutionary democracy in Russia, the class contradictions continued to have their effect in the form of class struggle.

The longer the alliance between the revolutionary democracy and the bourgeoisie lasted and the firmer it became, the more it fettered the revolutionary forces of this country. The renewal and the reconstruction of the country on a higher plateau seemed to move further and further into the distance. There were no thorough social reforms in favor of the proletariat, the peasantry and the petit bourgeoisie. Even the safeguarding of the political heritage of the February Revolution by a Constituent Assembly was postponed from month to month. There was no decisive action to realize the demand of revolutionary democracy: A peace without annexations and indemnities with the guaranteed right of the self-determination of nations. To be sure, given the circumstances of the times, it would have been difficult to carry out these redeeming deeds whose effects should not have been to favor one group of belligerent states over the other and to place the beginnings of democratic development under the dragoon boots of the reactionary forces. However, the effect had to be looked upon from the point of view of further political development, and peace seemed to be the only successful means of overcoming the imperialism of all states and the *sine qua non* for Russia's revolution to change the country from the bottom up.

With increasing bitterness and even despair the broad Russian masses witnessed how one provisional government after another continued to waste the blood and the treasure of the people for imperialist desires to obtain world power. The myriad forms of the people's sufferings defy description. A change of mood could be detected among the workers, peasants and soldiers whose organization, the Workers and Soldiers Soviet, constituted the backbone of revolutionary democracy. It seemed detrimental to them to continue to share political power with the bourgeoisie. The need of the moment seemed to be to seize the entire governmental might with one's own hands. It was through this realization that the slogan triumphed which the left wing of Russian Social Democracy, the Party of the Bolsheviks,[2] had maintained from the very beginning. The leadership of the Soviets changed from the moderate to the radical Socialists whose influence is being strengthened by the similar left wing of the Social Revolutionaries, the Internationalists. Concepts turned into willpower and willpower became action.

The gigantic shadow of the Revolution hovered menacingly over Petrograd when in July the capital's proletariat rose up in order to force the then provisional government to stick to the announced peace formula. Bloodily suppressed in a manner worthy of Tsarism,[3] it, nevertheless, accomplished the expulsion of leading imperialists from the government as well as a more explicit explanation of the peace formula which was supposed to block the war-prolonging diplomatic game. And now at the beginning of November, the mighty Revolution has returned even more strongly. Inspired and guided by the slogans of the Bolsheviks,[4] the Petrograd Soviet led the working people against the Kerenski Government by raising the flag of rebellion. The All-Russian Congress of Workers' and Soldiers' Soviets received it from its hands and made it its own universal banner. The coalition government of revolutionary democracy and the imperialist bourgeoisie no longer exists.

The Bolsheviks have reached their goal in a bold assault which has no parallel in history.[5] Governmental power is in the hands of the Soviets. What has transpired is the revolutionary dictatorship of the proletariat or more correctly: The dictatorship of the working population because, around the industrial proletariat of the great modern economic centers of Russia (the axis of crystallization for the revolutionary forces) are grouped the peasants and petit-bourgeois citizens in their work garments and military uniforms. The idyll of revolution as the work of all strata of society is finished. The revolutionary democracy must maintain its power in a difficult civil war.

Do not these facts turn everything upside down that we learned and taught about the developmental maturity of societal phenomena and people as indispensible prerequisites for such an "upheaval" as is occuring in the East of this world? And must not the "backwardness" of the economic development of Russia and its masses doom from the beginning the insurrection of the Bolsheviks and thus the revolution itself? This is the opinion not only of the foreign Socialists but also of the moderate Social Democrats and Social Revolutionaries in Russia itself. . . . Three-quarters of Russia consists of agricultural lands. The great centers of capitalist industry that possess a modern proletariat are sparse and separated by long distances. The means of communication are still in their infancy. The proletarians themselves are still caught up in rural sentiments and rural thinking. The broad masses are illiterate. They are without strong organizations with well-filled treasuries and without political training by ballots, electoral campaigns and parliamentary speeches. What a frivolous sacrilege to demand the dictatorship of the proletariat under such circumstances!

As convincing as all of these arguments sound, they are in our opinion not accurate, even though we do not mean to deny the incredible difficulties which the above-mentioned conditions pose. The "necessary maturity" of phenomena or people for a revolution is a formula which receives content and life by historical reality and this historical reality cannot be pressed into preconceived schemata. Historical materialism is no collection of ready-made prescriptions by society doctors, quacks and druggists. It is the heretofore most perfect tool for the exploration, illumination and comprehension of the historical development of humankind. The development of the economy and the societal phenomena in Russia must be viewed within the context of that country and not compared to the countries of old European culture. Its development includes aspects of Asia, Europe and America. And if the Russian people did not experience the culture which in Central and Wetern Europe was primarily the achievement of the urban bourgeoisie (fine arts and especially architecture, the most socially oriented of all art forms, make this obvious), it also means that it is not encumbered with all of the bourgeois traditions and ties which, in our country, enervate the decisiveness of the masses. But setting all this aside, what is really important is: Phenomena and people are ready for revolution when the broad strata of the population find certain conditions intolerable and if they no longer believe in the ability and the desire of their superior ruling organs to be able to alleviate the unbearable burden. The revolution occurs when they solely trust in their own strength and are imbued with the feeling that:

> "The old primeval state of nature has returned,
> in which each human faces other humans."[6]

Among the followers of Cromwell, the number of illiterate singers of psalms was certainly large and very few conquerors of the Bastille were "literate" enough to even be able to read Pere Duchesne. The Russian proletarians and peasants are ripe for revolution and for the seizure of power because they want the revolution and state power and they are not afraid to fight for it.

The conquest of the entire political power in the Empire, the seizure of state power, is one thing. But the revolution cannot be content to bring about political changes in Russia. It must also hammer out a new economic and social philosophy. The social content of this revolution is its life blood. The government of the Soviets wants to give the land to the peasants. It wants to hand over to the working class the control over industrial production. It desires transformations which will encounter mountains of difficulties, but which will lend the greatest historical significance to the Bolsheviks, a significance not only within the framework of Russia but of the world. The most important prerequisite for the realization of the revolution is peace. The revolutionary government faithfully endeavors this peace, true to the principles which the Bolsheviks proclaimed to the masses ever since the outbreak of the war:

"Russia's proletariat stands in irreconcilable opposition not only to the imperialism of the Central Powers but the imperialism of all states including that of Russia. The proletariat of Russia feels the closest solidarity not only with the workers of the Entente Powers, but with the workers of the entire world, including the workers of the Central Powers."

Guided by this concept, the revolutionary government of Russia is determined to make peace. It has taken the initial steps towards an armistice without feeling any obligations towards the secret treaties by which Russian imperialism chained the land and the people to the chariot of war of West European imperialism.

Whatever may be the outcome of the bold struggle of the

Russian working class for power and peace: It has not been in vain. This struggle will create deep and ineffaceable marks upon history. Not just from its victory, which the proletarians of all countries passionately desire, but from the mere fact that it occurred, new creative impulses will radiate in all directions.

[Women's Supplement of the *Leipziger Volkszeitung*, November 30, 1917] □

1919

KARL LIEBKNECHT AND ROSA LUXEMBURG MUST REMAIN ALIVE

Wilhelmshöhe, January 19th, 1919
Post Degerloch At Stuttgart

Dear Miss Mathilde,[1] Dear Friend:

The horrendous news arrived yesterday morning. On the previous afternoon, the newspapers had reported the arrest of Karl and Rosa.[2] I had bad premonitions and I immediately sent telegrams to Haase and Mrs. Zietz, pleading with them to do everything possible to provide protection for the two of them. I also sent a special delivery letter to Eisner[3] urging him to make use of his official influence. In spite of illness, traffic difficulties and Rosa's warnings, I was going to travel to Berlin to move heaven and earth to protect these precious, irreplaceable human beings.

Then appeared the morning papers. Everything was finished! Oh, my dear Mathilde, you will understand what I have gone through since then, because even though you were never politically involved, you knew the two of them on a personal and human level much better than many of the political fighters did. You know only too well what has been done to them. That is why I am writing to you in this desperate hour. I am asking myself whether I am still alive and how I can possibly go on living after what has transpired! I want to cry and utter a scream which would shake up and topple the world. I cannot bear to think about the horrible fact: They are dead and assassinated under the most brutal circumstances. I cannot believe that life without Karl and Rosa should go on in its normal fashion and that the sun is shining outside. It seems to us that the sun has lost its luster and that time is standing still and not being able to advance beyond this horrible event. Oh Mathilde, Mathilde what we have lost!

Your sympathy is appreciated, but it cannot lessen our despair. For Rosa's sake we will try to put up with life without her, but whether we will be able to do so, whether it is not beyond our strength, remains to be seen. Our own despair reminds us of the grief of the other friends. What you must feel, dearest Mathilde and the poor incarcerated Leo[4] and the wretched Sonja, for whom Karl was her whole life's meaning.[5] And what about the ordinary, modest individuals who had worked and fought with them during recent times! We all join in our immense grief.

Mathilde, will we be able to live without the two of them, without Rosa? The attempt to do so will only make sense if I give to my life the following purpose: To work in their spirit among and with the masses and to make sure that the spirit of these murdered comrades will continue to be our guide. That is Rosa's testament as far as I am concerned. And part of that must be the collection and publication of Rosa's works. They constitute for us a precious, living testament that belongs to the masses. These works as well as the future revolutionary development will be a fitting monument to Rosa which will be much more permanent than ore. I will use all of my strength to make sure that Karl and Rosa will obtain this fitting monument in Socialist literature and in history.

Dearest friend, it is our task to see to it that not one little scrap of paper and not one line of Rosa's manuscripts will be scattered and carried off. None of the old and already printed works, articles, brochures, etc. must be allowed to disappear. You must watch with Argus-eyes that absolutely nothing of Rosa's intellectual and political estate will be confiscated under the pretext of judicial inquiries, house searches, etc. You will need a lawyer. I hope that you will have one that does not lack the proper intelligence and courage which are needed for this task! Rosa's spiritual testament must be defended; it belongs to the revolutionary proletariat. Unauthorized people, such as Kautsky & Co., too, must not be allowed to touch it. That would be a desecration of corpses. It is too bad that Leo is not free! We must also collect all of Rosa's old writings. I am afraid that Rosa behaved just like I do; it was sufficient for her to scatter her thoughts throughout the movement, distributing them in a wasteful manner without collecting them. That is why we have to search for this material in newspapers and periodicals. Of particular importance will be her writings during the last years and weeks.

Die Rote Fahne[6] will be for this revolution what the *Neue Rheinische Zeitung*[7] was for the Revolution of 1848—the leading voice of Socialism. The heart of the revolution beat within it.

The assassination of Karl and Rosa looks like a carefully prepared plot. The governmental mass murderers feared the unpleasantries and the revolutionary effect of a trial against the two. They feared the unquenchable fighting spirit of the two, which had been temporarily obstructed but had never been vanquished. They wanted to destroy the brave fighting arm, the illuminating, guiding brain and the passionately glowing heart of the revolution.

Karl and Rosa were assassinated. No! They will not only continue to live for us but they will and must remain alive for the masses for whom they sacrificed their bodies and souls. Can hearts like theirs cease to beat? Can minds like theirs stop to scintillate and to be creative? As soon as I am able to do so, I will come to Berlin to speak with you personally about a lot of things which can hardly be done in a letter. Tell the friends that I am supporting them more than ever. We have to clench our teeth and "carry on to the end." That is the exhortation of the dead to the living. I would be very grateful if you could send me some news. But make sure to send a registered letter. I received your last letter along with an 8-page letter from Rosa. Her letter had been written in the heat of battle under fire. It was such a sweet letter, typically Rosa and now—I must not think about it!

My dear Friend, please accept my apologies that I am so little in control of myself, but all of this has overwhelmed me. I kiss you in heartfelt friendship.

Your Clara Zetkin

[A letter to Mathilde Jacob, Rosa Luxemburg's secretary, Institute for Marxism-Leninism at the Central Committee of the Socialist Unity Party of Germany at Berlin. Archives.] □

1919

ROSA LUXEMBURG AND KARL LIEBKNECHT

I am the sword, I am the flame
I lit the way for you when it was dark
And when the battle raged, I fought in front
In the first row . . .
We have no time for mourning
The trumpets sound anew
A new fight looms . . .

Heinrich Heine[1]

The counterrevolution, which is blessed and supported by Ebert,[2] Scheidemann[3] and their accomplices has reached a new height of criminal action. In Berlin, it has progressed from the mass murder of revolutionary proletarians to the assassination of its best leaders. After their arrest, Comrades Liebknecht and Luxemburg were murdered in a cowardly and insidious fashion. Rosa Luxemburg's horrendous and barbaric murder will forever remain an indelible outrage for the Germans who always speak so vain-gloriously about their superior culture and good breeding.

The two assassinated leaders were with every fiber of their being, convinced ardent revolutionary fighters. Their beings were totally submerged in the mighty goal which history drew up for the class battles of the proletariat: The liberation of the exploited by the abrogation of capitalism and the construction of Socialism. With heart and soul and, at the same time, magnanimously and masterfully, they threw themselves into the thickest battles of the class struggle. Deeply convinced that its decisive battles would not be fought in parliaments but on the open fields of the revolution, there was never any doubt which of the two kinds of death, the death upon the sick bed or the death before the enemy, they would choose when the inevitable hour would strike. But these revolutionaries of the spirit and the deed always fought with open visors and with honest, chivalrous weapons. It is the bitter tragedy of their end that they did not die in open battle but that they were assassinated after the battle when they were disarmed and defenseless, by bestial marauders and pillagers and by despicable criminals. We are standing upon our Golgotha. It seems to us that the sun has lost its luster and has become dark and that the earth must erupt and cleave asunder. Will the curtain in the temple (decorated with Socialist oratorical metaphors) be rent apart and reveal to the proletarian masses the Holy of Holies of the Ebert-Scheidemannian counterrevolutionary policy: Capitalist property and the bourgeois system?

Rosa Luxemburg and Karl Liebknecht no longer with us! The revolutionary vanguard of the German working class has lost its most resolute, bold and strong leaders. The proletariat of all countries and international Socialism are most severely hit by this loss. Ever since August of 1914, when the majority of the Socialist and Workers' Parties of Germany, Austria, France and England disgracefully capitulated and even yoked the working class masses to the chariots of the war, Karl Liebknecht and Rosa Luxemburg represented the hope and the confidence of all those people who not only continued to cling to the precepts of international Socialism, but in accord with their convictions, endeavored to mobilize the masses for its battles. Karl Liebknecht and Rosa Luxemburg, these names constituted a program, the program of international Socialism. A program not merely consisting of withered and tired lip service, but of robust and unselfish willpower. Like the red banner of the International itself, they shone above the cowardly betrayal, the timid resignation, the lacerating doubt; in brief, all the disorder and confusion which the World War poured from its Pandora's Box upon the world proletariat and its Socialist vanguard.

Karl Liebknecht and Rosa Luxemburg belonged to the very few leading Socialists in Germany (one does not need the fingers of one hand to count them!) about whose attitude towards the imperalist world conflagration there was never even a shadow of doubt from the outset of the war until its final days. Everybody knew how those two felt about this conflict and their position was also honored abroad by all those comrades for whom the term international Socialism was not merely empty rhetoric. They were honored by those segments of the proletariat whose class feelings and class consciousness was still alive. The courage, toughness and self-abnegation which they displayed in throwing themselves against the gigantic tide of triumphing imperialism and the way they raised the unsoiled red banner of international Socialism above its murky waters, allowed the respect and sympathy for the Socialist movement of Germany and the belief in its renewal, to subsist. In all countries, the social patriots who served imperialism referred to Scheidemann and David.[4] The indecisive persons of the tame opposition who were not sure of their principles relied upon Kautsky. But whenever in France, England, Italy and Russia, proletarians desired to express their feelings of solidarity with their brothers of the entire world and with their brothers in Germany in particular, and whenever they wanted to identify themselves as international Socialists, they would exclaim: "Long Live Karl Liebknecht!"

And who could ever forget that in Germany, Karl Liebknecht was the first (and for a long time the only) Social Democrat who dared to break the evil constraint of party discipline which, from a subordinate means of achieving more effective action, had been elevated to become the idol Vitzliputzli to whom every action had to be sacrificed? And who could ever forget that he was the first (and for a long time the only) member of the Reichstag who spoke and acted as an international Socialist so that the real "German honor", the honor of German Socialism would be intact? The majority of the Social-Democratic Reichstag delegates approved the war credits for the fratricidal strife. They obscured and poisoned the judgment of the masses by adopting bourgeois slogans and shibboleths which denied the Socialist ideals.

The opposing minority remained submissively silent. Only Karl Liebknecht had the courage to stand up all by himself and fling his uncompromising "no" into the parliament and into the world.

Ringed by the fury of the bourgeois parties, reviled and slandered by the Social-Democratic Majority and deserted by the Minority, he transformed the Reichstag into a battleground against imperialism and capitalism, using every opportunity to expose the mortal enemies of the proletariat and to urge the exploited to rise up against them—until the day when the Reichstag practiced self-mutilation by giving up its proper right of parliamentary immunity by stripping Liebknecht's immunity as a deputy, handing him over as an alleged "traitor" to the hate-filled bourgeois class justice. This brave and furious fight revitalized the movement. It resurrected the flame in proletarian hearts and made proletarian fists become clenched in readiness to do battle. And Karl Liebknecht carried the fight to the place where it must be waged—to the masses. Both by speeches and by writings, he fought with imperialism over their souls until the day when bourgeois society took its revenge against the feared and hated enemy by sending him to a penitentiary. Why? Because as a draftee he had urged proletarians on the street to make May Day, in the name of international Socialism, a gigantic demonstration against the corrupting "cessation of party strife" and the ongoing genocide.[5] He also called for the removal of the criminal government. Neither danger nor persecution shook Karl Liebknecht's conviction or paralyzed his will to do battle. This is illustrated by his wonderfully proud speech before the military court (which is a classical example of what the defense of a political fighter should be) and his subsequent political activity confirmed it.

Filled with the spirit of international Socialism and able to evaluate the historical situation and its dangers with a profound and exact eye, Rosa Luxemburg had already proven herself as a long and brilliant fighter against imperialism when the World War broke out. The bankruptcy of the Social-Democratic leaders on August 4th was no shattering surprise for her. Without losing even a minute, she summoned up all of her energies in order to gather for resolute action all those forces within Social-Democracy that had remained loyal and firm. Her intention was to lead the straying proletarian masses back to the fold, to lead them from the corrupting war of the nations to the liberating class struggle.

When it came to the first protest against the Reichstag deputies and the Executive Committee of the Party who had spurned the Socialist ideals and principles, and when it came to the first challenge of international Socialism to imperialism and social patriotism, the number of parliamentarians who had privately criticized the Majority in a grandiloquent manner melted like March snow in the sun. Out of 20 people, only Karl Liebknecht together with Rosa Luxemburg, Franz Mehring and myself signed the protest.[6] What affected Rosa Luxemburg infinitely more was the silence and failure of the masses. With consuming urgency, she attempted to instill in them a clear knowledge of the situation, mainly self-confidence in their power and the determination to succeed. Disregarding the illnesses that plagued her at the time as well as the obstacles resulting from the state of siege, she made use of every opportunity to participate as orator or discussion leader at meetings and by personal contacts with male and female comrades within the Social-Democratic organizations to keep alive the Socialist spirit.

The Majority press polluted the proletariat both spiritually and morally. Its activity had to be countered. For this purpose, a Correspondence for Newspapers[7] was established which was written by Rosa Luxemburg, Franz Mehring and Comrade Karski.[8] This Correspondence published many valuable and brilliant contributions, particularly by Rosa Luxemburg. In spite of, or perhaps better, because of its value, it soon folded. Most of the newspapers did not dare to reprint articles from the Correspondence, fearing that to do so would brand them as subversive. The Minority papers feared that the content, which was finely honed like razor blades and consisted of passionate socialist phrases, would irritate the censors. Indeed, the censorship authorities did everything that was possible and impossible to prohibit the articles from the Correspondence or at least to mutilate those that appeared.

The opposition which was beginning to grow within the ranks of Social Democracy needed a leading organ which was destined for the advancing vanguard. It was supposed to be at the same time the awakening clarion call and the profound theoretical guide. It was designed to place the Opposition on the granite ground of firm fundamental International Socialism, plus to provide the correct guidelines for its practical activity. It was supposed to fuse what belonged together and to separate what should be cast off because clear concepts and firm action do not mix with foggy ideas and superficiality.

Together with the above-mentioned friends as well as others, Rosa Luxemburg sketched the plan for the publication of the *Internationale* and prepared the first issue. However, before she could conclude the editorial work, the authorities of the class state seized her. Rosa Luxemburg was suddenly arrested and jailed for one year for her above-mentioned fight against militarism in spite of the fact that she was suffering from the after-effects of a serious illness. Without paying any attention to the burden of work and the threatening persecution, Franz Mehring, the old man with the strength of an adolescent, took the place of the arrested one.[9] The first and only issue of *Internationale*, historic document of International Socialism, was able to appear but not without the indictment of Mehring, Comrade Luxemburg, Comrades Bertens and Pfeiffer at Düsseldorf for the most serious crimes against the bourgeois system and state.

The ruling class knew very well what they were doing when they locked up Rosa Luxemburg for one year. It knew very well what it was doing when after a year in jail and a "breathing spell" of several months (in reality no rest at all but a period of feverish activity), they took this "treasonous person" in protective custody and dragged her for two and a half years from jail to jail, at times under murderous conditions (like the police jail on Alexander Square in Berlin) which could break even the most robust health. Yet the ruling circles miscalculated when they thought that they had defeated this implacable enemy of the bourgeois system. What they could not grasp and what their system did not allow them to grasp was the unyielding, victorious strength of the revolutionary soul of a Rosa Luxemburg. The fire of her heart, whose great passion was Socialism, melted the locks and bolts and her iron will tore down the walls of the dungeon. Her bold, proud, imaginative and ingenious spirit scorned the chains and the myrmidons. It gathered the amplitude of the coursing world outside into the narrowness of her gloomy cell and enlivened the solitude with the phenomena of the historical events that were transpiring. It examined and illuminated them and discovered the correct path which served as directive and guide for those living on the outside. Besides the scholarly and literary activity which she was allowed to pursue, Rosa Luxemburg produced an amazing amount of political and revolutionary work, which had to be done in the face of thorough searches of her involuntary "home," worries about her belongings and her physical survival, innumerable instances of observation through the spy-hole, life in freezing semi-darkness and always the threat of being discovered and heavily punished. Day after day, it was a struggle of the revolutionary spirit and temperament against extraordinary obstacles, but her spirit and temperament emerged as victors. Martyrdom became heroism and sacrifice was turned into deed.

It was behind the jail walls that Rosa Luxemburg wrote the *Junius Pamphlet*[10] by which she exposed in a profound and illuminating manner, the roots and the character of imperialism which had triggered the World War. With unrelenting trenchancy, she dissolved all of the intoxicating, glittering patriotic slogans in the aqua fortis of reality and revealed its true character and its real aims. She recognized imperialism as the involuntary catalyst of world revolution and pointed out to the proletarians of all countries their great historical task: To unite on an international basis in order to make use of the existing opportunities to carry out the liberating act of pushing capitalism into the pit and to establish Socialism. True to the nature of its author, the *Junius Pamphlet* was to be the clarifying theoretical work serving as the indispensible prerequisite of the practical realization of the revolution. Thus it closed with tenets that proclaimed internationalism as the highest law of the proletarian class struggle.

The articles which Rosa Luxemburg wrote for the organs of the most extreme Socialist left, her contributions and stimuli for the "Spartacus Letters," her pamphlets etc. were written in the same spirit as the *Junius Pamphlet* and under the same circumstances. Her secret correspondence with trusted friends was a fresh and inexhaustible source of historical insight into the situation. It was a peerless exhortation to fight and to work.

November 9 opened the jail doors for Rosa Luxemburg and she regained her freedom during a revolution which she had so passionately desired. Shortly before her release, Karl Liebknecht had been freed from the penitentiary by an amnesty. The friendship between these comrades-in-arms was forged in the fire of that revolution. The revolution needed a voice which would awaken the masses, show them the direction and the aim of the struggle and reveal the dangerous activities of the counterrevolution which was working under the Socialist flag. It needed a voice which would warn of half measures and faintness and teach the masses to rely on their own strength. Karl Liebknecht and Rosa Luxemburg cooperated in founding *Die Rote Fahne*.

This is not the time to render a detailed account of this daily newspaper and its main precepts. As far as its characteristics and effect are concerned, *Die Rote Fahne*, as the organ of the revolution, was really a part of that revolution itself. Brimming over with strength and energy, incisive in its outlook, popular in its presentations, it took issue with all of the current questions and phenomena. Within *Die Rote Fahne* one feels the pulse beat of revolution and out of *Die Rote Fahne* emerges a fiery breath. *Die Rote Fahne* was Rosa Luxemburg. Its staff was small. Every member of the staff had to fill many other positions in the revolutionary struggle. The main burden of work rested upon Rosa Luxemburg's shoulders and it was that well-armed, passionate revolutionary woman who put her stamp on the paper.

Karl Liebknecht's forte was the spoken word. He lived and worked in gatherings and demonstrations. He gave expression to whatever the masses felt and whatever constituted their grief and their desire. He carried the banner of the revolution and of International Socialism without growing tired or weak. It is just incredible what the two murdered comrades accomplished during the two months of the revolution. In addition to editorial work, pamphlets, speeches and participation at demonstrations, there were almost constant conferences with individuals, business transactions and much more. It was a feverish, all-consuming haste which turned night into day. Everything was determined by the lightning-like speed of the events accompanying the rapidly unfolding revolution. There was no peace or rest to be had in the comfortable home which Karl Liebknecht's high-minded wife had offered in friendship to Rosa Luxemburg.[11] The path to that home was not only blocked by their utter devotion to duty, but also by the mortal hatred of their enemies. From the very first day of the revolution and on, long before the situation had turned into a bloody civil war, fanatics who had sworn to kill them were waiting in ambush for them. Constantly in flight, they continuously had to change their domicile. The fact that they did not collapse before they were assassinated was one of those "miracles" created by the strongest and purest revolutionary passion which was produced by the furious atmosphere of the revolution.

I considered it to be my duty towards the dead and the living to render at least an abridged and incomplete summary of what Karl Liebknecht and Rosa Luxemburg achieved during the World War and the two months of the revolution for the liberation of the proletariat. Much of their work has remained unknown to many people even though it is a marvelous example of resolute conviction and sacrificing willpower. I can only hint at the difficult times which descended upon these fighting international Socialists upon the outbreak of the World War.

Karl Liebknecht was one of the most diligent and respected orators and propagandists of Social-Democracy. As deputy of the Reichstag and the Prussian House of Representatives he had become aware of the limits of parliamentarianism and he regarded it as his main task to address the masses from the window of the "high houses." In the conflict which has raged during the past fifteen years in the Social-Democratic camp in respect to principles, tactics and means of struggle, he emerged as an adherent of the Left Wing. The German and International Socialist Youth Movement owes him significant stimuli and energetic promotion. Much clearer and more keenly than most of the Social-Democratic leaders, he recognized the dangers of militarism for the proletarian class struggle and demanded that it must be obstructed by the dam of an organized campaign of anti-militaristic propaganda among the young people. His own anti-militaristic propaganda, which resulted in his trial for high treason and will remain a shameful page in the history of German class justice, led to Liebknecht's conviction and incarceration for one and a half years.[12] In the years before 1914, he stood at the forefront of the fight against imperialism in order to call upon the massess to resist the growing danger of a world war.

And Rosa Luxemburg? Hardly eighteen years old, she had to flee her homeland Russian Poland, and flee to Switzerland because of her revolutionary outlook.[13] Besides her thorough and far-reaching studies of the social sciences and the best literature of Scientific Socialism from all countries, she ardently participated in building up the young Socialist movement in Poland, which was split in several directions. Rosa Luxemburg fought with her characteristic energy and acumen to overcome the petit-bourgeois, nationalist and semi-anarchist currents in International Socialism. Thanks to her superior mind and personality, she soon belonged with the most influential leaders, honored by some and slandered as well as hated by others. According to her historical precepts, it was the German proletariat which was destined to fight the next great decisive battle for Socialism. Her fiery revolutionary heart drove her to prepare for and participate in this battle. By a phony marriage (soon dissolved after it had accomplished its purpose) she acquired the citizenship of the Reich and thereafter she was able to make

Germany her place of work and struggle.[14] She devoted herself body and soul to the cause of the proletariat.

Thus it is that only one comprehensive scholarly work by Rosa Luxemburg appeared in print: *The Accumulation of Capital.*[15] A manuscript constituting a continuation of this highly significant book was concluded by Rosa Luxemburg in jail. If I am not mistaken, she also prepared a series of scholarly essays for publication while she was imprisoned. Of genuine scholarship is her doctoral dissertation, "The Industrial Development of Poland" as well as the pamphlet *Mass Strike,*[16] in which pulsates her revolutionary temperament. A similar blend of scholarship and fighting spirit distinguishes the many articles with which she enriched and enlivened *Die Neue Zeit* at an earlier time. Her articles in the old Dresden *Sächsische Arbeiter-Zeitung,* the *Leipziger Volkszeitung,* the *Gleichheit* and the *Vorwärts* lack the ephemeral nature of other writings that appear on a daily basis. At the party school at Berlin where she taught, she was highly respected even by those who fought her ideas.

Ever since she set foot on German soil, she threw herself with energy and endurance into the fight against all opportunistic and revisionist currents. She fought in the press, at meetings and at party congresses for the revolution and its corresponding tactics. There was no controversy in which Rosa Luxemburg was not deeply involved. The party congresses and the masses of the country listened to her when she appeared before them as a propagandist.

The gigantic work of revolutionizing the German proletariat was not enough for the sense of duty of a Rosa Luxemburg. She remained the intellectual head of the Social-Democratic Party of Poland which held high the internationalism of the proletarian class struggle. Her position brought her much work, many worries and a lot of responsibilities. When the proletarians of the Russian Empire rose up against Tsarism and capitalism in 1905, Rosa Luxemburg thought of herself as most fortunate to be able to share this fight. Surrounded by difficulties and dangers, she hurried to Warsaw, where after several months of hectic activities, she became the victim of the victorious counterrevolution and was thrown into a horrible prison. An escape saved her from an even worse fate. Hidden near St. Petersburg along the Finno-Russian frontier, she continued her activities until she was able to return to Germany to resume the good old fight.[17] Just as her life work was international, so was her influence. Rosa Luxemburg was a leading figure of the Second International whose voice carried great weight.

How inadequate is all of this dry information when one attempts to show the rich and beautiful humanity of Karl Liebknecht and Rosa Luxemburg! It was exactly from this humanity that the two pioneers of Socialism drew their strength and it was this humanity which gave their lives and activities the glamor, the color and the warmth that they reflected. Karl Liebknecht was the worthy son of a great father who wanted no other fame than to forge ahead as "a soldier of the revolution." Karl was indeed a heroic vanguard soldier of the revolution. He possessed the magnificent, impetuous and exuberant temperament of a born fighter which was characterized by vigorous daring and stubborn perseverance. Within him pulsated the blood of the faithful which could move mountains. He possessed the proud courage to face alone a world of enemies. Dangers and sacrifices did not perturb him and calumnies and slanders slid off him like water. To risk his position and his life for his convictions was a matter of course for him. Like his father,[18] his life was marked by its Spartan modesty and plainness, yet he was full of kindness towards others. When he was fighting, Karl Liebknecht felt no needs whatsoever because the battle itself was for him exhilaration and ambrosia.

His thoroughly chivalrous character became incensed at every injustice and he always considered the affairs of the weak, the disadvantaged and the suppressed to be his own.

Rosa Luxemburg was a person of such incredible willpower as only a few people in this world could rival. Fierce self-control held back the flaming interior of her being and hid it under a cover of external composure and tranquility. Since she was able to control herself so well, she was able to form and direct others. Her sensitive nature needed a protective barrier against the outside world. A seeming coolness and self-contained seclusion really hid tender, deep and rich sentiments which did not just concern themselves with human beings but, in a pantheistic sense, recognized the unity of all living matter. The "bloody Rosa," exhausted and overwhelmed by work, was capable of turning around on a road in order to pick up a caterpillar that had lost its way and to take it to a new source of nourishment. She never showed indifference towards human needs and she always found the time and the patience to listen to those who needed her advice and help. She gladly did without in order to aid others. As hard as she was towards herself, she was most forgiving towards her friends whose sorrows and worries bothered her more than her own sufferings. As far as her friendships were concerned, she was loyal, devoted, sacrificing and full of tender care. What a charming hostess, sparkling with life and spirit, this "unapproachable fanatic" could be within the circle of her closest friends! Self-discipline and noble pride had augmented her capability of putting up with suffering that she bore with closed lips. In an incorporeal manner, she had put everything coarse behind her. The tiny, fragile Rosa had become the embodiment of unparalleled energy. She required of herself the ultimate and she attained it. When she seemed ready to collapse under the strain of asking too much of herself, she "recovered" by carrying out even greater accomplishments. She seemed to be growing wings during times of work and battle. Only rarely did she say: "I cannot do it." All the more frequently she exclaimed: "I have to do it." Weak health and unfavorable external circumstances exercised no control over her. Surrounded by difficulties and dangers, she always remained true to herself. Limiting outside barriers were overcome by her internal freedom.

The lament for the murdered victims becomes an accusation: We accuse the counterrevolutionaries of having murdered Karl Liebknecht and Rosa Luxemburg according to a well-prepared plan. We accuse: The blood of the horribly murdered sticks to the souls of Ebert, Scheidemann, Landsberg and Noske.[19] They have conjured up a civil war by their deeds and sins of omission. They created (and let others create) the atmosphere which has led to the assassination of Karl Liebknecht and Rosa Luxemburg. They looked with benevolence upon Stampfer and his cohorts who daily described the Spartacists as common criminals and directed the wrath of the possessing classes (that felt threatened) upon Rosa Luxemburg and Karl Liebknecht as the alleged leaders of robbers and murderers. They tolerated the distribution of hundreds of thousands of leaflets which read: Beat Karl Liebknecht and Rosa Luxemburg to death! Hang Karl Liebknecht and Rosa Luxemburg from a lamp post! They offered cannons, mortars and tens of thousands of soldiers to protect the rolls of paper, printing presses etc. of Messrs. Mosse, Scherl and Ullstein. They had only the outspread arms of an officer, but not enough accompanying soldiers to protect the two arrested prisoners.[20] The Eberts and Scheidemanns may use all available juridical formulae to try to prove their innocence when it comes to this foul murder. They may order the most painstaking investigation of this disgraceful event and they may promise the most severe punishment for the guilty persons. They are and they will remain responsible for this tremendous assassination. Just as all of the scents of Araby were unable to remove Banquo's blood from Lady Macbeth's tiny hand, the blood of the murdered martyrs will forever stick to the counterrevolutionary wrists of these men. The time will come when their own government will choke in this blood.

The assassins' hands were able only to slay the bodies of these fiery fighters. The murdered ones are not really dead. Their hearts continue to pulsate throughout history and their spirits shine beyond these dark, yet not hopeless days. The proletariat will inherit the great legacy which Karl Liebknecht and Rosa Luxemburg have left behind. The murdered martyrs are alive, they will be the victors of the future. Out of their bones, their avengers will arise who will carry out and complete the revolution.

[*Leipziger Volkszeitung* February 3, 1919] □

1926

IN THE MUSLIM WOMEN'S CLUB

A symbol for the broad Oriental women's masses are the Muslim Women's Clubs of the Soviet Republics. Their creation and development are of great historical significance.

In the Orient, the working women who passionately desire a transformation of social conditions that will lead to their liberation are beginning to stir and to act. The lowest of the low, who had been pushed into the deepest depths of social enslavement by traditions, laws and religious decrees, are rising. Diffident and wounded in body and soul, they are nevertheless rising steadily in order to achieve freedom and equality. Lenin correctly judged this event as having the greatest historical significance. He was always most sensitive to even the faintest stirrings of revolutionary energies and he evaluated them always within the framework of the general social transformation of this world. Even if the stirrings of the Oriental women masses appear only as faint lightning at this time, they are the harbinger of the approaching thunderstorm. They confirm the fact that the proletarian revolution will indeed turn out to be a world revolution in which even the last suppressed and enslaved individual will free himself by his own strength. The Muslim Women's Clubs in the Soviet Republics are not the tender breeding grounds for suffragette tendencies but the gathering places and schools for the revolutionary forces.

The Muslim Women's Club of Tiflis[1] was founded by the Communist Party and is the special work of its women's division. It was founded in the knowledge that the establishment of the Soviet system had profoundly stirred the psyche of Muslim women. It symbolizes for them the transformation of their lives since Soviet laws know of no domination of men over women and of no prerogative of one sex over the other. Instead, this club proclaims the full equality of women in all social fields and proves that the Soviets are eager to realize this equality. These women demand passionately that they can realize their new legal status by participating in the transformation of society, building a new structure which will accommodate the talents of the working women. Up till now, however, the demands of the majority of the awakening Muslim women are still being obstructed by age-old prejudices. Thus most of them shrink from asserting their positions alongside their men folk. Between their desire and its realization stands the locked door of the harem. The female and male comrades at Tiflis became convinced that they must create a halfway house for the Muslim women between their secluded domestic existence and the meeting halls. It had to be a place where deep longing would mature into a clear consciousness and will to fight. Guided by the realization that the revolutionary reconstruction of Georgia would be impossible if it had to be achieved against the will and without the cooperation of the Muslim women masses, they created such a site in organizing the Muslim Women's Club.

It was the first creation of this kind which I was to encounter and I was consequently very excited as I headed for this Club. Its members had been notified of my visit; otherwise, I would only have been able to inspect the building and talk to a small number of female Muslim comrades. I was interested, however, in obtaining an impression of the entire community and perhaps even to go beyond that by assessing the impact of the Club upon other women's clubs. Thus I was certainly being expected. The sidewalk and the street around the Club were filled with Muslim women, all of whom had discarded the veil. The car had to slow down to a snail's pace and it never quite reached the entrance. Being more pushed and lifted up than walking, I finally made it to the corridor, up the winding staircase and into the large central room of the Club. Here, too, was the same pushing and shoving, in stifled air. The scene reminded one of the stirrings of an ant heap.

When the Club was founded in 1923, it consisted of forty members and constituted an undeniable success. The Soviets gave it the amount of space which corresponded to its original membership. The establishment of the Club was such a radical innovation that nobody expected a rapid development, but then the unexpected happened. The propaganda for the Club fell on fertile soil. Hardly a year has passed and the organization already has two-hundred members and additional numbers of Muslim women are applying for membership all the time. There is no doubt that the Soviet government will eventually donate a larger edifice to the Club. However, that new building will have to be situated in a different location so that its influence can reach the large masses of Muslim women. The transfer of the Club will not be as easy as it seems.

Due to the Club's nature, only women were present when I arrived. They were women belonging to the various Muslim mountain and steppe people of Transcaucasia. The bright electric light fell upon their multicolored and richly embroidered veils, which, without covering any faces, served to enhance the gracefulness of their figures and movements. Even more interesting and attractive than their colorful exotic garments were the expressions of absolute rapture on their faces. It was clear that a revelatory message had reached these women who were stirred to the depths of their beings. Every one of them had acquired a new consciousness which was straining to find expression. This feeling united them all, extending far beyond the confines of the Club and even beyond the borders of the country. The proletarian revolution is consoling the old woman as she is entering the twilight of her life; it is calling the mature woman to a new life full of struggle and work, and it exhorts the young girl that is still half a child to prepare herself for the succession.

The assembled women sang the "International." I have heard that Communist hymn of battle and hope sung many hundreds of times with the same unshakable faith and revolutionary readiness by Russian male and female proletarians. But never have I heard the words and melody sung more solemnly and enchantingly than when it came from the mouths of the Muslim women and girls at Tiflis. Their hearts and their whole being were reflected in that song. They sang the "International" in the same mood that a pious Protestant receives the Lord's Supper and is deeply moved by the conviction that by taking the wine and the oblate, he is "in touch with his Lord Jesus Christ and his God." They are overwhelmed and inspired by the feeling that his song deals with recognition of their humanity and human dignity. They realize that this song means the recognition of their total equality with men, which makes them the equals of millions upon millions of human beings around the world.

The above-mentioned mood clearly emerged from the fervent speeches that some of the Muslim women gave at the Club.

Among them was a young female comrade who could hardly speak for excitement. Indescribable joy about their new evaluation and position as women and their incorporation in the globe-circling community of freedom fighters, intermingles with ardent gratitude for the redeeming work of the proletarian revolution and the Soviet system. Sacred oaths are heard which pledge the construction and protection of the Soviet Republics as well as service to the world revolution. But the memories of unspeakable suffering, humiliations, and bitterness also emerge from their speeches. Shall this horror ever return and become the crushing fate of the blossoming daughter? The attentively listening audience passionately exclaims: "Better to die than to suffer such a fate once more!" Strong applause greets this passionate outburst.

One of the speakers burst out: "How was our life before the revolution? Our fathers sold us like young lambs when we were hardly ten or twelve years old—sometimes even younger. Our husbands demanded our affection and love, even when they seemed to us revolting. When our husbands were in the mood for it, they beat us with clubs or whips. We had to serve them day and night like slaves. When they grew tired of us, they told us to go to hell. They rented us out as mistresses to their friends. They starved us when it suited their fancy. They took away our dearest daughters who were the joy of our eyes and the aid for our weak arms. They sold them just as they had bought us. No mullah came to our aid when we were in need. Where could we have found a judge who would have given us legal aid?

"But now, my dear sisters, how everything has changed! The revolution arrived like a mighty thunderstorm. It has smashed injustice and slavery. It has brought justice and freedom to the poor and oppressed. Our father can no longer take us when we are young and force us upon the bed of a strange husband. We are able to select our husband and he must never again become our master; rather he shall be our friend and comrade. We want to work and to fight next to him and help to construct a new society. A new life must begin for everybody. The Soviets have written a new law. It states that we are human beings just like men are and that we are free and have the same rights as they do. We, too, can select the people, both men and women, that we would like to be sent to the Soviets. And we, ourselves, can work in them. When we have grievances toward our husband, a neighbor or a boss, we take them to the People's Court. It will side with us if we are in the right. Nobody asks us what prophet we follow: Mohammet, Moses or Christ. The Soviets brought us salvation. Eternal gratitude to them!"

The mood and the spirit of the gathering is explained to me by the trained women comrades who have worked for a long time among the Muslim women of Tiflis. These women, with few exceptions, belonged to the lowest strata of the population. Most of them came before the Revolution, lured to Tiflis by the hope that they could find there easier and more amenable living conditions than they had found in their native mountains and steppes. The men became peddlers, day laborers, servants and carriers or whatever menial occupation they could find outside of the home. The wife remained with the children in the miserable hut. With the migration to the city, she has lost the old economic foundations of her existence. Far removed from her former cabin or tent as well as her fields and herds, she lacks even the most primitive means and possibilities for productive work. She can no longer meet even the demands of her own household. Everything has to be purchased and she has no money to buy anything. Only her husband has money. As a consequence of this change, the Muslim women lost their significance in the eyes of their husbands as co-workers preserving the family. The economic basis of the old patriarchal family was shattered. The dominance of the man within the patriarchate, however, continued and under the most unfavorable conditions. Women felt more than ever that they were slave-like, pieces of property of their husbands. Customs, tradition, language and religion separated them from the rest of the urban population, even the poor people. Their misery, loneliness and despair took on extreme forms. they were like leaves that had been torn off a branch with which the wind is playing. In the literal sense of the word, the Revolution came as a redeemer to the Muslim women of Tiflis. Alongside of it, unhoped-for and overwhelming events entered their lives.

The female comrades explain the greatest significance of the Women's Clubs for the Muslim women of the city. It is here that the ones that have the greatest energy, talent and thirst for knowledge gather in order to obtain their first political and social training. It is here that they are able to acquire knowledge of various kinds. Some of them join the Communist Party in order to train themselves to become propagandists or organizers of their co-religionists. The Club, however, is also a place of refuge for all those Muslim women that need counsel and aid when they want to defend themselves against an injustice or try to save themselves from sinking into misery and obscurantism. The Club contains "Sections for Cultural Work" where white-haired women sit next to budding young girls and attempt with touching zeal to draw letters and to learn how to read. Courses and lectures convey the elementary knowledge of the natural and social sciences. At certain hours during the day, three comrades who have legal expertise are present at the Club to assist with juridical problems. They are particularly appreciated. The proclamation of legal equality cannot, of course, overcome all at once with a magic wand the traditional attitude of men towards the female sex which has developed over the centuries. Very often the women have to fight to obtain justice and that means going to court. The Club also teaches courses in the repairing and sewing of clothes and in embroidering. Most of the urbanized Muslim women have not learned the needlework of their mothers and the younger ones hardly know how to hold a needle.

Naturally (as the female comrades strongly emphasize), it is the aim of the Communists to incorporate the female masses into the Socialist economy. This is, however, very difficult as long as Georgia's modern industry is still in its infancy. It will grow rapidly once the first big electric power plant along the Kura River near Tiflis is ready, a plant which the Soviet government is building right now. In the meantime, the Women's Section of the Communist Party helps out in individual cases to obtain jobs for Muslim women.[2] Some of them work in the carton factory, others in the tobacco and textile industries. After the necessary move of the Club to larger accommodations, the women comrades plan to set up women artels there, which are women collectives. The work in production collectives will raise the self-confidence and feeling of solidarity among the Muslim women and thus contribute to their understanding of Communism as well as the development of the Club. Already it has become a powerful magnet which attracts many Muslim women from the city and its environs. Its influence reaches far beyond the official 200 members. This supposition is no exaggeration because there are about ten women in support of every official member so that when it comes to important questions and events, the Club has the support of the majority of Muslim women. Every Club member is an advertisement for the Club and carries its message with energy, fervidness and even fanatic religious zeal to friends and relatives.

When the teachers and administrators of the Club went to a side room in order to show me the instructional material and the cupboards and boxes which were filled with hand-embroidered materials, the crowd of Muslim women also pushed into the room. All of them felt the desire to share in the admiration of the Club's activities and to show the joy about their accomplishments: "This is the instructional book which illustrates how people used to work before the Revolution;" "On this blackboard the teacher shows how many illiterates there still are in the Soviet Union;" "Here it shows how we must take care of our infants;" "I have written this ;" "I helped to embroider this large blanket and this blouse was made by me;" "I can sew shirts like these." Such exclamations, which resound all around me, express the tie which each individual feels with the work and the learning of the collective. In another side room, legal advisors are literally swamped.

One wants to show me that the Club is also a place for entertainment and for joy. The piano is being played and the dancing begins. The first dance is executed by the five year old daughter of a female comrade and her figure, face and garment remind me of how, as a child, I had imagined the Queen of Sheba and the Semiramis to have looked. The little girl is a charming creature with dark curls and big, burning eyes. Her graceful movements and the expressions on her face adapt themselves amazingly fast to the changing rhythmns and character of the music. She is evidently the spoiled little darling of the club. Then young girls are dancing, for the most part singly, but at times as couples. The gracefulness of their movements is far removed from the Oriental dances which one usually sees in our part of the world. These dances are passionate and yet chaste and they differ totally from the ones one sees in the West. There is no provocative display of the body but rather a joyful expression of life and movement.

The dances constitute only a brief episode of the evening. The Revolution, the awakened "new life" steps once again into the foreground of their feelings and thoughts. The questions, exclamations, speeches and assurances which breathe the spirit of international revolutionary solidarity, all demonstrate how far the formerly narrow horizons of the Muslim women have been extended. The feeling of solidarity has come like a revelation of salvation over the rising women of the Orient and it has given them fiery energy. They know and believe: "In this sign thou shalt conquer!".

When I was leaving the Club, the "International" was heard again both within the building and out in the street, sung by the Muslim women of Tiflis. The newspapers were full of news of the attempts of mighty capitalist groups and their bourgeois governments to prevent the threatening thunderstorm of the proletarian revolution and the mighty historical transformation of this globe. "And yet it moves, because we will move it." This oath, this article of faith resounds from the depths of this world.

[Clara Zetkin "In The Liberated Caucasus" Berlin and Vienna, 1926, p.p. 80-87.] □

Clara Zetkin (1). with Nadezhda Krupskaya,
Lenin's wife and colleague, Moscow, ca. 1929.

1932

SAVE THE SCOTTSBORO BLACK YOUTHS

Comrades and friends of the MOPR[1] and all those who still possess a humane mind and heart, unite in order to prevent a particularly incredible and heinous judicial crime which, without your decisive and quick action, will enter the annals of judicial crimes in the United States which are already redundant with horrible outrages!

The protest and revulsion over Sacco and Vanzetti[2] (two innocent individuals who after a correct trial of bourgeois class justice were burned upon the modern pyre of the electric chair) have not yet totally ebbed, when the executioners want to use this means of torture and murder once again in order to kill, at one strike, eight more innocent victims.

In the State of Alabama, of nine young Blacks who have hardly emerged from adolescence (the oldest is 20 years old!), one received "only" lifelong imprisonment whereas the eight others have been condemned to death.

This judgment was made even though it has been clearly determined that they did not commit the crime of which they stand accused, namely, the rape of two white prostitutes. The accusation is a conscious lie which was designed for sinister purposes by landowners and manufacturers. These forces want to incinerate these Black youths in order to terrorize the Black masses which are rising up against their exploitation and are beginning to form a common front with their white brothers and sisters against hunger, imperialist wars and bloody white terror.

From the very beginning, the serious indictment lacked any basis and could not withstand any serious investigation. One of the prostitutes finally admitted that her initial accusation had been false.[3] The judges, however, totally ignored this fact. The most despicable race hatred of white against Black, this lowest expression of arrogance and low human and cultural values, has awakened the beast of lynching. This beast is traversing the

State of Alabama and is demanding victims. For its gratification, eight Black youths are supposed to be incinerated on the modern pyre.

The Supreme Court of Alabama has not yet spoken.[4] That is why there has not yet been an appeal to the Supreme Court of the United States concerning this despicable verdict of lowest racial hatred. Yet the atmosphere of racial hatred and lynching brutality, which marked the trial and the judge's verdict, raise the fear that the confirmation of the bloody verdict by the Supreme Court of Alabama will come so late and the execution so rapidly, that there will not be any time to take the matter to the Supreme Court of the United States of America.

In the face of this horrendous possibility, you must act immediately and with all of your energy. No time must be wasted and every minute must be used so that eight young lives will be spared the possibility of being burned in the electric chair.

Comrades and Friends of the MOPR of all countries! It is clear that you will continue with all of your power and devotion to support the demand: "Let us get the eight Black youths off the electric chair and out of prison. Let us also free the brave and innocently convicted labor leaders Tom Mooney and Warren Billings[5] along with the Harlan miners[6] and all other political prisoners." Yes, you will accomplish the seemingly impossible and increase your unselfish and energetic effort to save the eight Black youths. Thus you remain the firm, unshakable vanguard in the fight against the threatening crime of racial hatred, lynch justice and exploitative greed. In order to prevent the judicial murder of eight Black youths, the strong and invincible forces of the masses must be employed.

All those of you who still possess a humane mind and heart! Let us save these eight young men from the executioner and the pyre of the electric chair. Their only crime has been that they were born with Black skins. Speak and act! In your front ranks there will be innumerable, unbiased and humane individuals from the United States of America. They have not forgotten that there existed in the United States, men and women with highly developed spirits and characters who, risking their reputation, their social positions, their health and not uncommonly their lives, fought for the end of Black slavery and for the liberation and equality of their Black brothers and sisters. The wonderful example which was set by these great deceased people must not only remain enshrined in the paper of scholarly works, but in the living deeds of people. The history of the United States contains forever the deeds of heroic men and women who, fearlessly lifting high the banner of liberation and equality for all the downtrodden and despised people, have fought in the mass battle for human rights against deep-rooted hatred and bias. It must not happen that alongside these luminous pages of history appears an augmentation of the dark, blood-stained chronicles of lynchings and judicial crimes by the murder of eight Black youths. Think of the indescribable suffering and horror which must be caused by their long investigatory confinement. Every day and every hour they are confronted by the burning question whether tomorrow or the day after tomorrow, the executioner will cross the threshhold of their cell in order to sacrifice the eight selected victims upon the altar of race hatred.

MOPR Comrades, MOPR Friends, all of you who still maintain a humane mind and heart. Raise your voices! Act! The strong, irresistible shout of the gigantic, innumerable masses must overcome the verdict of race hatred of the judge. It must drown out the scream of the lynching beast. The hands of the gigantic, innumerable masses must be clenched into one gigantic fist which will tear up this judgment and topple the electric chair. Every person that remains silent in this battle for the salvation of the eight Blacks, and perhaps even steps aside in a resigned, nonchalant manner, must share the guilt of a heinous crime which would become an indelible mark of shame in the history of the United States and humankind.

The battle for the rescue of these eight young lives from the torture and murder of the electric chair, is part of the worldwide historical struggle between unbiased, cultured humanity and narrow-minded, brutal and bloody race hatred whose uncivilized, barbaric roots, reach into the past. In this struggle, humaneness must emerge victoriously. Its victory is certain if everybody, consistently and courageously, will do his best. Let us work and fight with devotion! Let us work and fight, therefore, also for a strong MOPR, which is steeled in the fight against the White terror. Long live the international solidarity of the workers of all races and nations!

[*MOPR* Periodical for the Struggle and the Labor of the International Red Help 1932, Nr. 4, pp. 1-3.] □

1932

FASCISM MUST BE DEFEATED

The Opening Address of
The Honorary President
Of the Reichstag.[1]

Ladies and Gentlemen! The Reichstag is meeting in a situation in which the crisis of collapsing capitalism is showering the broad laboring masses of Germany with a hailstorm of the most terrible suffering. The millions of unemployed, who are starving either with or without the beggar's allowance of social welfare, will be joined by additional millions during the autumn and winter. Increased hunger is also the fate of all the other people who happen to be on social welfare. Given their low wages, those who are still working cannot replace the muscular and nervous energy which the ever-increasing rationalization of industry is extracting from them nor can they, of course, have their cultural needs met. The restrictions on collective bargaining and labor mediation boards will further depress the already depressed wages. Growing numbers of artisans and small tradesmen as well as small and middling peasants are being ruined. The collapse of the economy and the shrinking of the subsidies for cultural activities are destroying the economic basis of existence of all those who work with their minds. The field of activity for their knowledge is constantly narrowing. The conflagration which has been set off in the East (and which is being fanned mightily by the West, in part, in order to destroy the Soviet Union and its Socialist construction) could eventually cause a destruction and horror in Germany which would pale the havoc wrought by the last world war.

The political power in Germany has been seized at this time by a Presidial Cabinet[2] which was formed by the exclusion of the

Reichstag as the servant of trustified monopoly capitalism and big agriculture and whose driving force consists of the Reichswehr generals. (Communist delegates' shouts of "very good").

In spite of the omnipotence of the Presidial Cabinet, it has until now totally failed in both its domestic and foreign policy. Its domestic policy is distinguished, like that of its predecessors, by emergency legislation which creates emergencies by increasing the emergencies which already exist.

At the same time, the Cabinet impugns the right of the masses to combat this suffering. For the government, those in need consist of big landowners, bankrupt industrialists, big bankers, shipyard owners and unscrupulous speculators. Its tax, tariff and trade policies take from the broad strata of the working population in order to reward the small special interest groups. It worsens the crisis by putting restrictions on consumption as well as on import and export goods. Its foreign policy harms the interests of the working people (Communist shouts of "very true"). It is guided by imperialist designs and allows Germany to waver irresolutely and dilettantishly between unabashed subservience and sabre-rattling, an attitude which makes Germany more and more dependent upon the great powers of the Versailles Treaty. (Communist shouts of "very true"). Such a policy damages its relationship with the Soviet Union, the one state which by its honest peace policy and its economic rise, constitutes a support for the German working class. (Communist shouts of "how true!").

The Presidial Cabinet bears full responsibility for the assassinations of the past weeks because of its lifting of the uniform ban on the Nazi Storm Troopers (SA) and its beneficent attitude towards the fascist civil war units. It tries in vain to make people forget about its moral and political guilt by its strife with its allies over the distribution of state power, but the spilled blood will tie it forever to the fascist assassins.

The impotence of the Reichstag and the omnipotence of the Presidial Cabinet are symbolic of the decline of bourgeois liberalism and the collapse of the system of production. This decay can also be detected within the reformist Social-Democracy, which both in theory and practice stands upon the rotten ground of the bourgeois social system. The policy of the Papen-Schleicher Government is merely the undisguised continuation of the Bruning Government (that had been tolerated by the

Social Democrats) which had, in turn, been preceded by the example-setting policy of the Social-Democrats. (Communist shouts of "very good"). The policy of "the lesser evil" strengthens the feeling of power of the reactionary forces and is supposed to create the greatest of all evils: the passivity of the masses. They are to be persuaded not to make any use of their full power outside of Parliament. Thus the significance of Parliament for the class struggle of the proletariat is also diminished. If Parliament today, within limits, can be used for the workers' struggle, it is only because it has the support of the powerful masses outside of its walls.

Before the Reichstag can take issue with the special questions of the day, it must address itself to its central task: The toppling of the Reich's government which, in violation of the constitution, threatens to push aside the Reichstag completely. The Reichstag could indict the Reich's President and the Reich's Ministers for violation of the constitution and in case of further violations to take them before the State Court at Leipzig. To take them before this high court, however, would be to accuse the devil before his grandmother. (Shouts of "very true" and applause on the part of the Communist delegates).

It is obvious, of course, that a parliamentary decision will not be able to break a power which is based on the Reichswehr and all the other supporting agencies of the bourgeois state as well as the terror of the fascists, the cowardice of bourgeois liberalism and the passivity of large sections of the proletariat. The toppling of the government in the Reichstag can only be a signal for the mobilization and seizure of power by the broad masses outside of Parliament. (Communist shouts of "very true"). The aim in this battle must be to employ the full weight of the economic and social accomplishments of the workers as well as their great numbers.

The battle must be fought particularly in order to defeat fascism, which intends to destroy with blood and iron all class expressions of the workers. Our enemies know very well that the least amount of strength of the proletariat is derived from the number of parliamentary seats. Its strength rather is anchored in its political, trade union and cultural organizations.

The example of Belgium shows the workers, that even during the severest economic depression, a mass strike proves an effective weapon, provided that its usage is backed up by the determination and willingness to sacrifice of the masses who do not shrink from enlarging the battle and using force to repel the force used by the enemy. (Shouts of "very true" by the Communist delegates). The extraparliamentary muscle-flexing of the working class, however, must not be limited to the toppling of a government which has violated the constitution. It must go beyond the goal of the moment to prepare itself for the overthrow of the bourgeois state and its basis which is the capitalist system. All attempts to alleviate the crisis while the capitalist system still prevails can only worsen the disaster. Intervention by the state has failed because the bourgeois state does not control the economy, but the capitalist economy controls the state. (Shouts of "very true" from the Communist deputies). As the power apparatus of the possessing class, it can only operate to its advantage and at the expense of the producing and consuming masses. A planned economy on the basis of capitalism is a contradiction in terms. Such attempts are all defeated by the private ownership of the means of production. A planned economy is only possible once the private ownership of the means of production has been abolished. The way to overcome the economic crises and all threats of imperialist wars is solely by the proletarian revolution (shouts of "bravo" by the Communists) which will do away with the private ownership of production and thus guarantee a planned economy.

The great world historical proof of all of this happens to be the Russian Revolution. It has demonstrated that the workers possess the strength to defeat all of its enemies, the capitalists in its own country and the imperialist robbers from abroad. It has torn up slave treaties like the Treaty of Versailles. (Shouts of "very true" by the Communists).

The Soviet state also confirms the fact that the workers possess the maturity to construct a new economic system in which a higher economic development of society can occur without devastating crises because the cause of the anarchic method of production has been destroyed—the private ownership of the means of production.

The fight of the laboring masses against the disastrous sufferings of the present is, at the same time, the fight for their full liberation. The glances of the masses must be steadily directed towards this luminous goal which must not be shrouded by the illusion of a liberating democracy. The masses must not allow themselves to be frightened by the brutal use of force by which capitalism seeks its survival in the form of new world wars and fascist civil strife.

The most important immediate task is the formation of a United Front of all workers in order to turn back fascism (Communist shouts of "very true") in order to preserve for the enslaved and exploited, the force and power of their organization as well as to maintain their own physical existence. Before this compelling historical necessity, all inhibiting and dividing political, trade union, religious and ideological opinions must take a back seat. All those who feel themselves threatened, all those who suffer and all those who long for liberation must belong to the United Front against fascism and its representatives in the government. The self-assertion of the workers vis-a-vis fascism is the next indispensible prerequisite for the United Front in the battle against crises and imperialist wars and their cause, the capitalist means of production. The revolt of millions of laboring men and women in Germany against hunger, slavery, fascist murder and imperialist wars is an expression of the indestructible destiny of the workers of the entire world. This international community of fate must become an iron fighting community of the workers in regions where capitalism still prevails (Communist shouts of "very true"), a fighting community which will connect them to the vanguard of their brothers and sisters in the Soviet Union. The strikes and revolts in various countries are flaming signs which tell the fighters in Germany that they do not stand alone. Everywhere the disinherited and oppressed people are beginning to move towards a seizure of power. The United Front of workers, which is also constituting itself in Germany, must not lack the millions of women, who still bear the chains of sex slavery (Communist shouts of "very good"), and are therefore exposed to the most oppressive class slavery. The youths that want to blossom and mature must fight in the very front ranks. Today they face no other prospects but blind obedience and exploitation in the ranks of the obligatory Labor Service. All those who work with their minds and augment the prosperity and culture of society by their knowledge and diligence, but who in today's bourgeois society have become superfluous, also belong in this United Front. Those who, as salary and wage slaves, are tribute-paying dependents of capitalism and simultaneously constitute preservers and victims of capitalism, also belong in the United Front.

I am opening this Congress in the fulfillment of my duties as honorary president and in the hope that despite my current infirmities, I may yet have the fortune to open as honorary president the first Soviet Congress of a Soviet Germany.[3]

["Minutes of the Reichstag During the VI Electoral Period, 1932" Volume 454, Berlin 1932, pp. 1-3] □

1933

THE TOILERS AGAINST WAR

"No more war!" This abominable massacre of the peoples must be the last of its kind! This passionate outcry from untold millions of people rang out even during the imperialist struggle for power of 1914-18 and grew stronger after its termination; a cry of agonized suffering, an annihilating indictment against the terrible mass murder and the devastation of the world by the competitive struggle of the capitalists who held sway in the belligerent countries, a solemn vow for the future.

"No more war!"—the cry rang out in many languages both in the defeated and in the victorious countries, for in both camps vast masses of the population bore personal wounds which would never heal and the far-reaching disasters which accompanied the war and followed it assumed a menacing appearance.

"No more war!" So declared the men who had fought fearlessly at the front in the mad belief that they were "defending the fatherland." That which brought this cry for peace to their lips was not only the memory of the extreme privations they had borne or of the superhuman exertions they had made, but the thought of moments of abominable inhumanity in this fratricidal war, of cruelty against the civilian population of the "enemy." Many industrial and office workers, government employees and professional men became painfully aware after the years spent in war service that they had lost a considerable part of their professional skill and of the pleasure they found in work, or came back to find their posts occupied by women. Many small traders and small peasants also came home as enemies of war; during their absence their businesses had declined, become bankrupt, gone to rack and ruin.

"No more war!" This again was the piercing cry which rose from uncountable numbers of women. How could they forget the agonies and martyrdom of which they had almost always been the victims in the districts where the fury of war was let loose through the invasion of hostile troops, or the crash of bombs and shells, which turned their houses into a heap of ruins, and devastated their gardens, fields and woods? In the "secluded hinterland" of the years of slaughter, mothers remembered the nights spent in sleepless weeping and agonized anxiety for the health and lives of their sons who were away fighting; wives remembered the times when they had to slave in hard bondage to get bread for their children and to educate them in their spare time. The wives of poor peasants rose in protest against new wars, which left the villages with no one but children and old people besides themselves to do the ploughing, sowing and harvesting and to bear the whole brunt of agricultural labour. The women who were actively employed in industry, in transport and in other branches of social activity, were not anxious to see the return of those conditions under which, as "emergency helpers on the economic and administrative front," they were exposed to a murderous exploitation of their nervous and muscular power, even the scanty protection which the law normally provided being then removed. This was true, above all, of women in the war and munitions industries, who, besides having their labor power and vital activity squeezed out of them to the full, were exposed to the danger of being blown to pieces when filling bombs and shells, or of perishing as victims in the poisonous hells of the murderous chemical industry. . . .

The World War of 1914-18, with the vividness of a lightning flash, revealed that capitalism is on the declining curve of its historical existence, that it has become a fatal obstacle to the liberation of the proletarians, propertyless and small owners and creative workers of all kinds, a fatal obstacle to the higher development of the whole of humanity. Subsequent events have confirmed this verdict of condemnation; it has been strengthened by the all-destroying world economic crisis. But condemned capitalism is struggling with savage tenacity against its end. Imperialist wars, world war, appear to the leading and ruling groups of the bourgeoisie as the last means for upholding the social order which has to be sacred for its enslaved, exploited victims, because it grants to the big owners gold, power and unlimited enjoyment of life. Imperialist wars are equivalent in meaning to murder of peoples and world devastation. What does that matter to the "predominating" big leaders of capitalist industry? It does not impair their digestion that every year millions of workers are killed or crippled for life on the battlefield of labor or succumb prematurely to occupational diseases as a result of the murderous squeezing out of their labor power and of inadequate provision of the needs of life. Why should the rulers shrink from ordering further millions of the superfluous, who in any case could become dangerous, into the gigantic slaughterhouse of imperialist wars in order that they might massacre one another there in fratricidal struggle?

The struggle of the workers against imperialist wars is a life and death struggle against bloodsucking capitalism, for the salvation of socialism. It strives for the firm union of all toilers who are no longer willing to bear the oppressive fetters of capitalist slavery and plunder. Differences of occupation, political party, organization or religious views must not be allowed to act as barriers between them. The struggle against imperialist wars is waged for the great goal of the emancipation of all of them.... This struggle is so far-reaching in significance that it is not merely the cause and duty of the class-conscious exploited workers, but is rather the cause and duty of all who aim at the advance of humanity to freedom and culture. Under the slogan "for socialist world freedom, for socialist world peace" they will range themselves as valuable allies in the ranks of the fighters, in the army of which the unvacillating main columns consist of workers.

The imperialist wars intensify the old historical command to the workers, that they must overcome their enemy in irreconcilable, determined revolutionary class struggle. Nationally and internationally, they press forward with the utmost energy, class against class, on one side the downtrodden and oppressed, on the other side the oppressors and exploiters of every capitalist country and of the whole world of capitalist rule. Power is measured against power. This dry statement of facts must stimulate the workers to throw their whole power into the struggle against imperialist wars without the slightest hesitation or reserve. On their side they have the encouragement and promise of victory represented by the strong, invincible power of historic development which is leading towards the death of capitalism and the unfolding of the social creative power of socialism. In struggle the workers must attain the heights of the objective historical development. The imperialist wars which, according to the desire of the ruling moneybags, are to preserve the life of capitalism, will contribute to accelerating its end if they heighten the power of resistance and the readiness of the workers to act for its destruction. Their decisive onslaught against imperialist murder of the peoples and world destruction is equivalent to a great significant step towards the conquest of state power which gives the workers the power to erect under the leadership of the world proletariat a social order without enslavement and exploitation of man by man.

[Extract from the pamphlet, Clara Zetkin, *The Toilers Against War*, New York, 1934, pages 11-12, 125-28.[1]] □

NOTES

FOREWORD

1. Frederick Engels, *The Origin of the Family, Private Property and the State,* New York, 1970, pp. 137-38.
2. V.I. Lenin, *The Emancipation of Women,* New York, 1966, p. 81
3. Clara Zetkin, *Social Democracy and Woman Suffrage,* p. 15.
4. Ibid., p. 16
5. Batya Weinbaum, *The Curious Courtship of Women's Liberation & Socialism,* Boston, 1978.
6. Clara Zetkin, *The Toilers Against War,* New York, 1934, p. 73.

INTRODUCTION

1. Luise Dornemann, *Clara Zetkin: Ein Lebensbild,* Berlin, 1957, pp.27-29,32-33.
2. Karen Honeycutt, "Clara Zetkin: A Left-Wing Socialist and Feminist in Wilhelmine Germany," unpublished Ph.D. thesis, Columbia University, 1975, pp. 22-23,28-29.
3. Jacqueline Strain, "Feminism and Political Radicalism in the German Social Democratic Movement, 1890-1914," unpublished Ph.D. thesis, University of California, Berkeley, 1975, p. 26; Dornemann, *op.cit.,* pp. 13-15.
4. Dornemann, *op.cit.,* pp. 20-23.
5. Honeycutt, *op.cit.,* pp. 30-35; Clara Zetkin, "Auguste Schmidt," *Gleichheit* 12(July,1902): 109-10.
6. C.G.L. Alexander, *Aus Clara Zetkins Leben und Werk,* Berlin, 1927,pp.4-5.

   Ferdinand Lassalle (1825-1864) was the German lawyer and labor leader who founded the General German Workers Union in 1863, and was criticized by Marx as an advocate of opportunism in German Social-Democracy. For a detailed characterization of Lassalle by Marx, *see* his letter to Kugelmann, February 23,1865, in *The Selected Correspondence of Karl Marx and Frederick Engels, 1846-1895,* New York, 1942, pp. 193-97.
7. Alexander, *op.cit.,* p. 5. Wilhelm Liebknecht (1826-1900) was one of the founders and leaders of the German Social-Democratic Party, and became editor of the party paper, *Vorwärts.* Liebknecht was one of the first to enter the Reichstag as a Socialist.

8. Honeycutt, *op.cit.*, p. 39-42.
9. Alexander, *op.cit.*, p.5.
10. Dornemann, *op.cit.*, pp. 43-48.
11. J. Belli, *Die rote Feldpost untern Sozialistengesetz,* Stuttgart, 1919.
12. Alexander, *op.cit.*, pp. 7-8; Jane Slaughter and Robert Kern, editors, *European Women on the Left: Socialism, Feminism, and the Problems Faced by Political Women, 1880 to the Present,* Westport, Conn., 1981, p. 12.
13. Clara wrote for *Der Sozialdemokrat, Le Socialiste, Die Neue Zeit,* and *Berliner Volkstribüne.*
    Many of the articles for the party press were anonymous or signed with the name Ossip Zetkin, but they were the product of both Clara and Ossip. After 1886 they were increasingly the work of Clara alone.
14. Dornemann, *op.cit.*, pp. 56-71; Honeycutt, *op.cit.*, pp.46-57.
15. Dornemann, *op.cit.*, pp. 85-90.
16. Alexander, *op.cit.*, pp. 14-17.
17. Jean H. Quartert, *Reluctant Feminists in German Social Democracy, 1885-1917,* Princeton, N.J., 1979, p.67.
18. August Bebel, *Aus meinen Leben,* Stuttgart, 1911, 1: 102; 2: 259-65,403; Robert Michels, "August Bebel," *Archiv für Sozialwissenschaft und Sozialpolitik* 27(1913): 680-86.
19. August Bebel, *Woman and Socialism,* New York, 1910,pp. 1-34,105, 116,466-73.
20. *Ibid.*, p.7.
21. Protocol concerning the Proccedings of the Party Congress... Held at Gotha. . . 1896, Berlin, 1896; *See* p. 79.
22. Dornemann, *op.cit.*,pp. 71-80.
23. *Protocol of the International Workingmen's Congress at Paris. Held from July 14th until July 20, 1889,* Nürnberg, 1890,pp.80-85. For the complete text of Zetkin's speech, *see* pp. 45-50.
24. Engels insisted in 1885 "that the working woman needs special protection against capitalist exploitation because of her special physiological functions seems obvious to me." (*Karl Marx-Friedrich Engels Werke,* Berlin, 1958-68,vol.36,p.341.)
25. *Protocol of the International Workingmen's Congress at Paris,*pp. 214-16.
26. Strain, *op.cit.*, pp. 47-48.
27. For a discussion of Edward Bellamy and his utopian socialist novel, see Philip S. Foner, *History of the Labor Movement in the United States* 2(New York,1955): 44-46.
28. Dornemann, *op.cit.*, pp. 89-93,107. There is some question as to whether or not Clara Zetkin received a salary during her early years as editor of *Gleichheit.* Anna Blos maintains she received no salary whereas Luise Dornemann and Karen Honeycutt write that she received a modest salary of 240 marks per month.(Anna Blos, ed., *Die Frauenfrage in Lichte der Sozialismus,* Dresden, 1930, p. 24; Honeycutt, *op.cit.*, p. 123.)
29. "Probenummer," *Gleichheit 1* (December20,1891): 1. English translation in Honeycutt, *op.cit.*, p. 122.
30. "An die Leserinnen und Leser," *Gleichheit* 8(January 5,1898):1; English translation in Honeycutt, *op.cit.*, p. 124.

31. Honeycutt, *op.cit.*,p.124.
32. Strain, *op.cit.*, pp. 148-49.
33. *Gleichheit*, July 13,1892, p.120; Feb. 8,1893,pp. 20-23; Aug.4, 1897, p.126.
34. *Ibid.*, Aug. 2,1899, p. 128; Strain, *op.cit.*, p.54.
35. Werner Thönnessen, *The Emancipation of Women: The Rise and Decline of the Women's Movement in German Social Democracy, 1863-1933*, London, 1973, p. 49-50.
36. *Ibid.*, p. 61.
37. Honeycutt, *op.cit.*, pp. 293-95.
38. Hilde Lion, *Zur Sociologie der Frauenbewegung. Die sozialistische und die katolische Frauenbewegung*, Berlin, 1926,p.157.
39. Dornemann, *op.cit.*, pp. 170-71.
40. Alexander, *op.cit.*, pp. 25-26.
41. *Ibid.*, pp. 26-27.
42. *Gleichheit*, June 27,1894, p. 102; Honeycutt, *op.cit.*,p.173; Alexander, *op.cit.*, pp. 33-34.
43. Alexander, *op.cit.*, p.20.
44. Honeycutt, *op.cit.*, pp. 165-66
45. *Ibid.*, p.168.
46. *Gleichheit*, Feb. 20,1895, p.32.
47. Friedrich Engels to Victor Adler, January 28,1895, *Marx-Engels Werke*, vol.39, p. 400.
48. *Gleichheit*, Jan. 19,1901,pp. 10-12; Thönnessen, *op.cit.*, p. 163; Honeycutt, *op.cit.*, pp. 200-02.
49. *Gleichheit*, Aug. 3,1898, p.121; Thönnessen, *op.cit.*, p.65.
50. Amy Katleen Hackett, "The Politics of Feminism in Wilhelmine Germany, 1890-1918," unpublished Ph.D. dissertation, Columbia University, 1976, p. 206.
    In 1893 the SPD demanded women's suffrage in the Saxon Diet, and the following year it introduced a similar resolution in the Imperial Reichstag.
51. Hackett, *op.cit.*, pp. 210-12.
52. *Gleichheit*, Sept. 2,1907, pp. 387-89; Honeycutt, *op.cit.*p. 307.
53. *Internationale Sozialistenkongress zu Stuttgart. . . . 1907*, p.40; Honeycutt, *op.cit.*, pp. 306-07.
54. *Huitme Congres Socialiste International. . . Copenhagen. . . . 1910*, pp.490-91; Honeycutt, *op.cit.*, pp. 308-09.
55. Internationale Frauentag," in *Clara Zetkin: Reden und Schriften* 1(Berlin, 1957): 480; Philip S. Foner, *Women and the American Labor Movement: From World War I to the Present*, New York, 1890, pp. 158-59; Madeline Provinzano, "It All Began Right Here," *Daily World*, March 6, 1980.
56. Gerd Hohendorf, *Revolutionäre Schulpolitik und Marxistische Pädagogik im Lebenswerk Clara Zetkins*, Berlin, 1962,pp.11-12,146.
57. Karen Honeycutt, "Socialism and Feminism in Imperial Germany," *Signs* 5(1979): 35.
58. Dornemann, *op.cit.*, pp. 62-63; Honeycutt, *op.cit.*, pp. 326-29.
59. Thönnessen, *op.cit.*, p. 62.
60. A good example of this practice occurred in 1898 when Clara Zetkin vigorously criticized the central organ of the Party *(Vorwärts)* and

the Party executive at the Stuttgart Party conference. Auer replied, amidst laughter from the audience: "If that is the oppressed sex, then what on earth will happen when they are free and enjoy equal rights." (Thönnessen, *op.cit.*, p. 62.) Zetkin was not amused.

61. Thönnessen, *op.cit.*, p. 67.
62. Luise Zietz was born in 1865 in Holstein. Her father was a master weaver, but the family was poor and everyone had to work to make ends meet. At the age of fourteen, Luise entered domestic service. While she worked she educated herself, was admitted to the Froebelschule in Hamburg, and trained to be a kindergarten teacher. This ambition was terminated by her marriage to a dock worker. Through him she was introduced to Socialism and in 1892, she became a member of the Party. She emerged as an active speaker for the Party during the Hamburg workers' strike in late 1896, and became involved in work for the unions and the movement. Though her marriage failed, from 1897 on she was active in the Party as a popular speaker. From 1896 to 1908 she was sent to the Party Congress by one of the regular SPD organizations. In 1908 she became a member of the Party executive. (Franz Osterroth, *Biographisches Lexikon des Sozialismus*, (Hannover, 1960)1:340-43.
63. Osterroth, *op.cit.*, pp. 345-46.
64. Peter Gay, *The Dilemma of Democratic Socialism: Eduard Bernstein's Challenge to Marx*, New York, 1952, pp. 134-52.
65. Hohendorf, *op.cit.*, pp. 148-52.
66. Thönnessen, *op.cit.*, pp. 138-39.
67. Alexander, *op.cit.*, pp. 22-24; Honeycutt, *op.cit.*, pp. 402-03.
    Part of Clara Zetkin's battle against revisionism and reformism was her long feud with Lily Braun, the flamboyant and beautiful woman from the Prussian upper classes who came to Socialism from bourgeois feminism, a background which Braun found it difficult to overcome. Zetkin helped Braun after she joined the Socialist movement, and opened up the pages of *Gleichheit* for her articles. However, in *Die Frauenfrage*, her well-known book published in 1901, Braun completely neglected to discuss Zetkin's contributions. Zetkin, understandably upset, wrote to Kautsky condemning Braun as false, selfish, malicious. More important, she expressed her firm belief that Braun's views were the "latest blossoming of utopianism in its most dangerous, opportunistic form."(Julie Vogelstein, "Lily Braun: Ein Lebensbild," in Lily Braun, *Gesammelte Werke*, Berlin, 1923, vol. I, pp. CCX-CCXXXVI; Thönnessen, *op.cit.*, pp. 60-62; Strain, *op.cit.*, pp. 143-44. Honeycutt, "Clara Zetkin," devotes a few pages to the Zetkin-Braun controversy. *See* pp. 311-18.
68. "Unser Patriotismus," *Gleichheit*, May 27, June 24,1907, pp. 89-90, 99-100.
    In 1892 Zetkin editorialized vigorously in *Gleichheit* against the bill introduced into the Reichstag calling for a 90,000-man increase in the peacetime army. (*Gleichheit*, Oct. 19,1892,pp. 169-71; Dec.28,1892,pp. 212-13.) For the military bill, *see* J. Alden Nichols, *Germany After Bismarck: The Captive Era, 1890-1894*, Cambridge, Mass., 1958, pp. 214-15.

For Noske's pro-imperialism position, *see* his *Kolnialpolitik und Sozialdemokratie*, Stuttgart, 1914.

69. *Protokoll uber die Verhandlungen des Parteitages der Sozialdemokratischen Partei Deutschlands, abgehalten zu Jena, September 15, 1911*, Berlin, 1911,pp. 350-54, 470-72; Paul W. Avalone, "The Rise of Social Imperialism, in the German Socialist Party, 1890-1914," unpublished MA thesis, University of Wisconsin, Madison, 1975,pp.92-95.

The Moroccan crises occurred in 1905 and 1911. Germany, determined to achieve a place in Africa against rival French and British imperialism, created two European war scares in opposition to growing French influence in Morocco. In November, 1911, Germany finally consented to France's establishing a protectorate over Morocco in exchange for relatively minor concessions in West Africa.

70. Phillip S. Foner, *Karl Liebknecht and the United States*, Chicago, 1978, p. 28; F.L. Carsten, *War Against War: British and German Radical Movements in the First World War*, Berkeley and Los Angeles, 1982, p.35.
71. See letter of Clara Zetkin to Heleen Ankersmit, December 3rd, 1914, p.117.
72. Thönnessen, *op.cit.*, p. 79.
73. A minority of about six delegates from Russia and Poland voted against the resolution because while it condemned the war, it did not call for a break with the Second International. This position was adopted on the advice of V. I. Lenin, who was then living in Switzerland in exile. (Carsten, *op.cit.*, pp. 35-36.)
74. For the text of the manifesto, *see* pp.130-132.
75. In the same account the *Times* reported that Rosa Luxemburg was also being prosecuted for "alleged treasonable articles" (July 23,-1915).
76. Thönnessen, *op.cit.*, p. 80.
77. For the text of Zetkin's response, *see* pp.133-135.
78. See p. 141.
79. International Press Correspondence, No. 105, 1922, pp. 844, 849-50.
80. Dornemann, *op.cit.*, pp. 138-40; Honeycutt, *op.cit.*, p.457.
81. Robert F. Wheeler, "German Women and the Communist International: The Case of the Independent Social Democrats," *Central European History* 8 (June, 1975): 116.
82. Anise, "Making Revolutionists of Women: A Visit to the Women's Section of the Comintern," *Workers Monthly*, September, 1925, p. 506.
83. Clara Zetkin, *Lenin on the Woman Question*, New York,1934,pp. 3,13-16.
84. A number of writers who discuss Clara Zetkin's years in the Soviet Union make no mention of this work, and emphasize only that she was simply used to advance the interests of the Soviet Union. (For example of a totally negative approach to Zetkin's years in the Soviet Union, *see* Beatrice Farnsworth, *Aleksandra Koleontai: Socialism, Feminism, and the Bolshevik Revolution*, Stanford, Ca., 1982, pp.260-65.)
85. Dan T. Carter, *Scottsboro: A Tragedy of the American South*, Baton Rouge, La., 1969, pp. 128-30.

86. For the full text of the appeal, *see* pp. 167-169.
87. For the full test of the speech, *see* pp.170-175.
88. It was originally published in the Soviet Union under the title of *Imperialist War Against the Toiling Masses. The Toiling Masses Against Imperialist War,* Moscow, 1933. It was supposed to be published in time for International Anti-War Day, August 1, 1932, but a severe illness, including an attack of malaria, made it impossible for Clara Zetkin to complete the work in time. It was published under the title, *The Toilers Against War* by Workers Library Publishers, New York, 1934. It was also published under that title in England.
89. Clara Zetkin, *The Toilers Against War,* New York,1934, p.81.
90. *Ibid.*, pp. 127-28.
91. Quoted in Klara Zetkin, *Through Dictatorship to Democracy,* Glasgow, n.d., p.5. The work was translated into English by Eden and Cedar Paul.

FOR THE LIBERATION OF WOMEN

1. Clara Zetkin represented two groups at the Paris Congress: one was the workers associated with the *Berliner Volkstribüne,* and one from the working women of Berlin. (C.G.L. Alexander, *op.cit.,* p.14).
2. The verbatim report of the speech begins with the third paragraph.
3. *Women's work* refers to the entry of women into the industrial labor force.
4. In this period, Clara Zetkin rejected any form of special protection for working women such as laws prohibiting women from being employed in certain types of work deemed dangerous to females. The sole exception was in the case of pregnant women. As we have seen, she later changed her position.
5. The German Social-Democratic Party (SPD) was the party of German Social Democracy. It was organized in 1875 under the leadership of August Bebel and Wilhelm Liebknecht, the leading disciples of Karl Marx in Germany. The Marxists and Lassalleans joined to form the SPD.
6. Dr. Edward Aveling was one of the British delegates to the Congress. He married Eleanor Marx, Karl Marx's daughter, who was also a delegate.

WOMEN'S WORK AND THE ORGANIZATION OF TRADE UNIONS

1. A worldwide economic depression occurred in 1893. In the United States about three million people were without any means of earning a living in December, 1893.
2. In the United States there were 2,647,000 women gainfully employed in 1880 constituting 15.2 percent of the nation's work force. By 1890 there were over four million gainfully employed women making up 17.2 percent of the total labor force. This figure included almost 300,000 girls under fifteen years of age. (Philip S. Foner, *Women and the American Labor Movement: From Colonial Times to the Eve of World War I,* New York, 1979, p.186.)

3. In this connection it is interesting to note that Leonora M. Barry, the general investigator for the Knights of Labor's Department of Woman's Work, reached somewhat the same conclusion as did Clara Zetkin. In her reports of 1887,1888, and 1889, she also noted that workingwomen were partially responsible for their continued exploitation. "All this," Barry concluded, "is the result or effect of the environment and conditions surrounding women in the past and present, and can be removed only by constant agitation and education." (*Ibid.* pp. 204-05).
4. *Gleichheit* (Equality) was the socialist women's journal which Clara Zetkin edited from 1892-1917.

THE WOMEN'S RIGHTS' PETITION

1. The conflict between Clara Zetkin and the SPD leadership over her refusal to support bourgeois feminism came to a head over the Party's support for a petition drafted by the radical feminists, Minna Cauer and Lily von Gizycki, together with a member of the SPD, Adele Gehrard. The document called for an end to the assembly and association laws restricting the political activity of women in most German states. The SPD's Central organ and largest daily paper, *Vorwärts,* published the petition, together with a statement of support, recommending that Party members sign. Zetkin also reprinted the petition in *Gleichheit,* but accompanied it with a warning: "We decidedly advise every class conscious member of the proletariat against supporting this petition in any manner." Zetkin's position was that the petition of the radical feminists "breathe[d] a thoroughly bourgeois spirit" and stood "in the most glaring contradiction to our view." Among other things, Zetkin was angered by the failure of the middle-class women to seek a common understanding in advance with women of the working class, thus revealing, as she saw it, a contempt for lower class women. (Karen Honeycutt, *op. cit.,* pp.173-176.)
2. See p.24.
3. It was with great difficulty that Zetkin was able to secure publication of her letter in *Vorwärts*. Engels noted this fact in his letter to Victor Adler, January 28, 1895: "Luise is especially happy about the decisive rejection of the Women's League Petition. Take a look at Clara Zetkin's article in Thursday's *Vorwärts* supplement. Clara is correct and was able to have her article published in spite of all the efforts to squelch it. Bravo Clara!" (*Victor Adler's Essays, Speeches and Letters*. Published by the Executive Committee of the Social Democratic Workers' Party of German Austria. First issue: Victor Adler and Friedrich Engels, Vienna, 1922, p. 124.)
   Victor Adler (1852-1918) was the founder and leader of Austrian social democracy, and a member of the International Socialist Bureau.
   Clara Zetkin wrote a fifteen-page letter to Engels explaining in detail her reasons for her uncompromising attitude toward the bourgeois feminist petition.

A REPLY

1. The reference is to Ethical Culture Society feminists like Lily von Gizycki who had been conducting intense agitation among working class women. In her letter to Engels, Zetkin took the position that as long as the Ethical Culture women stayed in their own circle, one need not criticize them. But when they brought their bourgeois feminist ideas to the working class women, they had to be criticized. "Vigilance against the 'Ethical bacillus' was the more necessary," she maintained, "since already within the SPD, the tendency towards opportunism and reformism is rather great and grows with the expansion of the Party." (Honeycutt, *op.cit.*, p. 178.)
2. The author of this remark was not "this or that woman," but Wilhelm Liebknecht, chief editor of *Vorwärts*.

ONLY WITH THE PROLETARIAN WOMAN

1. Clara Zetkin's speech is considered the first major policy statement of the SPD on the woman question. It was published as a pamphlet and used extensively in agitation on the woman question. The Party Congress also adopted Clara Zetkin's resolution concerning propaganda among women. The resolution demanded that the Party increase organizational efforts among working class women and intensify its agitation for legislative protection of working women, for the appointment of female factory inspectors, for occupational courts for women workers, for active voting rights for women, for equal political rights, equal pay for equal work, equal educational opportunities, and equal status for women in private law.
2. Johann Jakob Bachofen (1815-1887), jurist and anthropologist whose book *Das Mutterrecht* ("Mother Right") published in 1886, presented the first attempt to advance a scientific history of the family as a social institution and suggested that mother right preceded father right. Bachofen adopted the views of U.S. anthropologist Lewis Henry Morgan on kinship.
3. Lewis Henry Morgan (1818-1881), lawyer who made a special study of kinship during his years of research among the American Indians. His famous work, *Ancient Society, or Researches in the Lines of Human Progress from Savagery through Barbarism to Civilization*, was published in 1877. Morgan's emphasis on property in cultural evolution influenced Marx and Engels.
4. The reference is to Engels' *Origin of the Family, Private Property and the State*, first published in 1884.
5. The reference is to Baron Stumm-Halberg (1836-1901), the most prominent Saar industrialist and a Free Conservative political leader.
6. The reference is to Bismarck's anti-socialist law of 1878. Under its terms all social-democratic, socialist, and communist associations, meetings, and publications could be forbidden or dissolved. The law provided that professional Socialist organizers, if found guilty of its violation, could be banned from certain towns or districts. In "imperiled" districts the government also received the power to lift the right of assembly and free political expression, and to expel persons who

seemed to endanger the public peace. Innkeepers, printers, and book dealers were threatened with the loss of their license if they violated the law.

7. August Bebel (1840-1913), one of the founders and leaders of the German Social Democratic Party and the Second International. He was sentenced with Wilhelm Liebknecht to two years' imprisonment for treason for opposing the Franco-Prussian War of 1870. For a discussion of Bebel's *Woman and Socialism*, see pp.21-23.
8. The reference is to Adelheid Popp, one of the leaders of the women's movement in Austrian Social Democracy.

PROTECT OUR CHILDREN

1. The "internal enemy" of the capitalists was the working class and the Socialists.
2. Frederick William III (1770-1840), King of Prussia from 1797.
3. The reference is to the Social-Democratic Party (or as it was originally called the Social-Democratic Workers' Party). By 1887 the Party had twelve seats in the federal parliament and its popular vote reached 9 percent of the total national vote.
4. Usually Junkers referred to the Prussian landed aristocracy, but here it is used to refer to ultrareactionary industrialists.
5. Adolph Stocker (1835-1909), conservative court chaplain who launched the Christian-Social Workers Party in 1878.

WHAT THE WOMEN OWE TO KARL MARX

1. Frederick Engels was born in 1820, in Barmen, Germany, the son of a religously-inclined, tyrannical owner of textile factories in Barmen. Despite pressure upon him to pursue a business career, Engels chose writing and radical journalism. He met Marx briefly in Cologne, but in the summer of 1844, the two struck up a permanent friendship which was to profoundly influence their lives and the whole course of scientific socialism. Engels worked in his father's business in Manchester for nineteen years, financially aiding the desperately poor Marx family. When he had accumulated enough capital for himself, he sold his share of the business and moved to London where he spent the last twenty-five years of his life writing his own important books and articles, editing Marx's works, and helping to direct the course of the Socialist movements in Europe and the United States. He died on August 5, 1895. Engels collaborated with Marx on a number of books and articles—among them, of course, *The Communist Manifesto* (1848), and wrote a number of prefaces to Marx's works.
2. The letter was sent from London, March 15, 1883 to Friedrich Adolph Sorge (1827-1906), who emigrated to the United States from Germany in 1852, joined the New York Communist Club in 1858, and actively corresponded with Marx and Engels. Sorge was one of the leaders of the local sections of the First International in the United States. After the General Council of the International was transferred to New York in 1872, Sorge became General Secretary. He was active in the formation of the Socialist Labor Party of the United States.

3. The principle of uniting upper-class and working-class women in a sisterhood that transcended class lines was an objective of the Women's Trade Union League established in the United States in 1903. While the principle was in evidence during the waistmakers' revolt of 1909, the sisterhood proved to be short-lived. (*See* Foner, *Women and the American Labor Movement*, pp. 343-44, and Nancy Schrom Dye, "Creating a Feminist Alliance: Sisterhood, Feminism or Unionism: The New York Women's Trade Union League and the Labor Movement," *Feminist Studies* 3(Fall, 1975): 111-25.)

WOMEN'S RIGHT TO VOTE

1. This was the first International Socialist Women's Conference and was attended by 59 women from 15 countries. It met at Stuttgart on August 17, 1907.
2. The reference is to the Russian Revolution of 1905.
3. Clara Zetkin was more critical of the Austrian Socialists, including Socialist women, for supporting the Party's tactic of not even mentioning women's suffrage during the campaigns in 1905 and 1906 for the extension of Austrian suffrage.
4. Limited suffrage included limiting the right to vote to women of property and wealth.

INTERNATIONAL WOMEN'S DAY

1. The proposal was adopted as a resolution. For the discussion of the origins of International Women's Day, *see* pp. 31-32.

PROLETARIAN WOMEN BE PREPARED

1. On June 28, 1914, the student Gavrilo Princip, a Serbian, killed Archduke Francis Ferdinand of Austria and his wife in the Bosnian capital of Sarajevo. Supported by Germany, Austro-Hungary delivered an ultimatum to Serbia, which she accepted but with several reservations. Rejecting the reservations the Hapsburg monarchy declared war on July 28. By the first week of August the war had spread to encompass Germany, France, Russia and other countries, bringing about the first World War.
2. The Triple Entente was a military alliance formed by Great Britain, France, and Russia. It was preceded by the Triple Alliance, uniting Germany, Austria-Hungary and Italy against France. In 1883 Romania was added to the Triple Alliance.
3. The reference is to the Inter-Parliamentary Conference at Bern., Switzerland, which was held from May 11 to May 12, 1913. The conference was arranged by members of the Swiss National Assembly who invited German and French Parliamentarians. The largest number of German participants consisted of Reichstag deputies of the Social-Democratic Party of Germany, among whom were August Bebel and Karl Liebknecht. The conference was to prepare a program against war propaganda and the unbearable increase in the burden of armament in both France and Germany.

4. The reference is to attacks by Rosa Luxemburg on German militarists in numerous articles and at meetings during the first half of 1914.

TO THE SOCIALIST WOMEN OF ALL COUNTRIES

1. The appeal was first published in the *Berner Tagwacht* and then distributed throughout Germany in December, 1914 in the form of a pamphlet. Censorship prevented its publication in *Gleichheit*.

LETTER TO HELEEN ANKERSMIT

1. Heleen Ankersmit (1872-1944) was a member of the Social-Democratic Workers' Party and later the Communist Party of Holland. A long-time comrade and friend of Clara Zetkin, she was an organizer and leader of the Dutch working class women's movement.
2. Clara Zetkin was elected at Stuttgart in 1907 as secretary of the International Women's Bureau of the Second International.
3. The appeal was "To the Socialist Women of All Countries," November, 1914. *See* pp.114-116.
4. The leaders of the German trade unions were the first Social-Democrats to support the government during the war. On August 2 they called off all strikes then in progress. On the following day the party's delegation in the Reichstag held its caucus in preparation for the meeting of the federal parliament on August 4. "In the hour of peril we shall not leave the fatherland in the lurch," went the statement as the SPD, despite the initial opposition of 14 deputies, voted to support the war effort. In the Reichstag the Social-Democrats joined with other parties in unanimously passing a credit of 5 billion marks. Even Karl Liebknecht yielded to party discipline and voted for the August 4th war credits, but this was to be the last time he would do so.
5. On August 2, 1914, before Germany was at war with France, the German government presented an ultimatum to Belgium demanding from the Belgian government that it should tolerate the passage of German troops. The Belgians would be treated as enemies in case it refused. On August 4, after the Belgians rejected the ultimatum, the Germans invaded Belgium.
6. At the caucus of the SPD's delegation in the Reichstag on August 3, 1914, 14 deputies, among them Hugo Haase (one of the two party chairmen), opposed the party's course in supporting the war. But in the end they yielded to party discipline, and Hasse even agreed to act as speaker for the party at the parliamentary session.
7. On November 12, 1914 *Justice,* published in England, printed a statement dated September 10, 1914, made by Rosa Luxemburg, Karl Liebknecht, Franz Mehring and Clara Zetkin, which stated that "we and many other German Social-Democrats regard the war from a standpoint that in no way corresponds to that" of the party leadership. They added: "The fact that we are under martial law makes it impossible for us at present to defend our views publicly."
8. Hugo Haase (1863-1919) succeeded August Bebel as leader of the Social-Democratic Party. Although he held pacifist views during the

war he submitted to majority discipline and voted for war credits. He resigned as party head in 1915 and became head of the Independent Social-Democratic Party (USPD) in 1916. Haase was one of the USPD ministers in the coalition government set up in November, 1918 following the Kaiser's abdication. He resigned at the end of December in protest against the government's counterrevolutionary course. He was murdered in 1919.

9. Literally: Let us return to our cheep. The phrase here means: Let us get back to our main subject.
10. The reference is to Luise Zietz. For a biographical sketch, *see* pp. 184n.62.
11. Angelica Balabanov was one of the delegates to the first International Socialist Women's Conference in Stuttgart in 1907. She represented the Italian movement and served as a principal translator. (*See* Angelica Balabanov, *My Life as a Rebel* (New York, 1938), p.80.
12. As a member of the Reichstag, Karl Liebknecht could not be arrested for voting and speaking against the war. He was therefore conscripted into the army in an effort to silence him. But there, too, Liebknecht continued to fight against the war.
13. On November 30, 1914 the SPD parliamentary delegates decided by a vote of 82 to 17 to vote for the new war credits. Then on December 2 Karl Liebknecht voted against the war credits. He gave as his reason that the war was "an imperialist war, a war for the capitalist domination of the world market.... The war is not a German defensive war... ." (Heinz Wohlgemuth, *Karl Liebknecht: Eine Biographie* (Berlin, 1973),pp. 174-75.)

    After this Liebknecht, Zetkin, Luxemburg, and Mehring issued a declaration asserting that the war was imperialistic in origin, and would lead to capitalistic expansion and annexation. It was an idle dream to hope that the war could be transformed into one of defense. Rather it had to be opposed and brought to an early end.

WOMEN OF THE WORKING PEOPLE

1. Clara Zetkin wrote this manifesto, which was adopted by a women's conference she convened as the secretary of the International Socialist Women. See also p. 37.

TO THE SOCIALIST WOMEN OF ALL COUNTRIES

1. In May, 1917 the SPD Executive removed Clara Zetkin as editor of *Gleichheit* because of her outspoken criticism of the Party's support of the German war effort.
2. Under the auspices of the Independent Socialists the "Frauenbeilage" (Women's Supplement) of the *Leipziger Volkszeitung* was founded, and Clara Zetkin was placed in charge.
3. In March, 1916, eighteen of the twenty Socialist deputies in the Reichstag who had voted against the fourth war loan, formed the Socialist Collaboration Group under the leadership of Hugo Haase, Wilhelm Dittmann, and Georg Lebedau. In January, 1917, a conference called by the Group met with representatives from all over

Germany and issued a manifesto attacking the capitalist governments on both sides for having failed to formulate war aims. During Easter, 1917 the opposition Socialists held a Congress in Gotha where they founded the Independent Social-Democratic Party.

THE BATTLE FOR POWER AND PEACE IN RUSSIA

1. On March 15 (March 2, old style), the Czar abdicated, and the thousand-year-old Russian monarchy came to an end. The recently dissolved Duma set up a Provisional Committee to maintain order and establish some democratic reforms. The same day leaders of the Petrograd workers and a rebellious garrison created the Petrograd Soviet of Workers' and Soldiers' Deputies, an unofficial but representative body elected by factories and regiments. Similar soviets were quickly set up all over Russia. The Duma Committee established the Provisional Government headed by Prince Georgy Lvov as prime minister, with Alexander Kerensky, a Duma deputy of the moderate Socialist Labour Group as Minister of Justice.
2. The word Bolsheviks is derived from the Russian word meaning majority. At the London Congress of Russian Social-Democratic Labor Party in 1903, there was a split on the question of what kind of revolutionary organization should be built. The Bolsheviks, led by V.I.Lenin, were in the majority; the Menshiviks were in the minority. Most of the leaders of the Bolshevik Party at the time of the March Revolution were in exile abroad or in Petrograd. Lenin returned from exile via Sweden and Finland, to Petrograd in the famous "sealed train" on April 16, 1917. Lenin immediately issued an open call for "All Power to the Soviets!"
3. Although the Bolsheviks grew in membership, the Party was outlawed following the mass demonstrations in Petrograd in July. Lenin went into hiding in Finland, and Kerensky replaced Prince Lvov as prime minister of the Provisional Government.
4. With their slogan, "Peace, Land, and Bread," the Bolsheviks gained more and more support among the peasants, workers, and soldiers. On October 20 (October 7), Lenin returned secretly to Petrograd to urge the policy of armed insurrection.
5. On the morning of November 7 (October 25) the Bolsheviks proclaimed the overthrow of the Provisional Government. That same night the Cabinet members were captured in the Winter Palace. The Second Congress of Soviets proclaimed the Soviets to be the ruling organs in Russia, headed by the Soviet Central Executive Committee and by the Council of People's Commissars as the Cabinet. Lenin was designated chairman of the Council of People's Commissars. After an abortive attempt to return to power was put down, Kerensky went into hiding, and the following year fled to England and then to the United States. By then the great October Revolution had fully triumphed.
6. Friedrich Schiller, *Wilhelm Tell,* Act II, Scene II.

KARL LIEBKNECHT AND ROSA LUXEMBURG

1. See p. 144.
2. Late in October, 1918 Karl Liebknecht was released from prison and in November, Rosa Luxemburg, who was being held without trial, was liberated. In November, Kaiser William II abdicated, and the Majority Social-Democrats proclaimed the German Republic. Meanwhile, the Spartacus League, headed by Liebknecht and Luxemburg, had issued a manifesto to the workers and soldiers demanding a socialist revolution. All over Germany revolutionary workers' and soldiers' councils were being formed. On November 11, 1918 the armistice was signed and World War I came to an end. On December 30, 1918 the Spartacus League held a convention and organized the Communist Party of Germany under the leadership of Liebknecht and Luxemburg.
   To crush the revolutionary movement, Gustav Noske, the Social-Democratic military expert, turned to the old army and used the reactionary *Freikorps* for this purpose. In the evening of January 15, 1919 Karl Liebknecht and Rosa Luxemburg were murdered by the officers of the *Freikorps* who were charged with delivering them to prison. A military tribunal absolved some of the persons involved and gave others light sentences, while helping them escape.
3. Kurt Eisner (1867-1919), German socialist and editor, member of the Independent Social-Democratic Party of Germany and President of Bavaria from November 7, 1918 until his assassination on February 21, 1919.
4. Leo Jogiches (1867-1919), lifelong revolutionary and one of the founders of Social-Democracy in Poland and Lithuania. He was one of the founding members of the Spartacus League in Germany a close friend of Rosa Luxemburg. He was arrested and assassinated in jail on March 10, 1919.
5. Sonja refers to Karl Liebknecht's wife.
6. *Die Rote Fahne* was the central organ of the Communist Party of Germany.
7. In March, 1848 Karl Marx returned to Cologne from Belgium and there founded the *Neue Rheinische Zeitung.* (The original *Rheinische Zeitung* of which Marx had been chief editor had been suppressed.) It remained in existence until after the May rising of 1849 in Dresden, the Rhenisch Provinces and South Germany, when the paper was finally suppressed. The last number, printed in red type, appeared on May 19, 1849.

ROSA LUXEMBURG AND KARL LIEBKNECHT

1. Heinrich Heine (1796-1856), German-Jewish poet and radical whose verses and prose writings dealt with romantic, humanitarian, and libertarian ideas. An expatriate who lived much of his life in Paris, Heine became a bitter critic of Prussian authoritarianism.
2. Friedrich Ebert (1870-1925), German Social-Democratic Party leader in the Reichstag who fully supported the government during World War I. Ebert entered the government in 1918 to suppress revolution.

He became premier of the provisional government and the first president of the Weimar Republic.

3. Philipp Scheidemann (1865-1937), Right-wing Social-Democratic leader in Germany who actively supported the war. He was appointed state secretary by Kaiser Wilhelm in 1918, but was unable to save the monarchy. He was minister in the Ebert coalition and worked to crush the revolutionary movement.
4. Eduard David (1863-1930), Right-wing member of German Social-Democracy and a leader of Bernsteinian Revisionism. A supporter and defender of German colonial expansionism, he vigorously supported Germany's participation in World War I as "a defensive war for national independence and the culture of Germany." David was the first president of the National Assembly in 1919.
5. On May 1, 1916 while Karl Liebknecht was on army leave in Berlin, he addressed a tremendous anti-War May Day demonstration in the great public square in front of the Kaiser's palace. In full uniform, Liebknecht called upon the German people to stop the war. "Our enemies," he cried, "are not the English, French, or Russian workers but the great German landed proprietors, the German capitalists, and their executive committee, the government."
   This time he was promptly arrested and tried for "attempted treason," "aggravated disobedience," and "contumacy to the authority of the state." He was found guilty, stripped of his Reichstag seat (he had already been expelled from the Social-Democratic Party), dishonorably discharged from the army, and given a two-and-one-half year prison sentence. Because he continued to denounce both the war and militarism during his appeal to a higher court, the sentence was increased to four years. (Wohlgemuth, *op.cit.*, pp. 235-354.)
6. For the protest *see* p. 120; 191n.7.
7. *Sozialdemokratissche Korrespondenz* appeared from December 1913 until May 1915.
8. Julian Marchlevski (1866-1925), prominent Polish economist, journalist and Socialist leader and founder, with Rosa Luxemburg and Leo Jogiches, of the Social Democracy of the Kingdom of Poland which became the Social Democratic Party of Poland and Lithuania. He was also one of the founders of the Spartacus League in Germany, and was President of the Communist University for National Minorities at Moscow from 1922 until his death in 1925.
9. In the spring of 1915 the first issue of *Die Internationale* appeared. It was immediately banned by the German government. Franz Mehring (1846-1919), German scholar and historian, biographer of Karl Marx. A left-wing Social Democrat, Mehring was a leading member of the Spartacus League.
10. When the war began Rosa Luxemburg had already been sentenced to a year in prison for an anti-war speech she had made earlier in 1914. In October her appeal was turned down, and although she was able to postpone serving the sentence for several months because of her health, she was finally imprisoned in February, 1915. The *Junius Pamphlet*, as it came to be known, was finished by April, 1915 and smuggled out of prison, but due to technical difficulties with finding a

printer, was not published until April, 1916. Its real title was *The Crisis of the German Social-Democracy*, but *Junius* was the pseudonym under which it was published.

11. While she was in prison Rosa Luxemburg sent many letters to Sonja Liebknecht, wife of Karl Liebknecht to keep her from despairing over her husband's cruel punishment.
12. In 1906 Karl Liebknecht delivered a course of lectures to the Young Socialist League, which he had helped found, on "Militarism and Anti-Militarism." Liebknecht's lectures were published in book form in 1907, which created an immediate sensation in Germany because of its exposure of the class function of capitalist militarism. The books were confiscated by the German authorities, and the author was tried at Leipzig for high treason. He was found guilty of treason and condemned to eighteen months in prison. While still in prison, he was elected to the Prussian Landtag by the workers of Berlin. (Wohlgemuth, *op.cit.*, pp.130-64.)
13. Rosa Luxemburg was born on March 5, 1871, in Zamosc, Russian Poland (now Poland), the youngest of five children of a lower middle class Jewish family. She learned Polish and German from her parents, and became involved in underground activities while still in high school. In 1889, with arrest imminent, she decided to leave Poland and at the end of the year she arrived in Zurich, which was to be her home for the next nine years. She enrolled at the University of Zurich—one of the few institutions which then admitted men and women on an equal basis—and studied mathematics and natural sciences. After a few years she shifted to the school of law, and in 1897 completed a dissertation on the industrial development of Poland, receiving her doctorate in political science. In Zurich she became involved in the international socialist movement. In 1892 she was one of the founding members of the Polish Socialist Party, the first attempt to unite all the various currents of Polish socialism into one organization. But together with Leo Jogiches, her lifelong political collaborator, she came into conflict with that organization's principal leaders. In 1894 she and a small group of Polish émigrés broke away from the PPS and formed the Social Democracy of the Kingdom of Poland, which five years later became the Social Democratic Party of Poland and Lithuania.
14. In 1897 Rosa Luxemburg moved to Germany where she began to play an active role in the SPD. She made a living as a journalist writing for the publications of the Party. But as long as she was a foreigner the German authorities could easily prevent her from being politically active. To meet this problem she married Gustav Lübeck and obtained German citizenship. A divorce was obtained five years later.
15. Published in German in 1913, the work describes imperialism as the result of a dynamic capitalism's expansion into underdeveloped areas of the world.
16. Rosa Luxemburg was deeply moved by the Russian Revolution of 1905. She went to Warsaw, participated in the struggle, and was imprisoned. *The Mass Strike, the Political Party and the Trade Unions* was written in August, 1906 in Finland, where Rosa Luxem-

burg went to recover from her imprisonment. In it she maintained that the mass strike was the single most important tool of the proletariat in attaining a Socialist victory.

17. Rosa Luxemburg returned to Germany and taught at the Social Democratic Party school in Berlin from 1907 to 1914. She tried unsuccessfully to win the SPD leadership to support the mass strike.
18. Karl Liebknecht's father was Wilhelm Liebknecht.
19. Otto Landsberg (1869-1942), one of the group of Majority Socialists in Germany who worked with Ebert, Scheidermann, and Noske to suppress the revolutionary movement.
20. According to reports in the bourgeois and Social-Democratic press, the soldiers of the Guard Cavalry Marksmen Division which had arrested Karl Liebknecht and Rosa Luxemburg, had tried to protect them afterwards. But revelations in the *Rote Fahne* forced the Social Democratic press to admit that the murder had been carried out by members of the Guard Cavalry Marksmen Division. Clara Zetkin was sick at Stuttgart at the time her two friends and comrades were assassinated in Berlin, and was unaware of the real circumstances of the murders.

IN THE MUSLIM WOMEN'S CLUB

1. Tiblis, Georgian Tblisi, is the capital of the Georgian Soviet Socialist Republic, in the southeast of the Soviet Union on the Kura river.
2. In Muslim tradition women are required to stay at home.

SAVE THE SCOTTSBORO BLACK YOUTHS

1. See pp. 15-16 and page 40.
2. Nicola Sacco and Bartolomeo Vanzetti, and Italian shoemaker and a fisherman who had emigrated to the United States and become involved in the radical movement., were arrested in 1921 and charged falsely with a robbery and murder in South Braintree, Massachusetts more than a year before. The anti-radical feeling of the time guaranteed that despite any real evidence, Sacco and Vanzetti would be found guilty. Despite tremendous defense activities and national and international protests, they were executed on the night of August 23, 1927.
3. Ruby Bates, one of the two prostitutes (the other was Victoria Price) wrote a letter to a boyfriend in which she said that the rape story was false, and that "those police man (sic) made me tell a lie." She also testified later in the second trial that the rape story was a lie.
4. On March 24, 1932 the Alabama Supreme Court upheld by a margin of six to one the conviction of all but one of the eight Scottsboro defendants. They granted Eugene Williams a new trial on the grounds that he was allegedly a juvenile at the time of his conviction. Chief Justice Anderson dissented, insisting that "they did not get a fair and impartial trial that is required and contemplated by our Constitution" (*Powell v. State*, 224 Ala.). On November 7, 1932, the Supreme Court of the United States reversed the lower verdict on the ground that the

defendants had had inadequate counsel. The Scottsboro youths were granted a new trial, but they remained in jail for years.

5. Thomas J. Mooney, a militant union organizer in San Francisco, was the target of open shop employers of that city. The opportunity to "get" Mooney presented itself during a Preparedness Day parade on July 22, 1916. A bomb was thrown into the ranks of the marchers, killing nine and wounding forty. A photograph showing Mooney and his wife a mile away from the scene of the explosion at the time of the incident was ignored, and the crime was fastened on Mooney and Warren Billings, another young labor leader. After a trial featured by perjured and purchased testimony, Mooney was sentenced to death and Billings to life imprisonment.
   Mass protest meetings were held, not only in the United States but in Europe as well. A series of labor protests in St. Petersburg, led by the Bolsheviks, played an important role in persuading President Woodrow Wilson to intervene and to urge the governor of California to commute Mooney's sentence of execution to life imprisonment.
6. The strike of coal miners in Harlan County, Ky., in 1931, led by the left-wing National Miners' Union, was met by evictions, blacklistings, raids on miners' homes, and arrest and imprisonment of miners on charges of criminal syndicalism. Harry Simms, a young NMU organizer, was shot to death by a company gunman who was given a deputy sheriff badge.

FASCISM MUST BE DEFEATED

1. In accordance with the tradition that each new Reichstag be convened by its oldest member, Clara Zetkin was entitled to open its first session on August 30, 1932.
2. Presidial Cabinet was the name for a government of the German Reich which ruled in a dictatorial manner, basing its authority not on the Reichstag, but on the powers of the Reich's President. Such a government ruled by emergency decrees. The Presidial Cabinets of Heinrich Brüning, Franz von Papen, and Kurt von Schleicher prepared the way for Hitler and the Nazis.
3. Clara Zetkin died on June 22, 1933.

THE TOILERS AGAINST WAR

1. See also p. 186 n. 88.

INDEX